The Consent of the Governed

The Consent
of the Governed

The Lockean Legacy in Early American Culture

Gillian Brown

HARVARD UNIVERSITY PRESS

Cambridge, Massachusetts

London, England   2001

Library of Congress Cataloging-in-Publication Data

Brown, Gillian.
    The consent of the governed : the Lockean legacy in early American culture /
Gillian Brown.
        p.   cm.
    Includes bibliographical references and index.
    ISBN 0-674-00298-9 (cloth : alk. paper)
    1. Political culture—United States—History—18th century.
    2. Political socialization—United States—History—18th century.
    3. Consensus (Social sciences)—United States—18th century.
    4. Locke, John, 1632–1704—Contributions in political science.
    5. Locke, John, 1632–1704—Influence. I. Title.
JK54.B76 2000
320'.01'1—dc21   00–059800

To Howard and Devon
and to the memory of Carol Kay

Contents

I

The Lockean Legacy

Introduction: The Informed
Consent of the Governed

This book goes back to some of the basics of early American culture: to the reading and writing of eighteenth-century colonists in North America; to the primers, readers, fables, fairy tales, political rhetoric, and novels through which Americans developed a sense of themselves as a sovereign people distinct from Britain. Through the process of learning to read and the experience of certain reading materials, the colonists came to think of themselves as Americans, as a people entitled, in the words of the Constitution, "to secure the blessings of liberty to ourselves and our posterity."[1]

Long before Revolutionary sermons and speeches, the ideal of self-determination resided intimately in the colonial imagination. The formation of Americans from British colonials (and other immigrants under British rule) proceeded according to Lockean reorientations of British habits of thought. Locke's reconceptualization of consent pervaded the colonies not only through editions of his works but also through schoolbooks and popular stories. When the founding fathers invoked Locke's *Second Treatise of Government* (1690), in which he presented the theory that government emanated from the people, they were marshalling an idea long familiar to Americans. In ratifying a new government based on Locke's principle that no one can be "subjected to the Political Power of another without his own Consent," Americans were legislating their childhood convictions.[2]

3

Locke formulated his political philosophy of consent in the context of his companion philosophies of knowledge and education, published in *An Essay Concerning Human Understanding* (1690) and *Some Thoughts Concerning Education* (1683). Americans knew Locke's ideas not only from these books, but also, and more profoundly, from the popular pedagogical modes and texts inspired by Locke's thought. Whether or not they knew Locke's writings, early Americans assimilated Lockean liberalism as they grew up. Reading thus crucially helped generate American national identity by circulating and typifying the acts of understanding in which Locke had anchored consent, the political principle by which a people forms and authorizes its government.[3]

The idea of persons ruling themselves, whether through a monarch or another form of leadership, notably arises in British political philosophy and experience. In this narrative dating back at least to the sixteenth century, government emerges from the consent of the governed. By authorizing government, consent provides a story of the origins of political systems as well as ongoing justification of existent organizations of power. Not surprisingly, then, consent is often the locus of critiques of power arrangements, as in the 1960s when the Vietnam War prompted many Americans to allege that their government was acting without their consent, or in still recurring charges by women and minorities about the exclusivity of consent.[4]

When eighteenth-century Americans included and wrote themselves into the history of the consent of the governed, they adjusted an old principle to sanction a new form of society, thus inaugurating a new history.[5] A commonplace in the British imagination, consent customarily rationalized, and continued to rationalize, the existent form of government, as we see in Hume's 1741 essay, "Of the First Principles of Government."[6] "Nothing is more surprising," Hume notes, "than to see the easiness with which the many are governed by the few; and to observe the implicit submission with which men resign their own sentiments and passions to those of their rulers" (32). Hume goes on to assert that because government rests on the people (with force on their side, according to Hume), "the governors have nothing to support them but opinion." It is "therefore on opinion only that government is founded" (32). Hume's phrasing simultaneously suggests the weight and whimsicality of opinion. In the gesture of attributing supremacy to opinion, Hume diminishes the actual role of opinion—"opinion only"—and thus the people's role in government. Governors must be responsive to the opinions of the governed, but for Hume, this obligation does not mean a perpetual receptivity to citizens' views. By defining opinion as "public interest, the right to power, and the right to property" (33), Hume limits the role of opinion to a barometer rather than a director of the government's performance. Shrewdly translating governmental accountability to the opinions of the governed into a matter of what we now call public relations, Hume argues against the principle of parliamentary members acting on the instructions of their constituents. His conservative opposition to a wider role for the governed in British government, which, he ominously predicts, "would soon reduce it to a pure republic," assumes that consent should function only to "cherish and improve our ancient government" (36).[7]

Hume's simultaneous acknowledgment and restriction of consent and opinion demonstrate what was by the eighteenth century a long-standing conservative usage of these concepts, one still plainly operative today. British subjects in the American colonies persisted in pressing the very issue that Hume was attempting to lay to rest in his account of consent and opinion: the responsibility of Parliament to the governed, no matter how distant the governed may be. Famously calling for no taxation without representation, American colonists wanted direct representation of their interests. To attach consent to the revisionary views of the governed, the colonists in British America relied on a much more comprehensive and dynamic model of consent and opinion: Locke's vision of opinion as itself a matter of consent.

Opinion, according to Locke, is one of the laws to which persons refer their actions. Along with divine and civic law, the "law of opinion" supplies a scale by which deeds can be evaluated.[8] Reliance on opinion follows the pattern of relation that Locke describes as fundamental to all operations of human understanding. As persons live, they regularly refer their experience to known standards. They relate their actions or the phenomena that they encounter to familiar rules of order, such as time, space, causality, and proportion. By reference to these rules, people identify and name objects and experiences. In the case of measuring more abstract matters, such as the quality of human behavior, the law of opinion helps to determine what is virtue and what is vice.

This standard, Locke emphasizes, derives from custom. What "passes for Vice in one Country" in another country "is counted a

Vertue, or at least not a Vice" (*Essay* 2, xxviii, 11). The variability of these terms from culture to culture demonstrates their local constitution, their emergence within local agreements and understandings. The law of opinion thus operates "by a secret and tacit consent" established in "the several Societies, Tribes, and Clubs of Men in the World, . . . whereby several actions come to find Credit or Disgrace amongst them, according to the Judgment, Maxims, or Fashions of that place" (*Essay* 2, xxviii, 10). Showing how consent operates in and composes the moral as well as civil laws that people make—they must agree on standards—Locke underscores the role of the people in constructing and reconstructing laws. The artifactuality of laws refers them back to their makers. Public opinion, in Locke's portrait, is just as subject to review and reformation as is government.

If, in tandem with civil laws, opinion—itself the product of judgment and agreement—measures and organizes human behavior, as Locke propounds, then forming, maintaining, and changing opinions are the crucial activities in a consensual society. Even Hume's assertion that "opinion only" rules grants an extensive scope to opinion (which he immediately seeks to restrict). In absorbing and applying Locke's comprehensive sense of consent, eighteenth-century Americans found a standard by which their opinions could establish a new system of laws. Locke's pairing of consent with opinion, which can range from the immobility of conviction to the mobility of speculation, highlights the central role of judgment in consent. Since consent works in conjunction with what people think even as it represents it, consent is always already informed. Occurring within the horizons of people's experience, consent inevitably involves relation to a given context. In any act of consent, of making social agreements, persons respond to and within an existing framework. Because consent is de facto informed, the means and matter used in informing persons are vital concerns for Locke. Informed consent means consent exercised with information, with knowledge that may be wrong, selective, biased, false, or incomplete. Today, we reiterate Locke's critical connection between the politics and pedagogy of society as we continue to debate what children should be taught, what scholars should study, teach, and perpetuate, and what information we should allow ourselves to encounter.

The issue of the public's relation to information has generated innumerable commentaries, especially since the eighteenth century. Perhaps the most influential late-twentieth-century contribution to this debate comes from Jürgen Habermas, who takes Locke's law of opinion as evidence for his conception of the critical public sphere.[9] Habermas views the eighteenth-century emergence of new communicative modes—the press, novels, cultural and literary criticism, coffeehouses, salons, book clubs, libraries, magazines—as the formation of what he calls a bourgeois public sphere. Distinct from both the state and the private domestic realms, this sphere sustained the critical thinking and expression that enabled the early modern revolutions and the establishment of liberal states. Habermas's work, which illuminates the pivotal informational changes taking place in the eighteenth century, has appealed to contemporary cultural critics and literary scholars because it attributes a powerful material status to the objects and practices that they study. Habermas usefully foregrounds the development of eighteenth-century print culture and public communicative institutions that usher in the modern era.[10] His narrative of this phenomenon, however, reveals more about his discomfort with the state of the twentieth century than it does about eighteenth-century operations of publicity. In his teleological presentation of the public sphere, modernity appears as a descent from a better time when public opinion mattered and even made revolutions. Locating criticism in a specific segment of public experience, Habermas in fact makes possible the disappearance of his critical public sphere. His report of the departure of this critical space and function provides the explanatory point for what is missing, or appears to be missing, in the present ethos of publicity.[11]

As even my very brief excursion through Hume and Locke and their eighteenth-century context shows, the composition and place of public opinion was not then, as it is not now, a settled matter. Public opinion is rather, to the extent that it can even be thought of in spatial terms, the site of competing interests and interpretations.[12] While Hume could relegate opinion to a removed and ineffectual public sentiment, Locke perceived opinion itself as an ongoing negotiation between individuals and the customs of their countries. Diverse and opposed political interests could figure in the defining, directing, and interpreting of public opinion. In my study of eighteenth-century pedagogical literature and style, the new presentations of information certainly affect public opinion, but do not absolutely determine its content. Thus, though I am tracing the revisionary process of early American reading, I would not idealize the communicative conditions of eighteenth-century Anglo-American culture. These conditions were the terms by which a people managed to institute a reimagined society. What Americans subsequently do, or do not do, with their society depends on how they engage the parameters in which they live.

To see the emergence of early American culture in the context of Lockean consent theory is not to establish, or reestablish, an originary account of American culture. Rather, I hope that this rereading of Locke, which distinguishes his thought from what I take to be recurrent liberal and antiliberal misunderstandings of it, clarifies the key point in Locke's liberalism: the citizen's continuous labor of crediting and discrediting ideas.[13] The citizen of the liberal state emerges in the processes of thought, which, in Locke's view, distinguish humans from other animals. Hence, the psychology and pedagogy of human understanding help delineate the state. Locke prescribes and supplies the cognitive provisions for the liberal state. Returning to Locke helps explain, both historically and conceptually, the connections between knowledge and consent that Americans forwarded as they claimed, applied, and adapted Locke's definition of consent.

Locke's significance in the making of the United States, once a cornerstone of American historiography, has since the 1960s become a feature of a discredited thesis. Twentieth-century postwar liberals dedicated to defending and promoting the liberal state against socialism and communism wrote celebratory histories of American liberal individualism. Even historians critical of liberalism paid respect to an American liberal heritage. Louis Hartz, for example, traced the Cold War–era liberal nation back to the formation of the United States, claiming a venerable genealogy for the twentieth-century American system.[14] The hallmark of this system is the rule of law, a law that protects individual rights. Challenging the liberal consensus thesis, other historians discovered in eighteenth-century America substantial evidence for a more communitarian vision operating in the emergence of the United States. Bernard Bailyn and Gordon Wood identified in early American political rhetoric a civic-mindedness. They discovered citizens committed to the public processes and duties of a liberal society. The attractive vision of civic republicanism advanced by Bailyn and Wood took on greater weight in the 1970s with the commanding work of J. G. A. Pocock, who elaborated the characteristics of republi-

canism that eighteenth-century Americans had inherited and implemented.[15] Unlike liberalism, which critics represent as dividing experience into political and personal spheres, republicanism offers a more
continuous view of the citizen and the state, one in which the citizen's
thoughts continually contribute to and communicate the sovereignty
of the people. The state formed by the people is not then a static or sol-
itary institution, but an instrument regularly exercised and directed by
the people through public channels. As Pocock puts it, "What mattered about a *repubblica* was that its authority should be *pubblica*."[16]

The historical recovery of ideals and customs of civic participation in
early America thus has highlighted the public communicative modes
that Habermas likewise finds significant. The public dimensions of citizens' opinions predominates also in Locke's psychology, which defines
all activities of human understanding as social conduct. Individual
judgments and choices cannot occur in isolation, but always proceed in
relation to existing conventions. Liberalism, as formulated by Locke,
registers the connection between personal and political spheres. The
most private and internal acts of individuals, those of their minds, acknowledge and engage with social standards. While contemporary critical descriptions of liberalism's detachment of the individual from the
state might apply to conditions of the late-twentieth-century liberal
nation, this account does not accurately represent Locke's view. Locke
imagines no fixed locus, private or public, for the mental operations of
persons because he regards individual deliberations as dynamic, always
interactive, even though issuing from a person's particular place in the
world.

In distinguishing Lockean thought from modern American political
liberalism and from the communitarian critique of that liberalism, I
mean to clarify how the civic sense registered by republicanism stems
from rather than repudiates Locke's liberal vision. My aim is not to re-
value liberalism or devalue republicanism, but to examine how certain
ideas coincide and cooperate in the eighteenth-century American understanding and usage of consent.[17] Persons acquire from experience
and education the ideas of self, society, the state, past, future, representation, and justice that inform their consent and that their consent endorses. The pervasiveness of Lockean pedagogy, therefore, helps explain the process of early American deliberations. While Lockean
models in no way predict or dictate American experience, they do point

us toward looking at the standards that early Americans encountered. Since that encounter commences with the earliest exercises of thought, my study starts with childhood.

Revisiting Locke makes clear that to understand the rise of the modern liberal state, we need to take into account the eighteenth-century appearance of new concepts of child development and their subsequent prominence in the imagination of consent. This book therefore begins by considering the implications of Locke's remarkable—and oddly unremarked—alignment of consent with childhood, which thereby links consent with frailty and contingency. Both the potentiality and insufficiency embodied in childhood pervade the primers, political treatises, and novels through which the colonists in eighteenth-century America were conceiving a new national identity. In the very conditions that seem to undercut self-determination (making liberal consent theory perpetually vulnerable to reproach), early Americans find the possibility of inventing themselves as members of their own social compact. My reading of the integral relation of consent to the ideas and ideals of childhood helps clarify the powers and limitations continually attached to consent in the American experience.

Tracking Locke's formulation of consent in his political, philosophical, psychological, and pedagogical writings, Chapter 1 illuminates the centrality of childhood to Lockean consent. Chapter 2 then traces the circulation of Lockean logic through pedagogy, looking closely at the most influential schoolbook in eighteenth-century America, the *New England Primer.* The confluence of Reformation religious and political principles in the *Primer* provided Americans with a strong sense of the importance of individual choice even as the text worked to direct this choice. Transmitting the Protestant value of individual interpretation, literacy thus plays a crucial part in the making of Americans.[18] The method of instructed choice presented in the *Primer* appears also in other popular grammars and spellers, which, following Locke's recommendation, regularly included fables as exemplary reading material. Chapter 3 examines the guidance furnished by fables, tracking the procedures of identification and determination upon which their morals rely. By the time Tom Paine wrote *Common Sense* (1776), the notion of the consensual child had come to figure familiarly in both the pedagogy and literary representation of children. As I demonstrate in Chapter 4, Paine's unprecedentedly successful political rhetoric draws on the prevailing account of the child circulated in the eighteenth-century revised editions of fairy tales. Like primers and fables, these old stories were recast in a Lockean mold to accent the values of individual judgment and self-determination.

At a conference in Edinburgh, where I recounted the Lockean paradigm of self-determination, a distinguished British scholar reminded me that Locke wrote his *Some Thoughts Concerning Education* for the sons of gentlemen. He then went on to muse, "Isn't it odd that Americans should think they could apply these ideas to *anyone?*" This, I think, is precisely the usefulness of Locke. I would suggest that those Americans excluded, either explicitly or implicitly, from the eighteenth-century narratives of individualism—women, Indians, slaves, Catholics, Jews, Muslims, and later immigrants to the continent—have continued to demonstrate the applicability of Locke's ideas to those whose perceived oddity has disqualified them from the full benefits of society. Indeed, opponents of equal rights for all members of American society have always recognized the possibility of subordinated persons advancing their claims. To prevent just such advances, conservatives customarily have tried to limit access to educational and economic opportunities. Prohibitions against teaching slaves to read, laws denying immigrants access to public education, and the repeal of low-interest student loans to the underprivileged are just a few prominent examples of the means by which American society excludes certain persons from the Lockean legacy. By the account of the British professor who found it strange that Americans applied Locke's ideas to their circumstances, none of us would qualify.

My exposition of the Lockean legacy in early American culture thus suggests other narratives to be unfolded and recorded as more and more so-called odd Americans claim their legacy. In this book, I can elaborate only the transformative logic by which some eighteenth-century persons became Americans. As Americans began to write and read stories about their new nation, they registered an array of anxieties about consent. From post-Revolutionary fiction emerged different portraits of consent: some nostalgic for British society, some laudatory of the United States, some desirous of further revisionary developments in American society. In many early American novels by both women and men, the fate of a woman typifies the abiding difficulties and inequities in even a liberal society.

Women in the late eighteenth century replace children as the proto-typical figures of consent. The feminization of consent signifies a shift in the focus of consent discourse from the possibilities of childhood experience to the constraints of adult experience. The difficulties of women, who never get to exercise consent, epitomize for the post-Revolutionary United States the omnipresent limits of consent. As novels explored the relation between women and consent, they also provided early Americans with another avenue of opinion through which they could continue to reimagine themselves. I thus turn in the second part of this book to some early American novels about women—specifically, to examinations of Hannah Foster's *The Coquette* (in Chapter 5) and Tabitha Tenney's *Female Quixotism* (in Chapter 6).

Because early American novels engaged Lockean contractual ideas of the self and society, I am interested in how American novelists employed British fictional conventions to explore the problematics of consent: questions of individual freedom and coercion, the status of testimony and evidence, the power of convention, the formalisms of law and custom. I also mean to convey the formal merits of the novels. The ready association of early American novels with early American politics, to which my own readings testify, has too often neglected the aesthetic merits of those novels. Those critics who take early American novels most seriously do so in political and sociological terms that justify the significance of this literature while admitting (or evading) an assumed aesthetic insignificance. Indeed, from the start, early American novels have seemed to embarrass critics, particularly because they appear imitative (and unsuccessfully so) of British novels. As Walter Channing lamented in 1815, "We have wanted literary enterprise, and have been sadly deficient in genuine intellectual courage."[19]

The fact that American novels employ British and European forms alerts readers to the distinctive formal choices and revisions that early American writers make as they use well-known conventions. In rewriting *Clarissa*, as they are often accused of doing, American novelists do not merely imitate a now standard novelistic form. Rather, they engage in the imaginative practice of mixing and rearranging conventions—a practice that the novel genre has always invited. It is in novelists' aesthetic decisions that the politics—sometimes reactionary, sometimes reformative, sometimes revisionary, and sometimes contradictory—of early American novels emerges. Thus seduction novels such as *Char-*

lotte Temple and *The Coquette* do not automatically signify the conservative attitudes toward women that some critics associate with seduction novels, or with the cultural moments in which seduction novels enjoy great popularity. Nor do these novels necessarily represent social critiques, as some feminist revisionary readings suggest. By ignoring the mechanics and formal features of early American novels, critics convert the question of these novels' politics, whatever they may be, into a taxonomic formalism that ironically disregards the aesthetic labors by and through which books engage politics.

Early American novels, then, are a postcolonial literature replete with gestures of imitation, appropriation, preservation, parody, duplication, subversion, and innovation.[20] The connections between British and American eighteenth-century novels throw into relief what is most characteristic of each national literary practice. Across national and geographical boundaries, novelists can find ways of making novelistic conventions represent their local interests.[21] The likeness of the early American novel to the British novel therefore signifies not an aesthetic inferiority, but instead the aesthetic value of particular formal choices. My study is particular to late-eighteenth-century American novels, and I analyze these novels in terms of their particularities. The particulars of literature include the formal matters of a genre or practice as much as they do historical circumstances, local geographies, and personal markers.

The early American novel's preoccupation with female experience recapitulates a primary interest of the British novel: the exploration of interiority through the case of a woman. American novels bring to the eighteenth-century representation of individual experience a different context, another set of opinions with which Americans can consider the problems of women and men depicted in the novels. Presenting familiar stories in a new perspective, as Hannah Foster does when she fictionalizes a news report about a seduced and abandoned woman, or as Tabitha Tenney does when she writes another version of both *Don Quixote* and *The Female Quixote*, early American novelists display the imaginative techniques of retelling.

Feminist criticism has attempted, with varying degrees of success, to retell literary and cultural history and to revise America's still unfolding history. My treatments of early novels demonstrate that the practice of feminist criticism in American society begins with the emergence of the nation and national culture. In the form of the novel, early American women found a means of representing their views, whether conservative or progressive. The presence of women's critical perspectives at the outset of the United States testifies to the way that even disenfranchised persons can insinuate themselves into the making of published opinion, becoming part of the background to which consent refers. If this Lockean chronology of attaining citizenship has proved all too long and arduous a process for women, blacks, American Indians, and nonwhite immigrants in the United States, the fact that certain men could much more quickly become Americans should alert us never to underestimate the force of obstructive opinions like misogyny and racism.[22]

The presence of the disenfranchised in the opinions informing consent dictates the vocabulary of consent. For the first part of this book, I represent the liberal subject as male, using primarily masculine pronouns. In the second part, I use primarily feminine pronouns, representing the liberal subject as female. My change in the gender of reference follows the feminization of consent that this study tracks. This feminization of consent recognizes women's disenfranchisement without necessarily advocating women's enfranchisement. Thus the eighteenth-century rhetorical narrative of consent in the United States registers the continuing subjection of women even as it makes women central figures in political and social discourse. Indeed, consent relies upon the presence of the disenfranchised, who mark the condition from which a consensual society distinguishes itself. So long as consent operates, consent recalls the unentitled. The image of imperiled women informs and accompanies consent as long as the unequal status of women persists.

1

The Child's Consent, the Child's Task

The United States was founded, or at least conceived to have been founded, on the principle of "the voluntary consent of a whole people" (*Federalist*, no. 85).[1] Under the concept of consent, society follows from and must fulfill the will of the individuals who compose it; polities exist legitimately only on the basis of the consent of the governed who have established government for their own protection. Following the principles of consent theory articulated and popularized through the writings of John Locke, the founders envisioned U.S. citizens as the source or "fountain" from which the authority of their government flowed.[2]

Long before the Constitution, British settlers in North America had used consent as the basis for forming local governments. The signers of the Mayflower Compact in 1620 decided that "there should be an association and agreement that we should combine together in one body, and to submit to such government and governours, as we should by common consent agree to make and choose."[3] For the Mayflower colonists, the establishment of government by consent signified not the now celebrated act of independence proclaimed by the Constitution, but an extension of their obedience to British rule. Having wandered outside their planned point of arrival within the territories of the Virginia Company, the Mayflower voyagers instituted a temporary government until they could obtain a royal charter for their community. In doing so, the settlers were following a long-standing tradition of re-

15

garding royal rule as emanating from the wishes of its subjects. The Mayflower Compact thus reenacted the relation of British subjects to the Crown as it furnished a surrogate form of subject-ruler relations. Since at least the sixteenth century, consent had provided both a principle and mechanism for establishing government, by which citizens routinely affirmed monarchical authority. Prior to Locke's liberalization of consent, with its contractual concept of consent that the founding fathers invoked and championed, consent usually functioned as a justification of Britain's parliamentary monarchy. Between 1620 and 1787, however, American colonists came to understand and employ consent in the antimonarchical and antihereditary terms developed by Locke, as the expression of the populace's will, prior to the institution of any government or monarchy.[4]

Locke's definition of consent furnished eighteenth-century Americans with the premise of each generation's right to authorize government. Rather than holding perpetual power, Locke argued, governmental authority requires regular confirmation by the governed, by every new generation of citizens. The continual ratification of government by its citizens sanctions and sustains it. Even if citizens are born and raised under a government they did not create, the doctrine of their originating authorization maintains, and can dissolve, that government. Consent theory thereby foregrounds the authority of the living, the rights of present and future generations. Thus, along with the familiar and venerable phrase "consent of the governed," the other most prominent idea in the founding of the United States is independence from the past, famously embodied in the figure of the rightfully rebellious child of autocratic parents. The characterization of colonial Americans as children wrongfully deprived of their rights and welfare pervades Revolutionary rhetoric and is inscribed in the documents of national founding. Jefferson permanently stamped this image on American history when in the Declaration of Independence he indicted the British for being "deaf to the voice of justice and consanguinity."[5]

The connection between consent and the rhetoric of generational rights so dramatically forged and wielded during the American Revolution originates in Locke's consent theory, which delineates the political principle of self-determination as the primary characteristic of individuals from birth. The individual thus becomes the crucial actor in history, and preparation of the individual for this major role begins in childhood. With the rise of individualism at the end of the seventeenth century comes a newly focused interest in childhood—in the under-standing, teaching, and rearing of the children who are to be liberal subjects. Published literature for and about children accordingly emerges in unprecedented numbers in the wake of Locke's reformula-tion of consent. Locke himself significantly set forth his portrait of the consensual subject in his educational and psychological writings as well as his political treatises. Probably even more widely read and circulated than the *Two Treatises of Government*, Locke's *Some Thoughts Concerning Education* provided colonists in North America with an account of the making of consensual subjects. The influence of Locke also permeated the education of American colonists, which increasingly incorporated the tenets of Lockean pedagogy. Schooled in the Lockean mode, early Americans eventually claimed the rights of individuals for which their education had equipped them.

In replacing earlier understandings and usages of consent with Lock-ean formulations, eighteenth-century Americans were registering and promoting the new account of children and their rights initiated by Locke, a new narrative of childhood that they themselves epitomized. The rise of the child, as a prominent rhetorical figure and as the subject of liberal pedagogy and psychology, therefore is a crucial phenomenon and context for understanding the emergence of the United States.[6] Every child's inevitable encounter with external authority encapsulates the recurrent problem of reconciling individual experience with social standards. Central to this drama experienced by every generation is the difficulty of accepting external authority, even when that authority de-rives from the individual. By going back to the basics of how consent theory operated in early American culture—and by extension, to the concepts of childhood underpinning consent—we can trace how the American affiliation with consent includes from the start an omnipres-ent anxiety about limits upon individual freedom.

The Consent of the Child

By the time consent becomes part of the carefully chosen vocabulary of the Constitution (and arguments supporting it), the term conveys not just the ideal but also the difficulties of self-determination. A large measure of doubt always has accompanied this liberal ideal of self-de-

termination. The very inclusion in the *Federalist Papers* of the specify-
ing adjective "voluntary" in the phrase "voluntary consent of a whole
people" suggests the uncertain relation of consent to individual freedom. The fact that consent—the preeminent act of individual authorization—requires the supplementation of volition implies that consent
by itself is not necessarily a self-determined act. In addition to appearing with the auxiliary of will, consent usually appears in affiliation with
knowledge and experience: as in the tandem concepts of informed consent and the age of consent. Consent would seem to become representative of agency only in conjunction with will and knowledge that the
self does not invariably possess.

The insufficiency of consent as an expression of agency has long provoked objections to liberal consent doctrine.[7] The need to augment
consent, however, is not at all a handicap in Locke's perspective—the
need for supplementation is in fact the condition of possibility for the
individual agent. Locke quite deliberately identified consent with a
quintessential state of insufficiency: childhood. Proponents of monarchy, such as Robert Filmer, whose patriarchal theory of hereditary
power and succession is the target of Locke's *Two Treatises of Government*, had argued that the natural subordination of children to parents
(that is, sons to fathers) exemplified the natural order of the subject's
relation to the monarch.[8] To advance the claims of present generations
against the arbitrary rule of monarchy, Locke roundly rejected the
monarchy-family analogy.

> These two *Powers, Political* and *Paternal*, are *so perfectly distinct* and
> separate; are built upon so different foundations, and given to so
> different Ends, that every Subject that is a Father, has as much a
> *Paternal Power* over his Children, as the Prince has over his; And
> every Prince that has Parents owes them as much filial Duty and
> Obedience as the meanest of his Subjects do to theirs; and can
> therefore contain not any part or degree of that kind of Dominion,
> which a Prince, or Magistrate has over his Subject.[9]

Because a prince's own paternal power and filial duty do not translate
into the subjection of his family members (or at least not the same kind
of subjection that political subjects experience), familial relations compose a different sphere from political relations. In the sphere of parent-

child relations, Locke finds no natural basis for subjection, but instead
a paradigm of the individual's freedom, "for *every Man's Children* being
by Nature as *free* as himself, or any of his Ancestors ever were, may,
whilst they are in that Freedom, choose what Society they will join
themselves to, what Common-wealth they will put themselves under"
(IV, 73, 10–14; Laslett, 333). Locke's political theory and psychology
crucially revised the idea of children's subordinate position by envi-
sioning that position as consensual—they are as free as their parents
and may choose their own society, their own commonwealth. Far from
signifying a natural order of subjection, the dependent condition of a
person's minority manifests the child's "express or tacit Consent" to
necessary parental governance (IV, 74, 17; Laslett, 335). Locke entitles
the child with the faculty and right of ratifying parental authority.[10]

Many have objected that no moment of consent exists for the child.
At what point, and in what form, does the child ratify the parent's authority? Locke answers this charge against the notion of the child's
consent with his delineation of tacit forms of consent, the nonexplicit
exercises of consent such as residence. To settle "how far any one shall
be looked on to have consented . . . where he has made no Expressions
of it at all" (VIII, 119, 11–12; Laslett, 365–366), Locke declares "that
every Man, that hath any Possession, or Enjoyment, of any part of the
dominions of any Government, doth thereby give his *tacit Consent*, and
is as far forth obliged to Obedience of the Laws of that Government,
during such Enjoyment, as any one under it." Such enjoyment can
be long-term, such as land ownership; short-term, such as taking "a
Lodging for only a Week"; or even as temporary and unmoored as
"travelling freely on the Highway" (VIII, 119, 13–22; Laslett, 366).[11]
Children, like adult citizens, follow the rules of the places where they
reside. Moreover, children clearly cannot choose where they live and
usually cannot live elsewhere. How can tacit consent, encompassing
the involuntary aspects of existence—such as physical incapacity—
within the voluntary, truly represent the force of individual will? Such
an understanding of the voluntary as a state constituted by limits seems
to make consent so general a faculty as to be inconsequential. If one's
existence is de facto consensual, what is the significance of the consensual?

Such questions point to the hypothetical character of consent—
which, as the political philosopher Hanna Pitkin has astutely pointed

out, far from invalidating the concept of consent, illuminates consent's operation as an explanation of political obligation.[12] While historically the rhetoric of consent has promoted a certain mythology of political origins, consent theory aims more directly to rationalize current relations to political authority. Consent is not an originary act or founding exercise, Pitkin emphasizes, but an ex post facto construction that evokes such a founding moment, affirming our acceptance of our present conditions. Consent in a liberal society such as the United States is the subjection that we acknowledge to our circumstances when we are not rebelling from or objecting to them. If consent marks our subjection, it nevertheless accents this subjection as a chosen state, or more precisely, as a state we can alter. By the principle of consent, we can reject or reform our obligations to the state. In Pitkin's reading of Lockean consent, consent only hypothetically signifies the founding of society; but this hypothetical account of the origins of government importantly assigns to citizens authority over their government. Whatever the actual origins of government, which usually can be known only conjecturally, the continuance of government depends upon the present citizens.

Pitkin's characterization of consent as hypothetical shifts critical emphasis from consent itself to the individuals who live in a consensual society. Rather than understanding consent as an originary story and justification of individual authority, Pitkin sees consent as a tool that persons use to express assent or dissent, a prerogative of each generation. In identifying consent with childhood, Locke crucially detached consent from heritage: "no Body can be under a Law, which is not promulgated to him" (VI, 57, 5–6; Laslett, 323). At birth, "every man hath" an "equal Right . . . to his Natural freedom, without being subject to the Will or Authority of any other Man" (VI, 54, 10–12; Laslett, 322). To distinguish government by consent from monarchical systems (which can claim to be consensual organizations), Locke must sever consent from conceptions of lineage and genealogy: consent must belong to each member of each generation independent of all other connections. Recognizing and protecting an embryonic form of agency in the child, Locke welds consent to the present: to the child's birth as well as to the child's successive stages of growth.

Recognition of the child's agency means that parental power is not a corollary to biological priority but a temporary obligation *"to preserve, nurture, and educate the Children,* [whom] they had begotten" (VI, 56, 11; Laslett, 323)—an obligation occasioned by biology but in no way inhering in the biological relation. The ability to procreate carries no political authority. Indeed, parental

> *power* so little belongs to the *Father* by any particular right of Na-
> ture, but only as he is Guardian of his Children, that when he quits
> his Care of them, he loses his power over them, which goes along
> with their Nourishment and Education, to which it is inseparably
> annexed, and it belongs as much to the *Foster-Father* of an exposed
> Child, as to the Natural father of another: So little power does the
> bare *act of begetting* give a Man over his Issue, if all his Care ends
> there, and this be all the Title he hath to the Name and Authority
> of a Father. (VI, 65, 1–9; Laslett, 328)

Mothers, who both bear and nurture children, have no greater claims of authority over children. As Locke points out, children are often, and particularly in America, "all left to the Mother . . . wholly under her Care and Provision," but this situation gives her no "Legislative Power over her Children" for that is solely "the proper *power of the magistrate.*" A father's or mother's command over "Children is but temporary and reaches not their Life or Property" (VI, 65, 12–26; Laslett, 328–329).[13] In Locke's reformulation of parent-child relations, parental authority, whether exercised by biological or adoptive parents, fathers or mothers, stems only from the child's basic needs and consists only in guardianship of the child's rights until the child has "arrived to the infranchisement of the years of discretion" (VI, 65, 32–33; Laslett, 329). Due to "the weak and helpless" condition of children, and to their initial lack of "Knowledge or Understanding" (VI, 56, 7; Laslett, 323), their "parents have a sort of Rule and Jurisdiction over them," but "'tis but a temporary one." Locke's uncharacteristically imprecise language here—"a sort of Rule"—underscores the qualified and strange nature of this passing parental power, a power destined to disappear. "The Bonds of this Subjection are like the Swaddling Cloths they are wrapt up in, and supported by, in the Weakness of their Infancy. Age and reason as they grow up, loosen them till at length they drop quite off, and leave a Man at his own free Disposal" (VI, 55, 2–9; Laslett, 322). "The *Power,* then, *that Parents have* over their Children, arises from that Duty which is incumbent on them, to take care of their Off-spring, during the imperfect state of Childhood. To inform the Mind, and govern the Actions of their yet ignorant Nonage, till reason shall take its Place, and ease them of that Trouble, is what the Children want, and the Parents bound to" (VI, 58, 1–6; Laslett, 324). Because the child is born ignorant—the full capacity to reason and thus consent is learned—the child needs parents for guidance as well as for sustenance and shelter. Parenting therefore inheres not in procreative abilities, in generation, but in nurture, in education. Once the parental function becomes an obligation, a moral response to and respect for a potentially rational creature, all relations and conditions, familial and political statuses, appear as provisional states. The provisionality of childhood suggests the possibility of changing conditions as it foregrounds the formative role that parents and children continually play in their society.

By depoliticizing—or more exactly, by privatizing—parental authority, and by defining it as not exclusively paternal, Locke deflates the natural claims upon which Filmer and other proponents of monarchy tried to justify monarchical power. At the same time, Locke in no way denies that the family operates as a cultural and political institution; indeed, patriarchalist accounts of government arise, according to Locke, because in practice civic arrangements have developed from familial organization.[14] As Locke acknowledges, it is "almost natural for children by a tacit, and scarce avoidable consent to make way for the father's authority and government" (VI, 75, 1–2; Laslett, 335). Though subjection to government may unavoidably follow from subjection to the father, it is equally inevitable that when the child acquires reason and will, he will be independent, free to direct himself. Even though the child initially lacks reason and will, he is born with property in himself—which is merely held in trust by the parent until the child can manage his own property, that is, himself. Since parental dominion extends no further than the child's minority, the child naturally checks the extent of his own subjection. The child's consent, then, ratifies his dependence on the parent as well as his future independence from the parent. Father and magistrate rule by the child's and citizen's consent. Granting to some degree the patriarchalist account of the emergence of government, Locke empties this development of predictive or prescriptive value, of any significance other than its plausibility as a description of a historical development. The key point for Locke is not that the child-parent relation offers a pattern for citizen-state relations, but that both sets of relations should be understood as consensual.

Locke's extension of consensuality to childhood thus works to ensure the rights of each generation "to choose what Society they will join themselves to" (VI, 73, 13–14; Laslett, 333), thereby allowing for changes in political and social practices. By severing individual status from the past, from connections established by blood or custom, Locke addresses the present state of individuals and attributes their conditions to their ongoing activities. Consent valorizes the role of persons in forming their government. And in proclaiming government as an invention of individuals, it suggests the malleability of government to reform.

From the prospect for change fostered in Lockean consent theory, colonial Americans developed their sense of independence from British rule. Thus when Jay Fleigelman characterizes the American Revolution as the culminating event of the eighteenth-century revolt against patriarchical authority, he is registering the profound political effect of Locke's redefinition of childhood.[15] With Locke's entitlement of the child come both the philosophy and procedures of consent that underpin the forming of democratic society. For the eighteenth century, the emergence of the new childhood performs a dynamically affirmative function: the figure of the consenting child validates the consensual state of adults that itself emanates from childhood. It might be said that the ideal of the consent of the child stands as the originary story of the American republic.[16]

The idea of the independence of the child was circulated in eighteenth-century America through popular stories about young people who seek to follow their own desires, such as *Clarissa* and *Robinson Crusoe*, and through a new children's literature in which parents are conspicuously absent, inept, or abusive. Standard books read by or to children in the colonies and the new nation included many versions of the tale of Tom Thumb, the tiny boy who saves his family from poverty and giants, and "The Children in the Wood," the original story of Hansel and Gretel, in which the children die because of the indifference of their parents and the cruelty of their guardian.[17]

Because the conception of the consensual child was a cornerstone in the founding of the United States, this figure attains a natural status, appearing as an emblem of freedom emanating from nature. Rather

than standing as the conceptual figure that Locke imagines, the consensual child quickly becomes a literal entity, a being endowed with the
full capacities and rights of self-determination. Within this conception
of childhood, Benjamin Franklin's *Autobiography* emerges as a proto-
typical narrative of individual accomplishment despite the quite remarkable combinations of luck, energy, and talent in Franklin's case.[18]
Not surprisingly, consent theory, which citizens quickly forgot was theoretical, appears an inadequate if not seriously inaccurate account of
the actual experience of individuals in the United States. People rarely
feel that they played, or play, any role in the founding of their society. Beyond the most obvious exceptional cases of American Indians,
women, and African Americans, the actual situations of many other
disenfranchised or disregarded persons, and of children themselves,
contradict the official historical portrait of a society built upon consent.
The contradiction, however, stems not from Lockean consent theory
but from the fact that people have naturalized consent into a political
foundation. Such an idealizing attitude toward political principles is
what Locke's frankly artificial notion of consent specifically rejects. So
thorough is the naturalization of the consensual child that anxieties
about individual freedom—fantasies of it, fears about it—always attend
the American liberal tradition.

Consent, Nature, and Artifice

To naturalize consent is to consider it a condition originating in nature,
a permanent characteristic of human life. In order to see how the liberal tradition of anxiety about individual freedom stems from a refusal
to understand, or a confusion about, the artificiality of consent, it is
useful to review Locke's view of the relation of nature to the question
of government. Although Locke is much quoted for his description of
"the state of nature," which he takes to precede society, he invokes nature as only a precondition rather than source of society.[19] From the
outset, the state of nature includes the presence and activities of humans. The striking feature about Locke's portrait of nature is its transitoriness: how quickly it is appropriated and augmented by people "for
the Support and Comfort of their being" (V, 26, 4; Laslett, 304). Individuals, according to Locke, continually act upon nature. By their activity, which Locke calls "labour," they make nature "a part of" them-

selves, the "property" of their persons (V, 27, 1–13; Laslett, 305–306). The resources of nature serve the individual who uses and annexes them. When Locke takes America as his primary example of the state of nature, he is never imagining the absence of proprietorship. Rather, he is referring to the fact that the American landscape is not all already owned as property to which successive generations are entitled; inhabitants there do not yet experience the same codified property relations that operate in Great Britain. Locke's references focus on the way the circumstances of America, as they were known to late-seventeenth-century England, illustrate the situation of the "first Commoners of the World" engaged in "the necessity of subsisting" (V, 46, 2–4; Laslett, 317–318). The Indian in America "who knows no Inclosure" may live outside the customs of property and government known to Europe, but he is still the proprietor of "The Fruit, or Venison" upon which he nourishes himself (V, 26, 12–15; Laslett, 305). Even in the earliest conditions of the human relation to nature, exemplified for Locke by the American Indian, the state of nature appears a social system structured by individual ownership.

As long as there were "plenty of natural Provisions," there was little cause for "Quarrels or Contentions about property" established by individual labor (V, 31, 12–17; Laslett, 308). But of course there were quarrels and contentions about property, which according to Locke had been always subject to regulation, even before social compacts. As soon as two individuals grasp an acorn or apple at the same time, the need arises for adjudication and for a common agreement to abide by the adjudication. Locke finds that the logic of labor in the state of nature furnishes this arbitration process. Because "God gave the World to Men in Common . . . for their benefit," and therefore "gave it to the use of the Industrious and Rational, (and labour was to be *his* title to it;) not to the Fancy or Covetousness of the Quarrelsom and Contentious," disputes over property could be resolved according "the measure of property"—by the "extent of Mens Labour" (V, 34, 1–6; 36, 1–2; Laslett, 309–310). In the case of an equality of labor, when individual claims to the fruits of nature exactly coincide, the individuals equally own the fruit. How they then use it—cutting it in half, sharing bites, or relinquishing it to the other—is a matter for them to determine. Only the introduction of a motive other than supplying one's needs, "the desire of having more than Men needed," would require a different system of governing (V, 37, 1–2; Laslett, 312). A form of government, then, already operates in the Lockean state of nature to regulate and adjudicate inevitable conflicts over the use of resources.

What Locke calls the law of nature is the "measure" that he sees operating upon conduct in the state of nature: the "Rule of Propriety, (viz.) that every Man should have as much as he could make use of" (V, 36, 1–15, 33–35; Laslett, 310–311). This rule derives not from an abstract principle of justice but from the capacities of persons. "The measure of Property, Nature has well set, by the extent of Men's labour, and the Conveniency of Life: No Man's labour could subdue, or appropriate all" (V, 36, 1–4; Laslett, 310). The exercises of labor and proprietorship can go only so far. When persons seek more than a sufficiency for their needs and when they devise means of extending and storing possessions in excess of their needs, the rule of propriety no longer holds. When this measure can no longer regulate individual acts of proprietorship, new laws become necessary and persons must agree to—must consent to—the new measures they honor.

Consent therefore registers conflict even as it redresses it through the establishment of accord. Lockean consent encapsulates a story of reconciliations, a narrative not of unchecked individuality but of continual checks to which individuals agree to comply. That consent recalls and reenacts the managing of disputes in the state of nature suggests that consent operates even before explicit social compacts. Only in this sense does Locke align consent with nature, a state that he characterizes as one of perpetual human industry regulated by a form of law.

It thus sometimes becomes difficult to distinguish the order of the state of nature from the order of formally governed societies; the difference lies not in a progression from no law to law, but in the instantiation of new practices to govern changes or variations in the handling of natural resources. For Locke, the mark of distinction is "the Invention of Money, and the tacit Agreement of men to put a value on it," which "introduced (by Consent) larger Possessions, and a Right to them" (V, 36, 37–39; Laslett, 311). Like all human inventions and arrangements, money develops in the course of laboring with natural resources. Because "the greatest part of *things really useful* to the Life of man, and such as the necessity of subsisting made the first Commoners of the World look after, as it does the Americans now, *are* generally things *of short duration*," they easily decay and perish. To prevent this waste of property, an individual could give or barter away "Plumbs that would have rotted in a Week, for Nuts that would last good for his eating a whole Year" (V, 46, 19–21; Laslett, 318). Other goods could be substituted for nuts, quite different objects such as "Gold, Silver, and Diamonds" if they were valued according to "Fancy or Agreement" (V, 46, 5–6; Laslett, 318). Then a person could "give his Nuts for a Piece of metal, pleased with its colour; or exchange his Sheep for Shells, or Wool for a sparkling Pebble or a Diamond." And thus "he might heap up as much of these durable things as he pleased." From this improvement upon the transitoriness of nature's productions, Locke concludes, *"came in the use of Money*, some lasting thing that Men might keep without spoiling, and that by mutual consent Men would take in exchange for the truly useful, but perishable Supports of Life" (V, 47, 1–4; Laslett, 318–319).

Stemming from labor and devised by humans, money introduces the means of preserving and enlarging possessions. The usefulness of nature now includes both its labor and commercial value. Hence an isolated society without any form of money need never leave the state of nature and its measures of property. Before money, Locke maintains, human society looked more like that of the American Indians: "In the beginning all the world was America, and more so than it is now; for no such thing as Money was any where known" (V, 49, 1–3; Laslett, 319). Initially invoking America as an example of the world under the rule of propriety, Locke immediately notes the differences between America and the state of nature. After all, America is part of a world in which money is a long-established feature; America in the seventeenth century is a set of European colonies, a site of encounters between different monetary systems. The point before money is no longer accessible but it is retained in the notion and practice of consent. Money can materialize only by consent; it "has its value only from the consent of men" (V, 50, 7–8; Laslett, 319). The presence and use of money thus bears witness to the accord by which people changed the terms and rules of the state of nature. In the artificiality of money, consent is most manifest.[20]

Consent, Agency, and Judgment

The familiar expectations of consent—that it be a natural, unbounded, and universal guarantee of self-determination—overlook the actual

features of Locke's consent theory, and hence its true radicalness: its refusal to naturalize human institutions. While Locke sought to establish
self-determination as a natural right, he understood perfectly that the
setting of any foundation is an imaginative exercise. It is the artificiality
of institutions, so well exemplified in the invention of money, that
makes them possible and replaceable. The strength of consent, as
Locke conceives it, is its artificiality. It is this perspective of Locke's
writings on consent that Elaine Scarry emphasizes in her recent study
of the centrality of the body in the discourse of consent. In highlighting
the prominence of the body in consent, Scarry seeks to recall the primacy of human activity in this process: that is, the imaginativeness and
artifactuality of consent. "The whole issue of consent," most manifest
in cases of medical consent, "by holding within it the notions of sovereignty and authorization, bears within it extremely *active* powers."
Moreover, as the example of the consenting anesthetized individual attests, "consent theory claims that it is by the will of the apparently passive that the active is brought into being."[21] Discovering activity within
what seems the most passive of human states—the unconsciousness
of an anesthetized patient—Scarry dramatically reasserts the human
agency in consent.

What Scarry calls the artifactual, and Pitkin calls the hypothetical,
character of consent opens the way for different imaginative exercises
of individuals in their society. Locke, though, defines individual agency
as fundamentally intellectual and therefore not necessarily issuing in
unmistakable acts of self-determination. In authorizing the ongoing
agency of individuals within and against society, Locke's consent theory
credits and demands the mental faculties of individuals, who must be
educated from childhood for their consensual office. Because the child
and the individual consent in the future—that is, make decisions in response to past and present events—consensuality consists in the individual's deliberative faculties, in what one might do. The eventuality of
childhood's end in adulthood aligns individual freedom with futurity,
an expectation granted by birthright. Independent agency is postponed
but certain, indeed certain by virtue of its postponement. Put another
way, agency is imaginative, outstripping and supplementing the present. Locke's reorientation of familial relations locates agency, and thus
individual freedom, in the putative realm: in the process of augmenta-
tions upon the present.

In the provisionality of childhood, then, Locke finds a paradigm of freedom, which he defines as the suspended state before the determination and implementation of an act. It is in the mind's "power to suspend the execution and satisfaction of any of its desires" that Locke situates "the source of all liberty." Liberty resides in mental suspension because this state affords us the opportunity to ponder and determine our actions: "For during this *suspension* of any desire before the *will* be determined to action, and the action (which follows that determination) done, we have opportunity to examine, view, and judge, of the good or evil of what we are going to do."[22]

Locating agency at a remove from actions, in the process prior to enactment, Locke envisions agency as always operative. There is nothing static or passive about the state of suspension—the "opportunity to examine, view, and judge" invites an energetic vigilance. This injunction to reflection and projection, to consider what might follow from what we are going to do, also underscores a temporal distance between agency and actions. In this interval, Locke imagines the self as ratifying its determinations.

Agency thus does not simply reside in the body, naturally developing with it, but inheres in the process of measuring what a body might do against some standard—in Locke's words, "good or evil." Law, whether religious or secular, supplies the standards of measurement, the horizons in which consent operates. It is law as well as bodily state that determine the span of childhood, stipulating the age of majority and the age of consent. Like childhood, consent then is both natural and statutory, a faculty and right originating from birth, defined and protected by law. In consent, persons appear forever filial: suspended between their desires and whatever cultural authority they do or will embody.

Consent, then, in the Lockean conception operative in eighteenth-century America, is a charge to the individual to confirm whether or not what he has willed, or is about to will, conforms to his best judgment. "And thus, by a due consideration and examining any good proposed, it is in our power, to raise our desires, in due proportion to the value of that good, whereby in its turn, and place, it may come to work upon the *will*, and be pursued" (*Essay* 2, xxi, 46). By exercising reason upon ourselves, we can "work upon" and improve ourselves. The state of self-reflection and continual judgment that Locke's formulation of the liberal individual generates requires continual review of one's relation to the effects of oneself, a continual self-corroboration. In the task of keeping one's relation to the world literally self-evident, all actions and effects are potential evidence. Lockean consent doctrine incites and obliges the self to substantiation, establishing the fundamental role of documentary techniques in the life of the individual. With the politicization and entitlement of childhood that underpin the formation of the liberal state, childhood education thus becomes a critical method through which individuals can comprehend and practice the task of composing themselves. Providing eighteenth-century Americans with such a method, Locke's *Thoughts Concerning Education* serves as the cardinal supplementary text to consent theory, as the key set of practical procedures for promoting consensual individuals.

Informing Consent

To teach individuals "to examine, view and judge of the good or evil of what [they] are going to do" (*Essay* 2, xxi, 47) means teaching them to use their minds associatively. In using their minds associatively, persons should be certain of the links that they make between ideas. Children accordingly must be taught to "often examine those ideas that they find linked together in their minds," and moreover, to "question whether this association of ideas be from visible agreement that is in the ideas themselves, or from the habitual and prevailing custom of the mind joining them thus together."[23] No easy charge, Locke's injunction to review and justify one's judgments requires "the most powerful incentives to the mind." Locke accordingly recommends appealing to children's sense of reputation, for "if you can get into children a love of credit and apprehension of shame and disgrace you have put into them the true principle which will constantly work and incline them to the right."[24] What makes reputation the true working principle of education is the fact that it operates as a witness and measure of conduct. Reputation, Locke avers, is "the testimony and applause that other people's reason, as it were by common consent, gives to virtuous and well-ordered actions." It is thus "the proper guide and encouragement to children, till they grow able to judge for themselves and find what is right by their own reason" (*Education*, section 51).[25]

Standing in loco parentis, reputation makes the child aware not only that he is subject to judgment, but also that the judgments defining his status derive from a consensual process. The public character of an individual originates from external accounts, harmonized into general approbation or reprobation. Signifying an agreement in judgments, reputation thus alerts the child to the terms in which self is constructed and confirmed. The child then can enter into an associative relation with an ideal of himself, with his desired self. Forming oneself is the primary object of the child's education; reforming in order to endorse oneself is the continuing task of the adult who succeeds the child.

Besides appealing to reputation, Locke advocates motivating children to attain skills and self-discipline by making learning and practice a game. Cozening the child to learn through play acknowledges both the importance of pleasure for the child and the intellectual value of play—the importance of what children already want to do and are doing. Locke's emphasis on the child's pleasure, now an article of faith in pedagogical theory and practice, validates the child's desire, respecting that desire in the process of trying to direct it. It is the child's impressionability to this educative process—the image of the child as blank slate—that is most often recalled and cited from Locke's formulation of childhood. Though this malleability—Locke also refers to the child as "wax, to be moulded and fashioned as one pleases" (*Education*, section 216)—is clearly crucial to Locke's concept of the individual, it works only in tandem with the individuality of the individual. Locke bases childhood education on the recognition of the child's individual character: his desires, pleasures, willfulness, pride, ambition, temperament, tastes, experiences, proclivities, abilities, and limitations.[26] "God has stampt certain Characters upon Men's minds, which, like their shapes, may perhaps be a little mended; but can hardly be totally alter'd, and transform'd into the contrary" (section 66). A parent or teacher must take into account the particularities of these features when appealing to a child's pleasure and pride. If Locke sees the child as a blank slate, receptive to inscriptions and reinscriptions, he also carefully notes that the process of inscribing the child-slate can take place only within the contours of its shape and constitution—"the various Tempers, different Inclinations, and particular Defaults, that are to be found in Children" (section 216).

Education, then, always involves recognizing the presence of personal traits and habits. Indeed, the child in Locke's treatise appears quite formidable, a creature whose willfulness must be regulated and directed. Of all the creatures on earth, none are "half so wilful and proud, or half so desirous to be Masters of themselves and others, as Man" (*Education*, section 35). To overcome this propensity, Locke therefore stresses that children "should be used to submit their Desires, and go without their Longings, even *from their very Cradles*" (section 38). "He that is not used to submit his Will to the Reason of others, when he is Young, will scarce hearken or submit to his own Reason, when he is of an Age to make use of it" (section 36). It is therefore crucial for parents to get children in the habit of submitting. Parents may even have to use physical force to gain their children's submission. Locke generally opposes the use of corporal punishment because he thinks it merely reinforces the child's already excessive preference for personal pleasure. Due to the "Natural Propensity to indulge Corporal and Present Pleasure, and to avoid pain at any rate," a child may temporarily submit to parental authority without developing any lasting respect for that authority. Locke nevertheless reserves this form of punishment as the last pedagogical resort for making children obey. When all other methods fail, beating is appropriate for children who exhibit "Obstinacy or Rebellion" toward parental authority because submission to the parent or tutor who embodies the standard of reasonability is the chief lesson of education (sections 48, 78).

While Locke upholds the authority of standards of reasonability, he stresses that such standards, like all forms of authority, are human contrivances, themselves subject to judgment and change. This is why Locke so dislikes maxims, conventional pieces of knowledge to be recited, and why his pedagogy so little relies on a set curriculum.[27] Despite the limits and imperfections of our knowledge, we still can and do guide our conduct by what we know. For example, "'tis of great use to the Sailor to know the length of his Line, though he cannot with it fathom all the depths of the Ocean. 'Tis well he knows, that it is long enough to reach the bottom, at such Places, as are necessary to direct his Voyage, and caution him against running upon Shoals, that may ruin him. Our Business here is not to know all things, but those which concern our Conduct. If we can find out those Measures, whereby a rational Creature put in that State, which Man is in, in this World, may, and ought to govern his Opinions, and Actions depending thereon, we need not be troubled that some other things escape our Knowledge" (*Essay* 1, i, 6). In the case of children, experience is a continual encounter between their desires and constraints upon those desires. To impress children with the reality and authority of constraints, it is necessary to make them obey the adults who articulate and implement the limitations upon individual behavior.

For the child to become accustomed to measuring and adjusting his conduct, he first must value and internalize proper social practices: the limits upon individual desires and acts. Locke approvingly cites the case of a "prudent and kind Mother" who mastered her daughter's repeated "stubborness" by eight successive beatings in a morning. The mother "had ever after a very ready Compliance and Obedience in all things from her Daughter" (*Education*, section 78). The nature of the child's repeated disobedience—she had resisted the instruction to leave her mother for her nurse—seems from a late-twentieth-century perspective not a matter of fault but a characteristic expression of dependence to be respected and gently assuaged.[28] For Locke, though, the child is less vulnerable to such feelings if properly taught from the start to control all desires and appetites. Yet Locke's schooling in self-denial seeks not to deny the fact of desire but to regulate or redirect it: toward more healthful foods, for example, or in the case of the little girl, from dependence to obedience. Locke respects the child's reality—her desires and feelings—but also ascribes to the child a vast capacity for managing these.

Locke's childrearing plan thus involves expanding the child's range of experience so that he or she may develop proper habits with which to negotiate all events. In the incident of the child who refuses to leave her mother, Locke doesn't disregard the child's sense of need but focuses on the force of will applied to serve that need. Redirecting that will toward pleasing (because obeying) the mother, and toward finding solace in the company of the nurse, Locke familiarizes the child with other sources of satisfaction. Self-regulation need not entail deprivation. By always attending to the child's pleasure, Locke redirects the child's desire toward other objects of fulfillment. This process of accustoming the child to both self-control and alternative means of fulfillment involves continually widening the frame of the child's experience. Locke's childrearing methods accordingly entail regularly exposing the child to various elements and experiences, physical and intellectual. Many of Locke's recommendations regarding children's health—he advocates plenty of open air, the lightest and loosest of

clothing, and hard beds—stress accustoming them to the varieties and
vicissitudes of the environment. "He that is used to hard Lodging at
home, will not miss his Sleep (where he has most need of it) in his
Travels abroad," Locke reasons (*Education*, section 22). In order that
"the Body may be brought to bear almost any Thing," Locke also recommends that from infancy the child "play in the Wind and the Sun
without a Hat," and that "his Feet be washed every day in cold Water;
and to have his Shoes so thin, that they might leak and let in Water,
when ever he comes near it" (sections 9, 7). The strength and vigor
achieved by the body will enable it best to "obey and execute the Orders of the Mind" (section 31) and "as the Strength of the Body lies
chiefly in being able to endure Hardships, so also does that of the
Mind" (section 33). Thus exposing the child to limits to be endured or
surmounted likewise will "set the Mind right, that on all Occasions it
may be disposed to consent to nothing, but what may be suitable to the
Dignity and Excellency of a rational Creature" (section 31). When the
little girl learns to control her desire and to choose alternative objects
of satisfaction, she has affirmed not just her mother's authority but also
her own consensuality, her own authority over herself. Within limits,
she discovers how to exercise power with propriety.

Encountering conflicts between personal desire and external standards, finding alternative objects as well as directions of desire, the
child simultaneously learns the elasticity as well as inevitability of limits. Locke's injunctions to harden body and mind are meant to cultivate
the greatest flexibility in the individual, the ability to manage any situation. Teaching the child to modify his or her behavior means enabling
the child to temper not just individual appetites but also the constraints
upon those appetites. More precisely, the child learns to experience
constraint as a benefit, as an opportunity for self-expression. By initiating and sustaining this dynamic between self and boundaries, the education of children equips them with the means of exercising their
eventual rights as citizens, their compliance with—or defiance of—customary authority. In retaining corporal punishment as a last resort for
the preservation of parental authority, "the last Remedy" (*Education*,
section 83) for a child's disobedience, Locke seems to uphold a far
more hierarchical relation of authority to the individual: the preeminence of parent over child. Yet even in, or especially in, the exercise of
corporal punishment, Locke emphasizes, the point is not to overwhelm

the child with physical force but to appeal to the child's sense of shame. "The shame of the Whipping, and not the Pain, should be the greatest part of the Punishment" because "the Smart of the Rod, if Shame accompanies it not, soon ceases, and is forgotten" (section 78). Efficacious beating must be aimed at the mind, to make the child sensible "of the Fault he has been guilty of" (section 87). Like chastisement and disapproving looks, physical punishment should arouse the child's awareness of disgrace, the shame of appearing in a negative light to others and himself. To heighten this aspect of beating as a general mark of low esteem, Locke emphasizes that the beatings must be conducted dispassionately and ideally by an intermediary rather than the parent. Not only do these provisions prevent the child from developing a sense of enmity toward the parent, but they also remind the child of the public realm of standards in which he is acting and being punished. Whipping in such a fashion then operates like reputation, which as Locke previously has remarked acts like "the Testimony and Applause that other People's Reason, as it were by a common Consent, gives to vertuous and well-ordered Actions" (section 61).[29]

Punishment as well as all the other activities of childhood education appeal to and direct children's associative faculties. When being punished—whether by word, look, withholding rewards, or whipping—the child is encouraged to consider his or her behavior in relation to how others see and evaluate that behavior. The child thus sees himself or herself according to external models and can adjust personal behavior to these models. Training the individual in associative processes, Locke affiliates the self with society. At the same time, Lockean pedagogy produces in that self-reflective and socially minded child the potential critic and reformer of society. The history of the emergence of American society from Anglo-American culture thus begins with the education of the children in the American colonies.[30]

2

The Liberal Lessons of the
New England Primer

Locke's *Thoughts Concerning Education* was probably the most widely read and instituted pedagogical theory in eighteenth-century Anglo-American culture. Lockean pedagogical principles appear prominently throughout eighteenth-century schoolbooks and fiction for children, often in stories of children who made their lives into moral and economic successes, such as *Goody Two-Shoes* and *Giles Gingerbread*, the prototypes of the later Horatio Alger tales.[1] Both Goody Two-Shoes and Giles Gingerbread significantly owe their successes to the fact that they valued and pursued their lessons. Giles actually embodies the importance of education by eating his pastry letters as soon as he learns them, becoming known as "the boy who lived upon learning."[2] An even more pronounced and comprehensive example of Lockean pedagogy can be found in the educational text often called the most important book in the eighteenth-century American nursery, the *New England Primer*.[3]

Alphabet Rhymes and Their Associations

"In Adam's fall / We sinned all," the opening line of the alphabet rhyme with which the *New England Primer* introduces children to language, would seem a classic statement of the heritability of the human condition. The first lesson taught to children along with the first letter is the belief in original sin. They learn that their existence derives from a certain history and that their nature is fundamentally sinful. The couplet encapsulates the child's genealogy as well as the logical connections attributed to that genealogy by Calvinist Christianity. One's membership in a historical community is established through an identification with an individual named Adam.

Yet the accompanying woodblock print pictures Adam, Eve, and the Serpent (with the apple and the tree), a trio of actors in the fateful event. This illustration casts the premier individual act as a drama of influence and interest. (See Figure 2.1.) Some editions of the *Primer* used a slightly different illustration in which Adam, the serpent, and the apple appear without Eve.[4] With or without Eve's presence, the story of Adam's fall appears not as a transgression of God's command— God is nowhere in the frame of Adam's activity—but as an encounter, still in progress, with both an object of temptation and a tempter or two. Here the reader's attention is drawn not to a sense of historical connections between Adam's sinfulness and his or her own condition but to the conditions of Adam's sin. In the picture, Adam's fall occurs in the presence and with the participation of both an intimate ally and an outsider. Also figured in the scene of temptation is the apple, the alluring forbidden object. Thus the picture presents the fall as a series of extenuating circumstances, or at least explanatory ones: Adam's act makes sense; it is fathomable because familiar.

The potential identity between the child and Adam lies not just in the commonality of sinfulness, and hence of mortality, but in the common experience of temptation: in the experiences of desiring things and following the persuasiveness of one's desire or others' advice. Adam appears as a counterpart to the child, not just its avatar; Adam's situation is the child's plight, the child's continual perplexities about doing what he wants and doing what he is told. From what the child has already been told, he knows that human conduct can be at odds with the voices of authority. Long before learning to read, the child has heard rules, admonitions, and information concerning behavior. It is to this stock of encounters in the child's experience that the mnemonic couplets of the *Primer* appeal as they join the inventory of what the child already knows. Thus the project of reading introduced by the *Primer* continues the oral and empirical processes with which the child is heretofore familiar. The story of Adam comes to the child in the

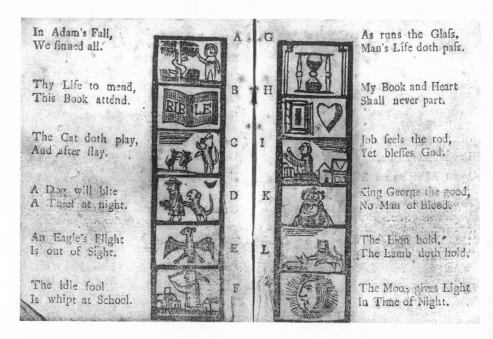

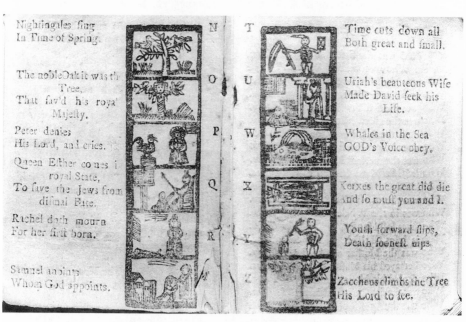

A | In Adam's Fall, We sinned all.
B | Thy Life to mend, This Book attend.
C | The Cat doth play, And after slay.
D | A Dog will bite A Thief at night.
E | An Eagle's Flight Is out of Sight.
F | The idle fool Is whipt at School.
G | As runs the Glass, Man's Life doth pass.
H | My Book and Heart Shall never part.
I | Job feels the rod, Yet blesses God.
K | King George the good, No Man of Blood.
L | The Lion bold, The Lamb doth hold.
M | The Moon gives Light In Time of Night.
N | Nightingales sing In Time of Spring.
O | The noble Oak it was the Tree, That sav'd his royal Majesty.
P | Peter denies His Lord, and cries.
Q | Queen Esther comes in royal State, To save the Jews from dismal Fate.
R | Rachel doth mourn For her first born.
S | Samuel anoints Whom God appoints.
T | Time cuts down all Both great and small.
U | Uriah's beauteous Wife Made David seek his Life.
W | Whales in the Sea GOD's Voice obey.
X | Xerxes the great did die And so must you and I.
Y | Youth forward slips, Death soonest nips.
Z | Zaccheus climbs the Tree His Lord to see.

Figure 2.1. Alphabet rhyme, the *New England Primer* (1756). Courtesy American Antiquarian Society.

child's context, as a subject to be compared and connected with himself and others.

Setting Adam's fall in the present tense, in the child's sense of reality, works to validate individual susceptibility to desire, to personal and public pressure, and to persuasion and argument. The couplet gives the child the example of Adam's weakness—the fact that Adam chose and acted wrongly, the fact that the child could do the same or otherwise. The child therefore can come to understand not only others but also himself as a potentially exemplary (or cautionary) figure. The child's association with Adam, developed in the association between the rhymes and the illustration, establishes the child as the significant actor in this narrative. If the rhyme is intended to inculcate in the child the knowledge of his membership in Christian community and history, its presentation with the illustration imparts a different, though not necessarily incongruent, lesson: the knowledge of his own capacities.

By looking at Adam, the child learns how to make associations, as he connects letters, words, and pictures with each other and with his prior experience and knowledge. The inclusion of the picture helps substantiate the ideas conveyed in the rhyme, supplying reality to the ancient story of Adam. In picturing Adam, the rhyme in the *Primer* acknowledges the child's perspective, the need to appeal to the child's frame of reference.[5] Books and lessons with pictures, Locke had advised, work best in teaching a child to read; the pictorial format "will entertain him much the better, and encourage him to read" (*Education*, section 156).[6] Besides the now canonical counsel to combine learning with play, this recommendation epitomizes Locke's epistemology. According to Locke, all ideas, the materials of what we know, derive from experience. It is "our Observation employ'd either about external sensible Objects; or about the internal Operations of our Minds, perceived and reflected on by ourselves" that "supplies our Understandings with all the materials of thinking" (*Essay* 2, i, 2). Because children have less experience, and a low stock of observations, they especially benefit from the materials supplied by pictures. Concepts presented in books often puzzle or dissatisfy children because "they have no Ideas of them; those ideas being not to be had from Sounds; but from the Things themselves, or their Pictures" (*Education*, section 156). Pictures can supplement the child's empirical experience, which is the foundation of knowledge. So "as soon as [the child] begins to spell, as many Pictures of Animals should be got him, as can be found, with the printed names to them, which at the same time will invite him to read, and Afford him Matter of Inquiry and Knowledge" (*Education*, section 156).[7]

As material substance of inquiry and knowledge, pictures provide the child with greater access to ideas by serving as objective correlatives. While Locke perhaps invested pictures with a questionable primacy, a kind of self-evident reality, his sense of the importance of pictures as translations of ideas into visible objects attests once again to the importance of association in Lockean pedagogy. Whether or not a picture accurately represents an idea, it furnishes the child with matter for comparison, with a figure as well as words to associate with an idea. Thus illustrations induce the process of examining and judging the links between ideas or between various representations of an idea. Since representations usually are conveyed orally to children, in certain tones, by figures of authority or importance, children always receive mediated representations of experience. Pictures make available a more direct apprehension of phenomena than others' words impart. Even as Locke supplies evidence for the child's knowledge, and encourages the child to rely on visual evidence, he presents evidence as another object of scrutiny, as an object requiring inquiry and validation. Pictures do not supply children with a simple positive sense of the world; rather, they introduce children to, as they assist them with, the task of thinking.

By exhibiting Adam as the child's counterpart rather than merely progenitor and patriarch, the alphabet rhyme illustration invites the child to consider Adam's act in terms of his own experience. Adam's appearance here differs markedly from both the seventeenth-century iconography of Adam as a patriarch as well as the nineteenth-century image of Adam as an emblem of individual innocence.[8] The aim of the illustrated rhyme is to make the child see the self as first distinct from custom and then in relation to it: Adam appears both as an individual familiar to the child's sense of personal experience and as an example of the generality of experience. Adam's history is the content of a customary recitation, but that content precedes the customary form in which it now resides. Seeing Adam apart from and within the frame of religious chronology, the child learns his own consensual relation to specific institutions and customs. He learns that he can reject or affirm the community into which he was born.

In seeing Adam's sin in light of his own experiences of temptation, the child also apprehends the principles of agency and consequentiality as at once immediate and historical. Already knowing the effects of many of his own acts, he can understand readily that Adam's act had consequences. The consequences of Adam's sin predictably are reiterated throughout the rhyme in the many references to mortality, ever-present reminders that "As runs the Glass / Man's life doth pass." These references come ever closer to the child as the letter *T* is conjoined with the reminder that "Time cuts down / Both great and small," and the letter *X* is coupled with the information that "Xerxes the great did die / And so must you and I." Finally, to link the child with the inevitability of mortality, the letter *Y* is marked by a rhyme that particularly relates death to the ephemerality of childhood: "Youth forward slips / Death soonest nips," or as in a rhyme version placed in later editions of the *Primer*, "While youth do cheer / Death may be near."

The fact of mortality stands not just as a feature of human experience but as one of many facts, both disturbing and reassuring, about natural phenomena that are conveyed in a series of pithy sayings such as "The Cat doth play / And after slay" and "The Lion bold / The Lamb doth hold," or "The Moon gives light / In time of night" and "Nightingales sing / In time of Spring." Sometimes these facts are neutral descriptions, as in the case of the couplet "An eagle's flight / Is out of sight," which appends the letter *E*. In other cases, the couplets transmit a sense of consequentiality that recapitulates the message of the child's susceptibility to sin and liability to punishment. The cultural order provides examples of crime and punishment—"A Dog will bite / A Thief at night" and, in a vignette closer to the child's experience, "The Idle Fool / Is whipt at School"—while the natural order illustrates proper subordination as "Whales in the Sea / God's Voice obey."

The *New England Primer* thus presents the child with a set of experiential and imaginative connections: an identification with Adam, a familiarity with facts of nature and an understanding of these facts and phenomena as emanating from God, and the moral and physical relations of cause and effect. While this presentation furnishes the child with an outline of the American Puritan doctrine of original sin and personal responsibility, the associative character of the presentation permits a very broad or loose interpretation of one's Puritan identity. This pedagogy of the alphabet roots the child more in the general val-

ues of Protestantism—individualism and self-discipline—than in a specifically Puritan character. There is no mention here of covenant and
election, the signifiers of the Puritans as God's chosen people. Following the Lockean tenet of cultivating the child's associative faculty, the
rhyme offers its sets of connections; rather than developing a distinctive portrait of these connections as the particular components of Puritan identity, the rhyme introduces the child to the fundamental techniques from which Reformation definitions of the self arise: reading
and interpretation. When the rhyme directly counsels the child, it recommends "Thy Life to Mend / This Book Attend." The accompanying woodblock displays an open book labeled "BIBLE" in large capital
letters. Preceding this recommended book, of course, is this book at
hand, or in hand, the *New England Primer.* As the *Primer* delineates
the alphabet, syllabication, and spelling, as well as presenting hymns,
prayers, Biblical stories, Puritan biography, and the reformed catechism, it supplies the child with the appropriate means and materials of
reading, and therefore of mending or remaking the self. Equipping the
child with the skills for approaching the Bible, the *Primer* also serves as
a prototype of the sacred book by introducing the child to some of the
features of Christian history and doctrine. Attending to the *Primer* establishes the crucial role of reading in the child's life, the connection
between self and books. "My Book and Heart / Shall never part" runs
the rhyme for the letter *H,* stating the intellectual requirements for
Protestant religious identity.

The very ambiguity of the referent for "this book" just described
demonstrates the potential difficulties of associative operations that
Locke described and eighteenth-century Americans encountered as
they employed those operations in their pedagogy. While the child
may link the *Primer* with the Bible, understanding both as "thy book,"
the difference between the two—the lesson of the supremacy of the
book that the child is to make his life's study—can get lost. To resolve
the ambiguity in favor of the Bible as the primary point of reference requires the child to examine the associated objects or ideas and to determine whether the link between them arises from what Locke called
"visible agreement" or from "prevailing or habitual custom." The picture of the book labeled "BIBLE" thus is a crucial pedagogical tactic to
produce visible agreement. At the same time, the *Primer,* visible and
palpable to the child, meets the standard of visibility and recogniz-

ability. In this critical exercise, the child still may not come to comprehend the unique significance of the Bible. Before appreciating the importance of the Bible, the child may need to see or hear more material,
such as the religious instruction of the reformed catechism that also
always appeared in the *Primer*. Thus, even as the *Primer* encourages
empiricism in the child, it constructs and supplies the conditions
and scope of observation. Following Lockean educational theory, the
Primer exhibits and utilizes the conventionality of empiricism: the customary ways by which vision is directed toward predetermined or desired conclusions. Pedagogy obviously always entails this conventionality since education strives to impart specific information and materials.
Locke's understanding of the conventional structure of experience and
perception (and hence education) shapes the pedagogical design of the
Primer, which acknowledges that reaching conclusions entails a continual consideration of conventions—even when the most conspicuous
traces of the customary are eliminated, and even when the child seems
to be proceeding solely according to his own cognitions.

Directing the Child

To respect and honor personal perception creates more work for the
individual, as Locke and the Puritans, political reformers, and Church
dissenters realized. At the same time, the shaping of this hard-working
reflective individual generates the production of more materials for
his observation. Information proliferates to supply the needs of the
consensual individual; as the continuous printings of the *New England
Primer* since the late seventeenth century show, the liberal individual
emerges in tandem with the expanding businesses of publishing and
pedagogy. Thus the activity of informing consent inaugurates the modern information age, with its attendant tensions about individual freedom and the influence of all the informational modes that surround the
individual. Eighteenth-century concerns with the propriety and utility
of literature (especially the effects of fiction), the advantages and disad-
vantages of imaginative activity, and moral and practical education—all
copiously documented and still central to American debates about personal freedom—register a keen sense of the power of informational
techniques. In the wake of Foucault's studies of the emergence and
functions of institutions of knowledge, many scholars of the eighteenth

century have emphasized the supervisory aspects of educating individuals.[9] In a similar vein, many twentieth-century critics of Puritanism stressed the repressive features of Puritan education and practice.[10] From a variety of twentieth-century perspectives, training persons to internalize certain principles of selfhood appears to undermine if not violate the ideal of self-determination.

Yet self-determination as Locke formulated it entails making the self an object of management while designating the individual as the rightful manager of himself. That managers themselves can be and are subject to external influence is an ongoing difficulty for individuals, but this difficulty is not a new paradigm of subjection. Rather it is the condition of all subjectivity, one significantly given to individuals themselves to govern and negotiate. This is why looking at oneself to appraise what one assimilates and endorses is the crucial activity of the modern liberal self. Thinkers in the liberal tradition are far more idealistic than Locke himself about what such self-consciousness can accomplish. Thus the liberal individual often appears to its critics as a fantasy of individual power and clarity.[11] The Lockean individual is not necessarily especially enlightened or well-equipped to conduct its appraisals, and in making those appraisals, this individual is limited by personal experience and particular circumstances, such as familial, social, religious, economic, and geographical stations. All such positions, however, are subject to scrutiny and change. Thus as the self becomes a primary object of investigation, so do the circumstances of the self. Concomitantly, the stakes rise in establishing the best circumstances of the self. Reform plans acquire a directive style of their own in opposition to the systems that they would replace. Precisely because the Puritans recognized and therefore feared the effectiveness of institutions like monarchy and papacy, they sought institutional foundations for their own alternative values.

Puritan parents, passionately committed to a specific spiritual identity, tried to establish in their children the same sense of character and purpose. They accordingly adopted the Lockean method of beginning to direct children's interests at a very early age. In his own pedagogical plan, Locke regularly stacks the deck presented to the child. He frankly sets out to bring the child into accord with the parents' wishes and values. If the child learns best by personal experience, the parents or teachers still can determine the shape and content of experience available to the child. Thus Locke sets obedience to adult authority as the primary lesson for the child. For Locke, this lesson does not contradict the child's entitlement to self-determination; instead, the child's compliance is a temporary condition, like physical and practical incapacities, that once surpassed will eventuate in independence. During the period of dependence and compliance, Locke aims to establish continuity between parents and children, to furnish a means of perpetuating values, thereby forestalling possible disruptions resulting from rearrangements of society by each new generation. Locke meets the risk of self-determination with education in self-determination. For the Puritans, who are spiritually as well as socially dedicated to Reformation principles of individuality, the risk of self-determination looms even larger: if a child deviates from parental commitments, the church society of the parents loses a member and the promise of the church's perpetuity. Indoctrinating children into church society, however, runs at odds with the tenet of individual freedom of interpretation that underwrites Reformation critiques of the institutions of church and monarchy. Bearing in mind their commitment to individual interpretation, American Puritans undertook indoctrination in the Lockean attitude: as a practical and precautionary measure to precede the inevitable moment when children will make and follow their own decisions. Yet from a Puritan perspective, from their historical standpoint of witnessing generational decreases in membership as well as departures from orthodox practices, Locke's pedagogy still permitted too much range for the child. By its very elasticity, its encouragement to the child to make connections and choices, the associative method cannot predict what conclusions the child will ultimately reach or maintain. Lockean pedagogy cannot ensure that the child will accept the supreme authority of the Bible, the *Primer,* or indeed any book.

To tighten the range of associations and more closely direct the child toward Puritan history and dogma, some mid- and late-eighteenth-century editions of the *New England Primer* use a slightly different rhyme alphabet in which the fact of death appears more personal and punitive. (See Figure 2.2.) In what has been called the evangelicized rhyme, the child encounters not just death, but death as an act of divine wrath.[12] God's destructiveness is manifest in the instances when "the deluge drown'd / the earth around" or when Lot "Saw fiery shower / On Sodom pour" or when "Proud Korah's Troop / Was swallowed up."

Figure 2.2. Evangelicized alphabet rhyme, the *New England Primer* (1767). Courtesy American Antiquarian Society.

To underscore further the terrible repercussions of sin, the alphabet rhyme includes analogues to Adam's disobedience, recalling Peter who "deny'd / His Lord and cry'd" and Vashti who for the sin of "Pride / was set aside." The earlier version of the rhyme had recounted instances of sinfulness but not as cause for punishment. The story of David's commission of adultery and murder—"Uriah's beauteous Wife / Made David seek his Life"—appears as a mere description of covetousness. In the admonitory style of the evangelicized *Primer* editions that appear from the mid to late eighteenth century, the consequences of such sins become paramount as the child is reminded of what happened to Sodom, Peter, and Vashti.

This series of cautionary tales carries weight, however, only because Christ died for human sins, thus providing the possibility of Christian salvation despite Adam's (and hence, everyone's) sinfulness. Thus in another significant change, the rhyme "Christ crucify'd / For sinners dy'd" replaces the cat at play couplet accompanying the letter *C.* To eliminate any ambiguity about what book to study, the couplet for the letter *B* now reads "Heaven to find / The Bible Mind." The hope for heaven offers a welcome alternative to the fear of punishment. To give the child reason and models for seeking redemption from the chronicles of sin, the *Primer* alphabet rhyme accordingly includes a series of verses of exemplary conduct: Job who "feels the Rod / Yet blesses God," Moses who "Israel's host / Led thro' the Sea," Noah who "did view / The old World and new," and Queen Esther who "saves the Jews." These examples encourage children to emulate admirable figures and, more importantly, to make them understand that they can shape themselves.[13]

Children as well as adults thus typify proper behavior in the evangelicized version of the rhyme: the revised alphabet recalls "Young Obadias, David, and Josias," who "all were pious," young pious Ruth who "Left all for Truth," young Samuel who "The Lord did fear," and "young Timothy" who "Learnt Sin to fly." More striking and memorable than these child exemplars are the children of the Protestant martyr John Rogers, who watch their father being burned at the stake in the picture that seems to have appeared in every edition of the *Primer.* (See Figure 2.3.) What stands out about this depiction of martyrdom is not just the exemplariness of the father, whose faith is elaborated in the accompanying "Advice to his Children" verses, but the witnessing role of

Figure 2.3. Woodblock, "The Martyrdom of John Rogers," the *New England Primer* (ca. 1780). By courtesy of the Trustees of the Boston Public Library.

the children.[14] Besides showing starkly the awfulness of the father's death—conjoined to a sense of the saintliness of the father's conduct and suffering—the picture foregrounds the presence of the children at this event. Their presence affirms the father's example, as they witness and internalize it. The child reader who encounters this scene thus can percieve himself in the position of observing and ratifying human behavior, including the behavior of his parents and himself.

In the woodblock of the Rogers family, the historical martyrdom appears a contemporary familial scene, making the events of Biblical history more immediate.[15] What also becomes immediate for the child reader is the potential reality of his or her own parents' deaths, an eventuality that every child must accept. Another purpose of the John Rogers story is to link the child reader with the Rogers children against the anti-Protestants who are so brutally killing their father. In linking Protestant identity to familial relations, the story and picture weld the child's filial feelings to the parent's religious identity.

To make this point, the *New England Primer* easily could have drawn on the rich seventeenth-century tradition of child piety narratives. In these narratives, best known through James Janeway's often published collection *A Token for Children*, exemplary children willingly go to early deaths that bring them into God's presence.[16] Though not martyrs for their faith, these children suffer pain and illness and the fear of death, and in the process manage to counsel and comfort their parents about losing them. Cotton Mather, among many other American Puritan ministers, contributed narratives of more pious children to this genre, calling his collection *A Token for the Children of New England.*[17] One of Mather's narratives chronicled the piety of his older brother Nathanael, who died at nineteen. Nathanael, like many of the much younger subjects of Mather's collection, diligently pursued his duty toward God, so much so that he neglected his health.[18] Most of these children seem not only to welcome but court death: thirteen-year-old John Clap of Scituate refused sustenance for six days, "with his teeth so shut, as they could not be opened" until he opened them to pray "Lord Jesus, receive my Spirit," and then died (10–11); similarly, when five-year-old Ann Greenough "fell sick at last of a Consumption, she would not by any Sports be diverted from the Thoughts of Death, wherein she took such pleasure, that she did not care to hear of anything else" (20–21). Another five-year-old, while playing with a top, suddenly "flung away his Top, and ran to his Mother, and said, 'O Mother, I must go to God, will you go with me?'"[19] Usually the children in these stories prefer to go to God alone, culminating a life-long pursuit of a private relationship with God. One of the foremost features of the piety narratives is the child's independent acceptance of religious duty, the self-determination of the child's spiritual pursuit. Janeway memorializes the autonomous exercises of piety by children such as Sarah Howley, who from the age of eight "was very much in secret Prayer" (3) and four-year-old Mary A., who was "wont to be much in secret Duty" (20). These children appear already in a different form of existence, already removed from the conventional activities of childhood.

As striking as these stories are—historians of children's literature and education almost routinely register horror at what they take to be the morbidity and grimness of this literature—they disappear over the course of the eighteenth century as publishers and pedagogues implemented the Lockean tactic of forming literature to please rather than frighten children. Yet the very severity of the child piety narratives would seem to recommend them to the mid-eighteenth-century American enterprise of setting children's education on more direct religious paths. Child exemplars, especially those in recent history and those who inhabited the same colonial America in which the readers of the *Primer* were growing up, would appear perfect subjects to include in the revised *Primer*s. The preference for continued usage of the John Rogers martyrdom story and picture marks the way in which this standard iconography of piety within a Lockean pedagogical ethos becomes a new and revised type of the seventeenth-century child piety narrative. Even better than the record of saintly colonial American children, the portrait of the Rogers children stresses the task that children should undertake: the duty of learning, remembering, and practicing their religion, a duty that they can learn from parents and that they must independently follow. Stories of children who die early may prepare children for the inevitability of death but they may also appear remote from the more immediate reality, from the lives that children are presently living.[20] More significantly, the portrait of the Rogers children captures the most immediate condition of the child reader, the state of witnessing and absorbing experience, or presentations of experience. Imaging the reader's position while encouraging the reader's identification with the watching Rogers children, the picture acknowledges the state of watchfulness and receptivity in which every child lives.

This recognition of the child's mental states manifests a more modern pedagogical strategy than the fear and consolation tactic of earlier child piety narratives. More exactly, the child piety narrative gets updated and intensified in the woodblock print of the Rogers family. The Lockean pedagogical possibilities discovered in the old picture are so generally recognized that by the end of the eighteenth century editors of the *Primer* often delete the accompanying text of John Rogers's *Advice to My Children*. The crucial aspect of the John Rogers martyrdom is now the witnessing function of children. What makes this role of children an effective way of linking them to Puritanism is its emphasis on individual encounters with experience, most often experience at a temporal and representational remove. Temporally removed from Roger's own acts, the child can forge connections to his example only through cognitive operations. By the exercise of individuality, the child forms a relation to the traditions into which he is born.

So it is not surprising that Jonathan Edwards, the most Lockean as well as orthodox of eighteenth-century Calvinists in America, defines the proper human relation to God and to God's creation as consensual, as "the cordial consent or union of being to Being in general."[21] Consent, in Edwards's formulation, consists in "propensity and union of heart to Being" (540), in the active posture of an "intelligent being" toward "being in general" (542). Accenting the individual's response to deity and creation, to the divine horizons of existence, Edwards reasserts the Protestant tradition of individuality, which is of course the context from which Locke's conception of consent also emerges.[22] In Locke's accounts of the cognitve processes of consent, Edwards found the empirical terms with which to describe and analyze religious experience.

To recognize and realize a consensual union with God, Edwards and other revivalists elaborated the Lockean evidentiary imperative in consent. Arguing that consent stems from judgments that humans make on a hopefully sound basis, Locke underscored the role of associations in judgments and the subsequent importance of testing, justifying, and adjusting associations. Edwards initially takes from Locke an elasticity about the coordinates of consent when he admits personal testimony, physical signs, and even circumstantial evidence, in addition to formal criteria (such as church requirements), as proofs for validating the individual's affiliation with God and the Christian community. The mass conversions of the Great Awakening in America therefore both relied on and raised questions about various kinds of evidence. Edwards, though an early instigator and celebrant of revivalist encounters in which individuals discovered intensely personal ties to God, remembers Locke's injunction to reflect on experience and judgment. Accordingly, Edwards was also one of the foremost skeptics and critics of the veracity of the dramatic conversionary experiences reported throughout the colonies. His efforts to define the "true nature of religious affections" address the problems generated by the consensual account of individual social and religious relations. By appealing to human judgment, consent raises the questions of how individuals arrive at their understandings, what standards they employ, what internal motivations and external influences operate in this process.[23] If religious feelings are to be distinctive registers of intimacy with God, they require differentiation from mass emotions to which all persons may be subject.

Edwards's insistence on the Calvinist dogma of election—God's predetermination of each individual's salvation—during a time when most Puritans were moving to more flexible notions of church membership that would keep children in the church largely by generational ties, reasserted God's sovereignty over social arrangements. For Edwards, the initial Protestant challenge to earthly authorities, ecclesiastical and political, affirms the primacy of the deity in human affairs. Edwards's adherence to early Puritan doctrine reflects his belief in the spiritual hierarchy that the Puritans originally strove to reinstate. The particularity of Puritan identity rests in the supremacy of God, a supremacy most vividly marked in the absolute dependence of humans upon God's will. While human subjugation manifests the almighty power of God, Edwards stresses that the subjugation is consensual. Individuals must and do follow their own interpretations of their relation to God. But in this process they must learn the inevitable lesson of uncertainty: no one can ever be absolutely sure of the rightness of his judgments. Certainty exists only in God. Though the fact of divine perfection and omnipotence qualifies the scope of individual authority, it never releases individuals from the responsibility to exercise their wills. God certainly limits the scope of human will, but within that limit humans do and must act and suffer consequences.[24]

In light of the capacity and responsibility for choice accorded the child in Lockean pedagogy and psychology, the Calvinist doctrine of original sin, which so distinguished and so troubled the American Puritan sense of identity, emerges as a mark of self-determination. By the grace of Christ, individuals could be saved, could have their own histories. Their agency in their salvation begins with their infancy, their arrival in the world as simultaneously limited and consensual creatures. The apparent morbidity, if not cruelty, of the child piety narrative embedded in the *New England Primer*, and in Edwards's own sermons, tends to obscure the empowerment of the child that such representations envision and propel.[25] The awfulness of that empowerment is the child's fundamental individuality, the child's aloneness. Unmooring children from the heritability of spiritual and socioeconomic rank (which in both cases means detaching children from parents) sets them on a precarious course equipped only with their own resources. Edwards assuages the difficulties of this condition with the reminder that the individual's dominion over himself or herself is only a subset of God's dominion. Placing children in the simultaneously terrifying and empowering ethos of the consequentiality of individual choice, Edwards provides them with the Puritan dogma of election that supplements as well as supercedes the provenance of individual choice. The child may be alone but nonetheless is—by the grace of God—divinely equipped for his tasks.

Congruent with the logic articulated by Edwards, the evangelicized rhymes remind children of the limits of their existence as they encourage children to exercise their powers within those limits. As the *Primer* rhyme conveys the primary tenets of Calvinist Christian doctrine, its very cautionary mode, augmented by pictures as well as by parental admonitions, alerts the child to the consequentiality of his own choices and acts, which is to say, to the importance of his own determinations: to the reputation he can attain. Though the child cannot help but be like Adam, he can still be like Obadias, David, and Josias—or Ruth, Samuel, and Timothy. These examplars, like the redemptive figure of Christ in the New Testament, suggest second acts to an Adamic human history, a chance to make better choices. The possibilities of choice also figure in other regular parts of *Primer*, most notably in the dialogue between a youth, Christ, and Satan in which a youth vacillates between obeying God's word and following the Devil's advice.[26] The young man takes the latter path but then wants to change his allegiance. Too late, he realizes the finality—and fatality—of his choice. As much as this dialogue teaches the lesson of making the right choice, it also makes clear that choice is not a state of perpetual options: choice is an action with inescapable obligations. Entitling the child to choice accustoms him to lawfulness, as the child learns the positive and negative effects of particular choices.

The Calvinistic edge to individuality recalled by Edwards and the evangelicized rhyme harmonizes with the Lockean injunction to review one's associations and judgments. Though Edwards's religious vision never gained endorsement, his use of Lockean principles instituted in American culture the centrality of individual experience. Thus the pedagogical modernization and religious returns of the *Primer* could proceed in tandem. The attempt to weld the readers of the

Primer to Puritanism coincides with other changes in the *Primer* that appeal to contemporary readers' immediate experience and affiliations. Along with the evangelicized alphabet rhymes, other rhymes and alphabets surface in the late-eighteenth-century editions. In the increasingly Americanized versions of the *Primer*, mentions of London become mentions of Boston and antimonarchical references begin to appear, such as "Kings should be good / Not men of Blood" or "Queens and Kings / Are gaudy things" or "Queens and Kings must / Lie in the Dust." After the Revolution, the letter *W* is most often associated with Washington, as in the couplet "By Washington / Great deeds were done." With the waning of orthodox Puritanism even after, or more likely due to, the mid-century evangelical movements, the more secular old alphabet rhymes reappear. By 1800, *New England Primer*s regularly included this alphabet:

> A was an Angler, and fished with a hook.
> B was a Blockhead, and ne'er learn'd his book.
> C The Cat doth play and after slay.[27]

The cat returns to the position in which Christ had been inserted. The Protestant tenets remain in the rhymes, as well as in the catechism, moral tales, and continued appearance of John Rogers and his children, but they are now parts of a less dogmatic format. The frame of reference in which children learn literacy and Protestant Christian beliefs is no longer Anglo-American history but American society, in which church and government are not integrally tied. What was once so closely identified with Puritanism—the individual's intellectual and spiritual consensuality—becomes the American range.

Over the course of the eighteenth century, Americans learned to read, write, and spell from the *New England Primer* or primers modeled after it. The Lockean educational techniques so effectively employed by the *Primer* therefore extended the principle of the child's consent far beyond the Puritans. New York Anglicans and Philadelphia Quakers reprinted the *New England Primer*, as did the Deist Ben Franklin; all found in it a pedagogy well suited to local circumstances and individual beliefs.[28] The Puritans rightly feared the generality and breadth of the *Primer*, which could serve so many individual perspectives. The cognitive process of consent taught by the *Primer* served the Puritan purpose of encouraging children to join the religious community of their parents, but this lesson could also be applied to other forms of membership and used by persons other than Puritan children.

That anyone could claim membership in God's chosen people is manifest in a moral anecdote included in *The Columbian Reading Book; or, Historical Preceptor,* a popular reader in the early republic. The brief story runs thus:

> A white man meeting an Indian asked him, "whose Indian are you?" To which the copper-faced genius replied, "I am God Almighty's Indian: whose Indian are you?"

This story appears as an example of "the retort courteous," and the Indian's social and intellectual facility is furthermore marked by the title "the Clever Indian" on the accompanying woodblock illustration of this encounter.[29]

While the anecdote shows the extensiveness of the liberal logic of social membership, it also marks the readiness with which race could be employed to uphold the exclusivity of society. The "copper-faced genius" makes his point as an anomaly; his exceptional acumen makes him the equal of the white man. Only by being a prodigy and an exemplar can the Indian qualify as one of God Almighty's children. When in the 1770s the slave girl Phillis Wheatley attracted public attention for her poetry, her achievement likewise was considered an exception to the general nature of her race. The case of the child prodigy, even more so than the figure of the consensual child, suggests the nonexclusivity of adult attributes. Wheatley's talent generated more interest for her assumed exceptionality from her race than for her actual exceptionality from her age group.[30] In this way, race could be invoked to uphold both racial and age distinctions. Since the eighteenth century, the use of age as a term of denigration has regularly accompanied notions of racial inferiority, as in representations of American Indians and blacks as children. But when persons are classed as children in this manner, the category of classification summons the pre-Lockean definition of children: the understanding of children as subordinates.[31]

Well into the nineteenth century, the *New England Primer* continued to furnish the foundations of literacy and intellection through which individuals could assess their world and articulate themselves. At the basis of these fundamentals lies the child's capacity and responsibility for choice. The identifications between words and pictures, models and self, past and present, initiated by the *Primer* set the child on a reflective course for making decisions. In the American Puritan implementation of Lockean pedagogy, the Lockean type of the consensual child thus emerges, prepared to ratify his membership in the religious-political society in which he is born. Long before the American Revolution, American Puritans discovered that the child may choose not to ratify that membership or may choose new identifications, to consent to new or other affiliations. Though the *Primer* supplied children with specific models and conditions of choice, thereby designating the materials as well as delimiting the scope of consent, no such liberal pedagogy could ever guarantee that the child's choices would conform to and confirm the parent's allegiances. The *Primer* thus bequeathed to Americans the Lockean legacy of self-determination and the ongoing task that comes with it: determining how we know if we are the we chronicled in Adam's fall, and deciding if we want to continue to regard ourselves as members of the all who identify themselves this way.

3

Fables and the Forming
of Americans

After the Revolution, American children still studied the *New England Primer,* now learning alphabet rhymes in which *W* referred to "Great Washington brave" who "His country did save."[1] Over the course of the eighteenth century the rhyme for *K* had changed from "King Charles the Good / No Man of Blood" to "Kings should be good / Not men of Blood" to the frankly antimonarchical statements "The British King / Lost States thirteen" and "Queens and Kings / Are gaudy things."[2] Even as editions of the *Primer* continued to convey the fundamentally Protestant inflections of the rhyme (evangelicized or unevangelicized), they presented new nationalist associations. Instead of displaying a portrait of one of the King Georges in the frontispiece, post-Revolutionary editions of the *Primer* showed portraits of John Hancock and Sam Adams as well as George Washington.[3] The project of teaching children an American identity proceeded through these revised primers and, on a larger scale, through the concerted production of distinctly American textbooks and reference guides—dictionaries, spellers, readers, geographies, histories, and arithmetics. Using American environment and experience as a frame of reference, these pedagogical books taught national affiliation along with basic cognitive skills.

Here we see the emergence of the now familiar correlation of American identity with an experience of the right books, the books deemed

best suited to prepare young persons for life as Americans. Current debates in and outside the academy over curricula, canons, and multicul-
turalism reiterate the nation's enduring faith in fiction's power to bring
persons to the places or positions that it represents. Sharp disagree-
ments exist over definitions of persons, places, and positions, but all
sides of these debates invoke and promote literary nationalism as they
advocate the forms of literature that they think best promulgate their
conceptions of American values.[4]

What often gets lost in these debates, and what immediately gets ob-
scured in the first round of this debate on national education, is the unpredictability of literary identifications. Presenting a reader with points
of association does not ensure that the reader credits and affirms the association. Moreover, the content of associations can and does alter. Just
as the alphabet rhymes register changes in values and commitments,
the content of children's readers consists of narratives already often
told and revised. Thus, the identification a reader makes with a literary
representation—an identification either desired or feared by social ar-
biters—is a connection to a variable if not evanescent entity. Models of
American identity are themselves changing imaginative patterns rather
than permanently set types. These patterns develop from new understandings or arrangements of old standards. Through the history of
different readings of a text, we can track the process of our cultural
patterns.

The realignments of referents in the primer alphabets exemplify just
one instance of a revisionary response to old texts. Besides the alphabet
rhymes, the most often employed and endorsed pedagogical forms in
eighteenth-century America included some of the most long-standing
educational genres. Fables and moral tales figure prominently in textbooks before and after the Revolution. As they continue to appear, they
vary in language and emphasis, sometimes dropping or adding endings.
These compact fictions, regularly retold and revised over many centuries, persist in the American curriculum; their status as one of our pedagogical resources bears witness now, as in the eighteenth century, to
the activities of interpretation and selection that stories both generate
and receive. In interpreting and selecting the lessons of fables, early
Americans put into practice the exercise of judgment recommended by
Locke. Their conclusions and choices emerge from, as they foreclose
on, a range of associations—the other perspectives always available in

reading that get occluded and forgotten. The fables recited to and read by eighteenth-century schoolchildren thus provide a record of the mental connections that come to be understood as characteristically American. The record shows how the forming of Americans depended upon the activities of associative thinking that fables instill, how the very idea of an American identity derived from not a strictly mimetic but a consensual model of identification.

Association and Identity

When the national conversation on education and American identity first began, in the 1770s and 1780s, cultural nationalists such as Noah Webster advocated and wrote schoolbooks "attentive to the political interest of America."[5] Sharing Webster's sense of the importance of an unique American language, history, and geography, Benjamin Rush urged his contemporaries "to adapt [their] modes of teaching to the peculiar form of [their] government."[6] In their educational plans, Webster and Rush envision the task of forming Americans as one of presenting youth with literature filled with what they deem American objects, features of American experience. In such representations of American society, young persons will find models to desire and copy.

Fables obviously do not feature American heroes or landscapes, and therefore might appear at odds with the cultural nationalist emphasis on the locality of identity. Yet fables demonstrate better than the insistent Americanism of late-eighteenth-century rhetoric how the actual evolution of American culture from colonies to confederation to nation over the course of the century proceeded from a belief in the changeability of the self's local affiliations. The sense of a distinctly American identity emerges not from schooling in American objects but from familiarity and engagement with both European and colonial cultural forms.[7] The texts through which Rush, Webster, and other eighteenth-century Americans learned language and social relations notably suggest a certain irrelevance of the local origins of both readers and representational objects.

As the differing versions of the *New England Primer* demonstrate, early American education follows the Lockean conception of identity development as an individual process of considering and applying universals. In Locke's view, persons inevitably and perpetually operate mimetically, which is to say in relation to representations. Persons also inevitably differ in their relations to representations. Whether they emulate, reject, or ignore a representation depends upon what associations an individual "Mind makes in it self either voluntarily, or by chance." Hence the ideas and responses generated by any representation come "in different Men to be very different, according to their different Inclinations, Educations, Interests, etc."[8] The standard mimetic correspondence that cultural nationalists envision is therefore a myth, a pattern that denies the features of individuality.

Locke, attentive to the varieties of individuality, provides a consensual model of relating to reading. In his view, the task of education is not to set and enforce connections but to afford the child the opportunity to form, consider, question, and finally, affirm connections. Because of what Locke calls the common "Disease" or "Madness" of making unreasonable connections of ideas "wholly owing to Chance or Custom," it is crucial "that those who have Children, or the charge of their Education, would think it worth their while diligently to watch, and carefully to prevent the undue Connexion of Ideas in the Minds of young People" (*Essay* 2, xxxiii, 3, 5, 8). To steer children away from making the wrong associations of ideas, Locke recommends "principling" them "in their tender years" to examine fully all associations, whatever their source—personal experience, ancient authority, custom, or chance.[9] Because books commonly function as sources of authority, "there is no part wherein the understanding needs a more careful and wary conduct than in the use of books" (*Conduct*, 55). Locke therefore stresses that reading be a testing of writers' associations of ideas: to read for knowledge and understanding is to "enter into their reasoning, examine their proofs, and then judge of the truth or falsehood, probability or improbability of what they advance" (*Conduct*, 57). By this account, a book is suitable for American children not because of the local character of its representations, but because of a quite different notion of recognizability: the book's intelligibility to children. "Some easy pleasant book" appropriate to the child's capacity, Locke advises, will both entertain and encourage the child to think.[10] The child unavoidably will bring local customs to her reading.

In line with Locke's advice, eighteenth-century books for children supplied models of associative thinking: words and pictures, rules and applications, questions and answers.[11] Clearly British Protestant in character, these books assumed the universality of Christianity. Their inclusion of imaginative literature—in the form of fables—conveyed an even more ancient and extensive literary tradition originating with the East Indians, Arabs, and Greeks. Learning from fables entails identifying oneself with or distinguishing oneself from literary figures, usually personified animals. The very generality of fables, their historic and geographical scope, invites readers or auditors to consider their local experience within the context of a general rule, according to an external standard that seems to transcend historical and cultural boundaries. The acceptance of an ancient proverb, though, may indicate merely the automatic respect that a student is instructed to muster for it, as in the case of memorizing catechism. Or acceptance (as well as rejection) of the fable's moral may signify the student's imaginative exploration of the fable's possible correlations with her own experience: a recontextualization of both the fable and the reader.[12]

The didactic effectiveness of the primers and readers thus depends upon an integration of two facets of mimesis: the appeal to reality by replicating or promoting a version of it, and the appeal to desire by introducing unfamiliar or different types and frames of experience. While the practice of publishing fables with accompanying moral interpretations would appear a doctrinaire pedagogical procedure of directing mimetic effects upon readers, this custom also can encourage readers to examine and evaluate not just the relation between themselves and a text, but also the relations within the text, between fable and moral. It is this intellectually stimulating quality of fables in general that leads Locke to "think *Aesop's Fables* the best" book to give children learning to read (*Education*, section 156).

Locke adds that the entertainment and enlightenment of children will be more certain if "the *Aesop's Fables* has pictures in it." For children to have ideas of unfamiliar objects, they must obtain the ideas from "the things themselves, or their Pictures." Therefore, as soon as children begin to spell, they should be supplied with "as many pictures of animals . . . as can be found" along with their printed names (*Education*, section 156). Because "diagrams drawn on Paper are Copies of the Ideas in the Mind, and not liable to the Uncertainty that Words carry in their Signification" (*Essay* 4, iii, 19), pictorial representations will help children make the right associations between ideas and words, and among ideas.[13] While Locke perhaps oversimplified the clarity of the

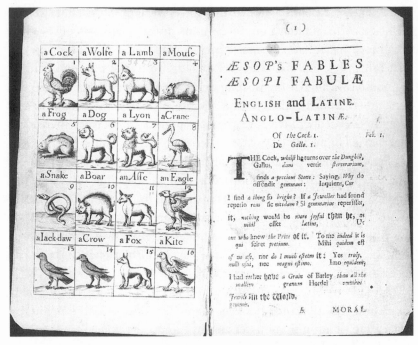

Figure 3.1. Frontispiece to Locke's edition of *Aesop's Fables in English and Latin* (London, 1703). The Pierpont Morgan Library, New York, PML 65064.

pictorial, his pedagogical method of using pictures is less significant as a registration of the inadequacies of words or superiority of pictures than as another instance of the associative exercises he promoted. The paradigm of fables and pictures provides occasions for matching, relating, and judging.[14] (See Figure 3.1.)

At the same time, the sight of fables with pictures draws attention to the continual encounter with and relations to representational forms that learning involves. Children and the adults that they become regularly experience and employ "copies" of ideas, whether words or pictures or representational forms. Thus fables introduce usages of representation, initiating the child into a lifelong procedure. As "Stories apt to delight and entertain a Child," fables "may yet afford useful Reflections" to an adult (*Education*, section 156).[15] Not only will children easily retain these stories but as adults they may continue to reflect on them. Registered and reproduced by memory, fables epitomize the ongoing work of understanding in sustaining identity.

Locke's definition of identity as a mental operation enables and informs the change in national correlatives that Americans were making in the late eighteenth century. The cultural distinctness of Americans that Webster and Rush were trying to institutionalize is imaginable only by virtue of the Lockean principle of identity as a process of making associations, testing them, and either affirming, rejecting, or redefining them. Fables thus furnished early Americans with a perfect medium for practicing the liberal representational logic of their new identity. The contribution of the fable to the making of Americans— defined as persons in a society of their own making—is to stage the cognitive maneuvers whereby an individual makes a judgment. In thinking through the lesson of a fable, and accepting if not approving its logic, the individual engages in the intellectual work of consent. The exercise of understanding a fable thus teaches the prototypical activity of a consensual society: the mental operations of association and determination whereby Americans know themselves as part of a society of like-minded beings committed to the concept of an American nation and people. To think of American cultural identity as an aim and effect of pedagogy, now as in the formative years of the United States, therefore requires acknowledging the workings of the assorted judgments that continually (though not necessarily continuously) compose American culture.

The Ingratitude of Snakes

In the fables that filled eighteenth-century schoolbooks, we can see the work of observing, identifying, comparing, evaluating, and judging that they enjoin. As early Americans learned, circulated, and retold different versions of the same fables, they exhibited reading in the Lockean mode, a reading that resulted in distinctly American forms of the ancient stories. Consider this Aesopian fable from the most popular speller used in eighteenth-century American schools before the Revolution, Dilworth's *A New Guide to the English Tongue*. (See Figure 3.2.)

Fable X. The Husbandsman and the Snake.

A good natured man being obliged to go out in frosty weather, on his return home found an adder almost frozen to death, which he brought home with him and laid before the fire.

As soon as the creature had received fresh life by the warmth,

Figure 3.2. "The Husbandman and the Snake," *Dilworth's New Guide to the English Tongue* (ca. 1751). Courtesy American Antiquarian Society.

and was come to herself, she began to hiss, and sly about the house, and at length killed one of the children.

Well, said the man, if this is the best return that you can make for my kind offices, you shall even share the same fate yourself; and so killed her immediately.

Following the text of this tale appears the moral, delineated to the reader as "The Interpretation":

Ingratitude is one of the blackest crimes that a man can be guilty of: It is hateful to God and man, and frequently brings upon such a graceless wretch all that mischief which he either did or thought to do to another.[16]

Clearly, getting this point from the fable is a matter of accepting convention, of committing to memory an association that might not initially arise. Ingratitude is not the first term that comes to mind when one encounters a killer snake. Indeed, a much more immediate and plausible meaning to take from the fable would be do not trust snakes. For the reader who fears snakes, this would be the *only* meaning. Even for the nonphobic reader, this would be the commonsensical point. It would also be the ready meaning for the reader schooled in scriptural imagery. Setting distance (if not enmity) between people and snakes would seem to be a reasonable conclusion, whether experientially or religiously motivated. Yet the moral supplied for this tale does exactly the opposite; it considers and characterizes the snake's actions within the context of human relations. Arriving at the designated moral interpretation depends upon an act of personification, in which the snake appears a figure of human agency whose "ingratitude is one of the blackest crimes that a *man* can be guilty of." Criminalizing the snake means according it agency, identifying it as human. Then the point is to reject the snake's behavior as a model of human behavior. The given interpretation directs the reader to identify with the snake in order to subsequently dissociate from this negative exemplar of agency.

Making the snake typify "one of the blackest crimes that a man can be guilty of," the fable exhibits two models of human behavior. The first model, described in the event of the good-natured man taking home the adder to warm it, presents the human capacity for sympathy and benevolence. Acting according to the golden rule of neighborliness, the man includes the snake within the ethos of civility. But in order for the civilities of sympathy and benevolence to succeed, an appropriate response must follow the man's charity: the proper return for this social exchange should be the snake's gratitude. It is not simply that the snake violates a certain understanding of social compact, but that as soon as she has "come to herself," that is, regained her animal character, she becomes a predator of humans. The snake's actions identify her as a dangerous creature—the man must kill it to protect himself and the rest of his family. Yet the man, his good nature now strained, still addresses the snake as human and in terms of social contract. He characterizes the snake's killing of the child as an ungrateful response—"the best return that you can make for my kind offices"—and thereby keeps the snake within the sphere of sociability.

A second model of conduct now emerges. For the sense of mutuality that the man's initial sympathy displays, he substitutes a different equilibrium, the symmetry of "the same fate"—a punishment befitting the crime. Invoking the code of "an eye for an eye," the man gives a return in kind. He thus upholds the principle of social order even as he switches to a different system of justice. The snake, when acting as a snake, appears most subject to human standards, though perhaps to what we would regard as a primitive standard. In the appended interpretation to this fable, the snake's ingratitude, "hateful to God and man," subjects it and all persons who behave similarly to the chance of retributive justice. For "such a graceless wretch" may eventually suffer "all that mischief which he either did or thought to do to another." Leaving retribution to chance, the fable does not finally endorse eye for an eye justice—though it certainly does not rule it out. It instead reinstates a principle of balance that accommodates human badness as well as goodness. To the virtue of charity, the fable adds the provision (and caveat) of punishment for violations of social ties. The punitive provision gains authority from the sense of fair play first introduced in the axiom that charity should elicit gratitude. Thus the fable concludes with a paraphrase and reiteration of the golden rule: do not do to others what you do not want done to yourself. The snake has revitalized the mimetic injunctions sustaining human society.

Persons and Animals

As children in eighteenth-century America read or heard the fable "Of the Husbandman and the Snake," as it appeared in Dilworth's *Guide*, they were encountering a version of the fable deriving from Locke's 1703 translation, rather than the version by Samuel Richardson that was more popular in Britain. These two different versions of the fable, which I will consider in detail later, counsel different attitudes toward the snake, or persons like it. To engage and direct the reader to specific points of view, all tellers of fables rely on the identifications established between readers and characters, on associations achieved through personification.

The alternating identification with and distance from the snake that the moral requires from the reader demonstrates the fundamental personifying exercise that fables induce, inspire, and exemplify. Personification initially appears a mimetic mechanism, which of course appeals to those who like fables as a mode of cultural didacticism. But personification, which entails the imaginative identifications of a person with other entities or objects, also involves the cognitive exercises that make fables so well suited to Locke's consensual pedagogy. Personification is a transfer between persons and nonpersons that proceeds in two different directions. On one course, objects take on life or personality; things or animals come to appear or behave as persons. On the other course, persons or human figures typify or embody some quality, thing, or idea. Persons become symbols, figurative materials. Both courses reveal an order of resemblance governing the definition of a person. In the first case, things or animals act or appear like persons: that is, they speak or think (or have a gender). Personified entities are endowed with characteristics that only humans possess. The discrepancy between, for instance, a cat and the human speech with which the Cat in the Hat is so rhythmically adept, or between a train and the virtuous effortfulness of the Little Engine That Could, highlights particular human skills and traits. These linguistic and moral human attributes appear more vivid when ascribed to nonhumans, and thus suggest the special distinction available to all those who really can possess such attributes. Resembling persons more than animals or machines, the facility of the Cat in the Hat or the Little Engine That Could furnishes persons with flattering models of themselves to imitate, or, as in the case of the murderous, ungrateful snake, with negative models of themselves to repudiate.

On the second path of personification, an idea, thing, or quality attains its clearest expression, its best representation, in an imaginary or idealized human form. Personified embodiment traditionally confers perfection upon the corporeal representative, presenting in the form of a person the perfect example of something incorporeal. For a body to epitomize some quality or idea, as Cupid personifies love or Santa Claus good cheer and beneficence, the body must be conceived to match what it symbolizes. Resembling what he or she typifies, the representative person suggests a proximity between persons and propensities. Again, just as the first path of personification shows a way for persons to choose to resemble models of themselves, the second path of personification likewise supplies paradigms of personhood. Persons embody magnified versions of human qualities with which they may associate, or from which they may dissociate. In the operations of personification, persons personify themselves in order to appraise and reconfigure the materials of personhood. Whether in human or nonhuman forms, personifications provide persons with portrayals of themselves, patterns to be imitated, avoided, or altered—or to be considered for appreciation, amusement, or criticism.[17]

Fables usually, though not always, follow the first course of personification as they furnish advice for social relations through stories of animals. In fact, the term fable has often been understood as animal story. The identification of fables with animals became so absolute by the end of the eighteenth century that the allegorical function of the animals could be forgotten, especially by critics of the pedagogical efficacy of fables. Thus John Franklin Jones declares in his preface to the *Analytical Spelling-Book* (1822):

> Something was wanted, in American schools to replace the lessons, which have been copied from book to book, since the reign of Queen Anne. It is the intention, in the present work, to advance principles suited to the rising generation, in the United States. Beasts, reptiles and insects are not represented in this volume, as the equals of rational beings; such a supposition is repugnant to nature, science, and correct moral sentiment. Most of the fables so long employed in schools, are particularly improper for small children, who should be taught by literal examples, before they can comprehend figures of rhetoric or draw inferences from remote hints. The fancy of converting inferior animals into "teachers of children," has been carried to ridiculous extravagance.[18]

Though he would proscribe the pedagogical use of Aesop, Jones does not manage altogether to refrain from anthropomorphizing animals in his own speller. He presents in place of animal stories the thirty-page "Story of Jack Halyard." Jack is an exemplary boy who teaches other boys to be virtuous. One day Jack and his friend Peter encounter a rattlesnake.

> [Peter] ran and screamed, as if the terrible creature was going to swallow him alive; but Jack like a hero, without being at all afraid, got a good stick and killed the snake. "These animals," said Jack, "are like tattling, mischief making people: they are very poison; but dangerous only when they creep in secret, and bite before they are seen."

Even Jack, Jones's replacement for animal teachers, cannot seem to avoid putting animal behavior in human terms.

Like-minded critics of fables denounced the appearance of both animals and inanimate objects as narrative protagonists in such popular works as *The Autobiography of a Mouse* and *The Adventures of a Pincushion*.[19] Besides not comprehending the representational nature of exemplarity, these advocates of the literal example missed the point that fables themselves continually distinguished between the human and nonhuman. As in the fable "Of the Husbandsman and the Snake," imagining human conduct in animal form only underscores the pervasiveness of rational discourse that children must learn and engage. In this light, the "pathetic fallacy" that Ruskin observed continuing to "form a great part of our modern view of nature" simply attests to the fact that humans operate in human terms (however inhumane those terms may be).[20]

One noxious habit of human behavior is to bestialize human enemies, competitors, or strangers. The animal representation of persons historically operates to dehumanize certain populations and to deny entitlements to such populations. Defining other humans as animals also denies those persons the imaginative capacities and relations whereby they can envision their rights. As an exclusion from what we might call the privilege of the pathetic fallacy, the bestialization of humans deprives them of the identifying faculty whereby persons know themselves. The personifications of animals in fables extend the attributes of humanity, thus producing the opposite effect. Though fables clearly can serve to uphold racial or sexual distinctions—when a race or sex is relegated to the animal condition—fables also can supply the subordinated with models of their own humanity: thinking, talking animals resemble persons engaged in asserting and protecting their interests. Aesop, according to legend, was a slave who used his ability to tell fables to preserve his welfare.[21]

The Varieties of Moral Interpretation

If personification threatens to undo distinctions between the human and nonhuman, fables regularly reinforce the borders and characteristics of the human world, particularly the titles and interests of individuals within that world. In one of the earliest extant translations of

Aesop's fable of the man and the snake (Phaedrus's Latin translation translated into English by S. A. Hanford), we can see the proper measures to maintain one's well-being against others most pithily formulated:

> One winter's day a farm-hand found a snake frozen stiff with the cold, and moved by compassion he picked it up and put it in his bosom. But with the warmth its natural instinct returned, and it gave its benefactor a fatal bite. As he died he said: "I have got what I deserve for taking pity on an evil creature."[22]

Rather than pointing out the ingratitude of the snake or endorsing the man's characterization of his fate as fair treatment—"I have got what I deserve"—the accompanying moral states that "This story shows that even the greatest kindness cannot change a bad nature." This version of the fable does not consider codes of justice even though the farm-hand ostensibly does so in his dying words. The moral differs from the man's own reasoning, concluding that "a bad nature" is immovable, unalterable. While there is a certain duplication in the two pronouncements—pity is met by evil, kindness is helpless before bad nature—the second view of the event generalizes the circumstances so as to make clear that the snake's behavior cannot even be considered within the social contract. Here is an instance of personification of the second kind, in which qualities attain their most distinctive form when embodied; the man's pity and the snake's evil are elevated to "the greatest kindness" and "bad nature." The moral defines evil as an absolute superior force in any encounter with good, with "even the greatest kindness." The encounter between the pitying man and the evil snake thus occurs outside the domain of justice. The best thing the man could have done was stop himself from thinking of the snake in human terms. His compassion was not just a tactical error but a fundamental mistake. Within the logic of self-preservation the man's fate is deserved—that is, emanating from his own failure to remember that the object of his pity was an evil or at least dangerous creature. The snakebite all too effectively reminds the man of the differences between persons and the objects of their identification. By describing those differences as fundamental and permanent in the case of men and some wild animals, the fable warns against misplaced sympathy. Reason, and in particular self-defensive reasoning, can and should check affective impulses when they lead us to overlook real and consequential distinctions.

In Locke's translation of the same fable, called "Of the Country-man and Snake," which appears in his 1703 edition of a Latin-English reader of *Aesop's Fables*, he similarly emphasizes the dangers of personification.[23] (See Figure 3.3.) Here, when the snake recovers its health and usual aggressive power—which Locke translates as poison—"the country-man, snatching up a stake, runs to him, and expostulates the Injury with him with words and blows." In Phaedrus's version of the fable, the man talks to himself, but here he expostulates with the snake as if the snake were human, asking "Whether he returned these thanks? Whether he would take away life from him, who gave him life." These expostulations raise the point about proper gratitude that the rendering of the fable in Dilworth's book also underscores. In Locke's rendition, though, the man does not die; he immediately sees the mistake in bringing the snake home and beats it. Locke thus shows the range of interpretation that the personifying imagination supplies. A new line of thought issues from Locke's staging of the relations between man and snake. The countryman's experience gives rise to a recognition of possible inequities in social relations: "Sometimes it happens, that they do harm to thee to whom thou hast done good, and they deserve ill of thee, of whom thou hast deserved well."

Moving directly from the encounter between the man and the snake to a discourse on social relations expressed in axiomatic form, a move initiated by the man's complaints about ingratitude, the moral in Locke's translation dispenses with the identifications generated by personification. It places the event in the realm of justice and judgment, restoring the principle of fair return that the snake's behavior had threatened to violate. This restoration interestingly first acknowledges the unfairness of the snake's behavior, validating the man's sense of injury. Having credited the man's account, the moral then goes further to justify the man's attacking the snake, stating "they deserve ill of thee, of whom thou hast deserved well." To develop a rationale of self-defense, the moral subsumes the snake into the category of those who "do harm to thee." The snake, translated into the hypothetical "they," becomes a deserving target, a figure for mitigating the horror of vio-

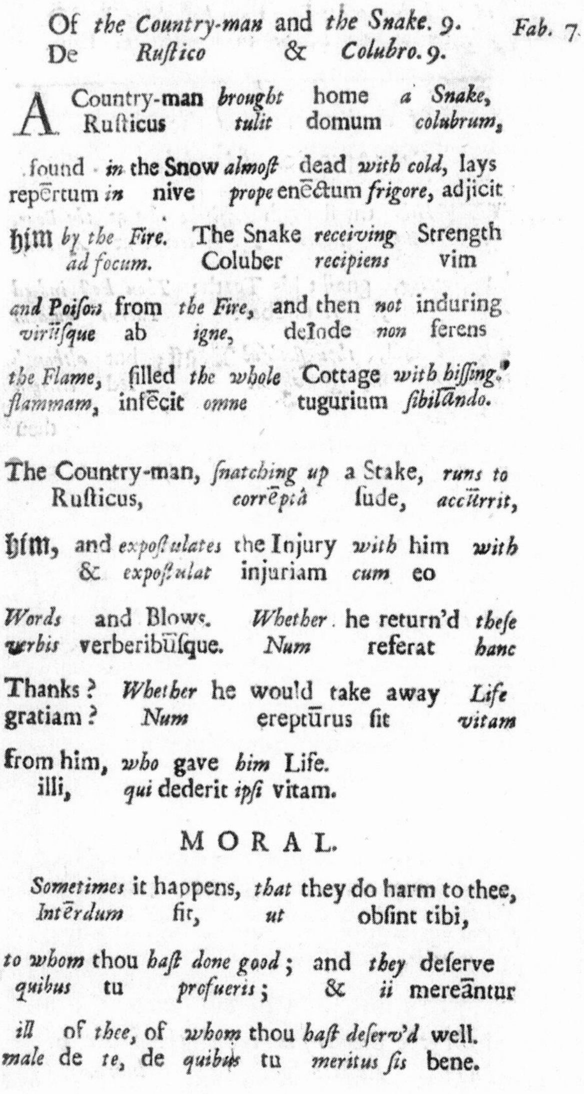

Of *the Country-man* and *the Snake.* 9.   *Fab.* 7.
De   *Ruſtico*   &   *Colubro.* 9.

A Country-**man** *brought* home *a Snake,*
   Ruſticus   *tulit* domum *colubrum,*

.found *in* the **Snow** *almoſt* dead *with cold,* lays
repērtum *in* nive *prope* enēctum *frigore,* adjicit

him *by the Fire.* The Snake *receiving* Strength
   ad focum.   Coluber *recipiens* vim

and **Poiſon** from *the Fire,* and then *not* induring
 viriiſque ab   igne,   deĩnde *non* ſerens

the Flame, filled *the whole* Cottage *with hiſſing.*
flammam, infēcit *omne*   tugurium *ſibilāndo.*

The Country-man, *ſnatching up* a Stake, *runs to*
    Ruſticus,   *corrēptā* ſude, *accūrrit,*

him, and *expoſtulates* the Injury *with* him *with*
    & *expoſtulat* injuriam *cum* eo

Words and Blows. *Whether.* he return'd *theſe*
verbis verberibūſque. *Num*   referat *hanc*

Thanks ? *Whether* he would take away *Life*
gratiam ? *Num*   ereptūrus ſit   *vitam*

from him, *who* gave *him* Life.
   illi,   *qui* dederit *ipſi* vitam.

MORAL.

Sometimes it happens, *that* they do harm to thee,
  Intērdum   fit,   *ut*   obſint tibi,

to whom thou *haſt done good ;* and *they* deſerve
 quibus tu   *profueris ;*   & *ii* mereāntur

ill of *thee,* of *whom* thou *haſt deſerv'd* well.
male de *te,* de *quibus* tu *meritus ſis* bene.

Figure 3.3. "Of the Country-man and the Snake," John Locke, *Aesop's Fables in English and Latin* (London, 1703). The Pierpont Morgan Library, New York, PML 65064.

lence in self-defense. Once the fable has dispensed with this personified creature, the abstract harmful "they" can also be eliminated. These harmful persons who replace the snake have no attributes other than their inimical nature, a threat to be dispelled. In a kind of deperson-ification of both snake and pronouns, the persons to whom "they" would refer have been placed outside the social contract. Attacking the snake, or a person in self-defense, is therefore not an act of retribution or a redress of injury but an appropriate, perhaps even unavoidable, reflex of self-preservation.

Acting according to the etiquette of social affiliation and exchange, the man has also acted in defense of that etiquette. The moral furnishes a restatement of fair play in which the unfair return of harm for good is balanced by a justified return of ill for the initial harm. This conclusion is not an endorsement of an eye for an eye justice, however, but a spe-cific judgment applied to an act in a specific context. The moral begins with the crucial qualifying "sometimes it happens," signaling that its endorsement of self-defense stems from a recognition of contingency. Not all acts of ingratitude appear life-threatening, but a hissing poison-ous snake is a clear danger to a man and is clearly beyond the scope of social appeals. Thus the moral's restoration and reinforcement of social justice points to the particularity of circumstances. We can credit and vindicate *this* man's actions; but all judgments are bounded by context and specificity. What first seems the generality of the moral turns out to be an expression of the importance of matching judgment to the par-ticulars of the case.

The particulars of the moral interpretation applied to the fable "Of the Husbandsman and the Snake" can operate alternatively to claim and promote a general rule, as in Samuel Richardson's version.[24] In Richardson's narrative, as in Hanford's translation of Phaedrus's rendi-tion, the countryman too late realizes the dangerous and unredeemable character of the snake:

A Countryman happened one hard winter to 'spy a Snake under a hedge, that was half frozen to death. The good-natured man took it up, and kept it in his bosom, till warmth brought it to life again; and so soon as ever it was in a condition to do mischief, it bit the very man that saved its life. Ah, thou ungrate-ful wretch! says he, is that venomous ill-nature of thine to be satisfied with nothing less than the ruin of thy preserver?

Even as the man recognizes the snake's inimical relation to humans—"that venomous ill-nature"—he attributes motivation to the snake, a perverse malicious intention. Assuming the snake's desire for "nothing less than" the man's "ruin," the countryman relates the incident as not simply a fatal human miscalculation about the bestial nature of snakes but as a revelation of the snake's active plot against the man. The snake appears vengeful as well as "ungrateful," determinedly destructive as well as unmindful of proper social relations. After reiterating the familiar tale with this emphasis on the snake's malevolence, Richardson appends to it a familiar moral:

> He that takes an ungrateful man into his bosom, is well nigh sure to be betrayed; and it is not charity, but folly, to think of obliging the common enemies of mankind.

Like the Phaedrus-Hanford moral, this interpretation emphasizes the folly of the man, admonishing us to know our enemies and act accordingly.[25] Those enemies are clearly not just wild animals but the ill-natured, ungrateful men personified by the venomous snake. The moral advises us to exclude such persons from the social exchanges of charity and obligation, emphasizing that our best defense against such persons lies in a prior knowledge of them, a knowledge that forewarns of their future acts. Knowing a man to be ungrateful amounts to knowing that you are "well nigh sure to be betrayed." This certainty of recidivism derives from the report of widespread examples of spiteful behavior, as Richardson elaborates in an accompanying "reflection" upon the moral:

> 'Tis no new thing for good-natured men to meet with ungrateful returns. How many examples have we seen with our own eyes, of men that have been relieved out of starving necessities, which have bereaved them both of spirit and strength to do mischief; who in requital have afterwards conspired against the life, honour, and fortune of their patrons and redeemers? Now all this is no more

than the proverb in a fable: save a thief from the gallows, and he'll cut your throat.

The frequency of ungrateful responses to good-natured acts—"'tis no new thing"—stands as a cumulative record of the chronic crimes of charity recipients. By establishing, or seeking to establish, a common truth, Richardson's reflection asserts the frequency and familiarity of ungrateful returns in order to make a universal case against objects of sympathy. Rather than moving toward individuation and its importance in matters of adjudication, as Locke's edition of the fable does, Richardson's version moves toward generalization about both past and future events. The accumulated evidence against the beneficiaries of our good nature (interestingly all hearsay) forms a record of recurrent—and thus seemingly predictable—vicious responses to charity.

Richardson's spectre of countless crimes against benefactors (crucially indeterminate in number) operates not only to check acts of benevolence but also to prevent and punish potential acts of malevolence. The reflection directs us to think of all the evil acts that ungrateful men have performed and could perform, and then to consider our sense of the reality and possibility of such acts as aptly encapsulated in the proverb "save a thief from the gallows, and he'll cut your throat." What begins as a warning against misplaced benevolence ends as justification of preventive and punitive measures against both actual and prospective harms. The thief being sent to the gallows has not (yet) committed the crime of murder with which Richardson's cautionary reflection has charged him. According to the preemptive logic developed in the fable, persons should maintain their security by eliminating potential evil before it ever happens: executing the thief saves your own life by making it impossible for the thief to become your murderer. Capital punishment here appears as a life insurance policy, a principle of self-protection.

To further intensify the threat of personal harm, and thus justify preventive measures, Richardson invokes the wisdom and authority of fables themselves: a proverbial statement to corroborate further the evidence of an alleged common experience.[26] Richardson thus moves from analogies between animals and humans to analogies between proverbs and proverbs, which additionally mirror and magnify the portrait of unredeemable criminality. This method of confirming a point by multiplying it reflects the authority that fables carry as accounts of human experience. To disagree with the adage "save a thief from the gallows and he'll cut your throat" is to discredit the moral that it is "folly to think of obliging the common enemies of mankind." Such disregard, Richardson warns, might be fatal. Depicting the perils of ignoring proverbial knowledge—loss of life, honour, and fortune; or having your throat cut—the Richardsonian version "Of the Husbandsman and the Snake" defends not just the necessity of uncompromising punishment of criminals but also the expertise of fables in cautionary thinking.[27]

Fables furnish a paradigmatic state of caution: as they continually exhibit the advantages of circumspection, discretion, and prudence, they encourage the exercise of thinking carefully and extensively. Whereas Locke elaborates the intellectual injunction of the fable into the (continual) task of considering the specifics of all the circumstances we encounter and judge, Richardson takes this injunction as sanction for a specific state of preparedness against the contingencies of human malice. Put another way, the fable as Locke relates it stresses reasoning within context; the fable as Richardson tells it constructs a context that then functions as a conviction, a certainty about our enemies and about our rightful responses to them. Locke keeps in view the horizon in which judgments form, while Richardson would make one judgment the entire horizon of understanding.

The same fable thus authorizes quite different, even diametrically opposed, positions. In Richardson's version, the implicit scare technique embedded in the fable's description of peril operates openly to rationalize a statutory formulation of criminality: once a criminal, always a criminal. This telling of the fable encourages an associational line of thinking from snake to criminal to criminality to more criminality. The different meanings and methods of thinking that Richardson and Locke draw from the fable demonstrate the significance of how one tells the fable, of how the fable's resources of intellectual and emotional appeal get employed by the teller. Fables do not work axiomatically; far from it. Instead they entail detailed work in form and content to achieve their axioms. The emergence of different moral interpretations of the countryman's encounter accordingly proceeds by new arrangements of the story.

The Snake's Perspective

Like many moral fables, the tale of the countryman and the snake re-appears in eighteenth-century and early nineteenth-century grammars and spellers, and in a later version incorporates and expounds the very issues it raises about interpretation and identification. Retitled "The Child and the Serpent" in Fiske's *The New-England Spelling-Book* (1802), the tale is now framed with a colloquy about itself:

> A child, playing with a tame serpent, said to it, My dear little animal, dost thou imagine I would be so familiar with thee if thy venom was not taken out; you serpents are the most perverse, ungrateful creatures. I remember to have read, that a good natured countryman found a serpent under a hedge, almost dead with cold. He took it up and warmed it in his breast; but it was scarcely come to life when it stung its benefactor, and the too charitable man died of the wound.

To the boy's recital of the familiar story, Fiske appends an alternative account, the story told from the snake's point of view.

> This is astonishing, said the serpent: how partial are your historians! Ours relate this history in a different manner. Your charitable peasant believed the serpent dead: its skin was beautifully variegated with different colours; he took it up and was hastening home in order to slay it.
> Now tell me whether the serpent was ungrateful?

The effect on the boy of this counterreading is to reaffirm his understanding of the standard reading. He immediately sees the snake as acting like an ingrate, exemplifying the very characteristics of ingratitude against which the tale warns. Having learned his lesson well, the boy can castigate and dismiss the snake. "Hold your tongue, replied the boy. Where is the ingrate who cannot find some excuse to justify himself?"

Surprisingly, the tale does not end here with the boy's reiteration and application of the moral he has learned. A supplementary instruction follows, which turns out to be a caveat against making judgments too quickly and too programmatically.

Well answered, interrupted the boy's father, who had listened to
the dialogue. Nevertheless, my son, if ever thou shouldest hear of
an instance of ingratitude baser than ordinary, forget not to examine every circumstance to the bottom, and be extremely backward
in fixing so foul a stain on any man's character.[28]

While the boy repeats the interpretation of the fable as an instance of
ingratitude, characterizing his snake according to the classification he
has learned, his father grants the possibility of another interpretation
such as the one the snake furnishes. Indeed, the father counsels sympathy of a kind as he expresses concern for the rights of persons to be protected from false accusations and characterizations. His concern with
the rights of the accused points to the problem of strictly formalist interpretations. The boy's readiness to fit all data about snakes into the
paradigm of ingratitude that he recalls from the fable could lead to
a mischaracterization. Since interpretations can become instrumental
representations, as the fable's account of the snake as ungrateful becomes the boy's standard of snakes, every judgment must be a careful
exercise of full consideration—examination of "every circumstance to
the bottom"—even, and especially, if the resultant judgment finally reiterates the standard interpretation.

Giving voice and perspective to the snake—here, significantly, a *tame*
and harmless snake—Fiske's version of the fable quickly moves from
personification to the rights of persons. Like Locke's movement from
personification to social discourse, this change in style directs the
reader to some new considerations. Even though the father's final
words affirm his son's conclusion, their caution against reflexive formalism lends some weight to the tame snake's testimony. That testimony is an explanation of the so-called ingratitude of the serpent as
self-defense. While the boy discounts this explanation as cynical self-
justification, the father defends the right to self-defense, particularly
when the charged crimes are "baser than ordinary." Thus the boy's
learning of the original fable's lesson is augmented by a new lesson, a
more complicated conception of justice requiring continual diligence
against rushing to judgment. Identifying the accused as "any man," the
father urges a potential resemblance between accuser and accused that
entitles the accused to the sympathy and protections of society. Staged
as a pedagogical exercise, Fiske's fable "The Child and the Serpent"
demonstrates the importance of regularly supplementing knowledge.

The fact that children may misapply or misunderstand fables provoked Rousseau's famous denunciation of them in *Emile*.

> Follow children learning their fables; and you will see that when
> they are in a position to apply them, they almost always do so in a
> way opposite to the author's intention, and that instead of looking
> within themselves for the shortcoming that one wants to cure or
> prevent, they tend to like the vice with which one takes advantage
> of others' shortcomings.

In their natural self-love *(amour-propre)*, Rousseau thinks, children invariably will emulate the winner of social contests. For example:

> In all the fables where the lion is one of the personages, since he is
> ordinarily the most brilliant, the child does not fail to make him-
> self a lion; and when he presides over some dividing up of por-
> tions, well instructed by his model, he takes great care to take ev-
> erything for himself. But when the gnat fells the lion, the situation
> is entirely different; the child is then no longer a lion; he is a gnat.
> He learns how one day to kill with stings those he would not dare
> to stand and attack. (115–116)[29]

What concerns Rousseau is not only that children will identify with
the lion—and this may be an identification with immoral behavior—
but also that they will change their identifications. In their erratic
mimeticism, children can readily get the wrong point from a fable.
Rousseau's account of children reading fables also assumes that self-interest is never the point or that self-interest is not a social virtue. Fables
do not generate virtues as Rousseau would like because they cannot
guarantee the reception of their dictates. As the scope and subtlety of
meaning that the various morals and epilogues to the fable of the countryman and the snake manifest, fables indeed inspire a variety of interpretations. And the long history of republishing fables demonstrates
the different meanings that fables may serve.[30]

What Rousseau rightly recognizes as the unpredictability of the fable's lesson is precisely what makes fables pedagogically efficacious in
Locke's view. For Locke, fables are exercises in thinking, incitements to
"reflection," rather than dictates of moral truth. By introducing the
process of making judgments, fables teach that meaning is conven-

tional but also consensual, formed in the individual's arrival at an agreement with a standard or a probability. If the reader is to accept the moral of a fable, he or she must trace the logic of the moral's relation to the tale. Though fables furnish set interpretations, if they are to make sense they must also compel the labor of reconstructing those interpretations, in a reenactment of their own advance to authority. Fables thus teach not simply their designated morals, but also the process of attaching a moral to a story. When a reader accepts or discounts, rather than simply memorizes, a moral, she affirms the authority of human understanding. We see in the father's addendum to the boy's restatement of a standard interpretation of "The Country-man and the Snake" the fable's capacity to incorporate the different and new understandings it might inspire—to represent its various readers.

The boy's readiness to discredit his pet snake's revisionary recitation of the fable risks limiting the fable's representative service. As they depict and adjudicate conflicting positions, fables of course can exclude or deny any divergent view from their forum just as the boy does and just as Rousseau wishes. When fables are taken to represent merely conventional views, they can operate with the formal efficiency that the boy displays. It is this sense of fables as surefire missives that William Bennett, one of our most outspoken and widely read contemporary cultural nationalists, invokes when he recommends reading moral fables as the best way to transmit and preserve American values. So sure is Bennett that fables carry indisputable meanings that he organizes them in his anthology *The Book of Virtues* under virtue headings such as self-discipline, compassion, responsibility, friendship, work, courage, perseverance, honesty, loyalty, and faith.[31]

In the Americanization of the fable that I have been tracing, transmission of an American social order occurs not through following statutes but by reviewing and ratifying the logic from which statutes emerge. Statutes and customs acquire authority when individuals reenact the deliberative processes of prior individuals. Through fables, then, Americans can recall and renew the contemplative process from which their identity putatively stems. As they read fables, they reenact the history through which they came to be the subjects of their particular society. This history is fundamentally a record of the exertions of individual reason and senses, as one of the first framers of the story, John Adams, stressed:

Although the detail of the formation of the American governments is at present little known or regarded in Europe or America, it may hereafter become an object of curiosity. It will never be pretended that any persons employed in that service had interviews with the gods or were in any degree under the inspiration of Heaven, more than those at work upon ships or houses, or laboring in merchandise or agriculture; it will forever be acknowledged that these governments were contrived merely by the use of reason and the senses, as Copley painted Chatham; West, Wolf; and Trumbull, Warren and Montgomery; as Dwight, Barlow, Trumbull, and Humphries composed their verse, and Belknap and Ramsay history; as Godfrey invented his quadrant, and Rittenhouse his planetarium; as Boylston practised inoculation, and Franklin electricity; as Paine exposed the mistakes of Raynal, and Jefferson those of Buffon.[32]

Adams here simultaneously celebrates the political constitution of the United States as a cultural achievement and establishes a catalogue of American cultural works. Highlighting the accomplishments of Americans in the arts, sciences, and criticism, Adams leaves out of the story the less congenial performances of reason and the senses that figured in the making of the nation. His selective narrative invokes the possibilities of mental energies, but finally reduces them to a nationalist inventory of achievement. Adams offers a fable of American accomplishment that citizens can read and retell without compunction.

While any telling of the story of national origins may omit the violence and destruction involved in the emergence, fables notably recapitulate the integrality of violence and civility. Whatever social proprieties and justifications fables may present, they also register aggression, suffering, and, quite often, death. As the tale "Of the Country-man and the Snake" attests, fables bear witness to the brutality and fatalities—as well as the ingenuity, art, and intellection—involved in forming and rationalizing a culture. Adams's litany of American invention promotes a narrative of American achievements—a chronicle fulfilling Webster's requirement of texts "attentive to the political interest of America"— which, like the myths of deific national origins that it displaces, is meant to inspire reverence "forever." By contrast, fables, retold tales from other lands and times, exercise rather than revere the reason and senses. What makes fables last is not the authority associated with their longevity, not the so-called universality of their messages, but their utility for diverse purposes and circumstances. Fables emblematize the reading capacities that sustain a consensual society. Whereas Adams, like Webster and Rush, would prescribe American culture, the fables that they read and we still read exemplify a procedure for describing and deliberating that culture. The continuing conflicts and inequities within American society lead many very different individuals to desire the certainty of cultural prescription. Yet whatever stories are presented or prescribed to us, the task of reading and rereading remains to us, whomever we may be.

4

Paine's Vindication of the Rights of Children

The Lockean alignment of the rights of individuals with the rights of children inaugurates the modern character of rights that we now take for granted; we expect our rights to reflect and serve our psychological and political welfare over time.[1] A now familiar modern style of depicting rights also emerges from Locke's conception of the consensual child. From the new prominence accorded childhood in the wake of Locke's formulations, eighteenth-century political rhetoric took the figure of the child as an emblem for humanity. Violation of parental duty toward children accordingly figures conspicuously in justificatory rhetorics of early modern republican revolutions. It is this eighteenth-century alignment of rights with children that made stories of Marie Antoinette's incest with her son effective antimonarchical polemics.[2] To describe a monarch as failing in or perverting parental relations was to suggest an unfitness for the larger parental task of governing subjects. To rally American colonists to revolt from the rule of Great Britain, Tom Paine's *Common Sense* accordingly characterized Americans as children fleeing from a tyrannical, monstrous parent, "not from the tender embraces of the mother, but from the cruelty of the monster" (84).[3] Paine's image of child abuse, which clearly remains potent in the American imagination of identity, draws on an iconography of abusive or insensitive parenthood familiar from widely read novels as well as from political philosophy and educational theories, an iconography

83

that children growing up in eighteenth-century America encountered early and often.[4]

Tom Thumb's Talents

From eighteenth-century literature, fictive and nonfictive, emerges the figure of the wronged child, perhaps best exemplified by Clarissa, whose parents refuse to acknowledge her feelings and rights. The situation of a young girl cruelly bound by her parents to an unwanted marriage nicely emblematized the right to self-determination, the right to choose one's own fate. Another popular character who typified the desirability of self-determination was Defoe's Crusoe. Crusoe regards his parents' opposition to his desire to go to sea as an expression of unwarranted authority, which he accordingly disobeys.[5] Both Clarissa and Crusoe encounter great dangers in their ventures of self-determination, which suggest the magnitude of difficulties faced by independently minded children, or by children in general. The figure of the wronged child also predominates in the emergent children's literature, most dramatically in the story of "The Children in the Wood," known today as "Hansel and Gretel," in which the parents or guardians of the children desert them, or in some versions of the story, murder them. Since the first printed appearances of the tale at the turn of the eighteenth century, popular American versions of "The Children in the Wood" most often followed a plot in which the uncle of two orphaned children arranges for their murder so that he can inherit their fortune. This rendition depicts the absolute denial of all the rights of children to property, life, and protection.[6] With the image of the wronged child, the case for individual rights gains a powerful affective appeal. In stories of children's suffering, the most extreme forms of affliction—starvation, imprisonment, violence, and death—foreground bodily harms feared by everyone. The child's greater vulnerability to harm and helplessness to overcome it summon an urgency to the redress of his conditions, an urgency that Paine musters in his portrayal of American colonists as suffering children.

Along with the figure of the wronged child emerges the figure of the empowered child, a strikingly self-determined individual. In the popular stories of Jack the Giant-killer and retellings of the ancient tale of Tom Thumb, tiny children manage amazing feats of courage and ingenuity.[7] A part of British folklore since at least medieval times, the tiny Tom Thumb performed heroic feats for which King Arthur knighted him. The figure of a tiny hero also long existed in Continental and Asian folklore.[8] At the end of the seventeenth century, Perrault recorded a version of Tom Thumb as a prototype of self-determination that would predominate during the next century. In Perrault's telling, which became the most translated and popular form of the story until nineteenth-century retellings by the Grimm brothers and Hans Christian Andersen, Tom is one of seven brothers of improvident parents. In a plot very similar to that employed in many versions of "The Children in the Wood" and "Hansel and Gretel," the parents try to abandon the children whom they can no longer support. Overhearing this plan, the resourceful Tom Thumb first thwarts the attempt at abandonment and then, when unable to avert another such attempt by his parents, overcomes the even more dangerous designs of an ogre who delights in eating little children. Perrault's "Little Tom Thumb" is all the more remarkable because he is the scapegoat of the family; his cleverness and courage save the family that has not treated him at all well. Not only does he save his brothers and himself from being eaten by the ogre, but he also steals the ogre's treasure, thus securing his family from financial worries. He steals the ogre's magical seven-league boots as well, which enable Tom to perform useful feats for the king. With his earnings from the king, Tom is able to add to the family fortune, and as Perrault concludes, "look well after himself."[9]

Tom, who is unable to rely on anyone except himself, and made even more singular by his tininess, nevertheless succeeds. Tom's heroism supplies a legendary realization of the capacities with which Locke endowed children. During the seventeenth and eighteenth centuries in England, the Tom Thumb story developed some additional sequences in which Tom dies but returns to life (after some time in Fairyland) to serve British royals of later generations.[10] Tom thus attains an immortal status; he becomes an enduring figure of heroic accomplishments who reminds a series of generations of his remarkable feats. It is Tom's pervasiveness as well as his smallness and canniness that make the name Tom Thumb a general term for child in the eighteenth century; it began to appear as such in titles of children's anthologies such as *Tommy Thumb's Songbook* and *Tom Thumb's Folio*, both collections of nursery rhymes.[11]

While tales of Tom Thumb and miniature heroes long antedate the eighteenth century, it is then that the figure of Tom Thumb became identified with the character of childhood, with the particular features of childhood that Locke's psychology and pedagogy introduced: effort, will, self-determination. Tom Thumb's achievements present in an entertaining way a chronology of attainments to which children can aspire.[12] The appeal of the tiny hero here depends upon as it converges with the sense of empowerment increasingly accorded children. Tom's ingenuity delights the reader by demonstrating an astonishing range of mental acuity in such a minute person. The apparent disproportionality of Tom works to favor his mind, foregounding the interior faculties of individuality. In Susan Stewart's study of narratives of the miniature, she observes how diminutive objects appeal to and celebrate the mind. Miniature forms and celebrations of the miniature, such as dolls, doll houses, toys, model railways, tableaux, and Tom Thumb weddings, offer an "experience of interiority" while exemplifying "the process by which that interior is constructed."[13] Her characterization, developed to explain modern adult preoccupations with miniature forms, helps clarify Tom Thumb's eighteenth-century significance as a model of the empowered child. Tom Thumb's diminutiveness invites an interest that turns on readers' imaginative comparisons of their experiences of size with Tom's situation. The story thus stages the reader's (or auditor's) critical distance and difference from the small protagonist with whom the reader may identify. Reading or hearing about Tom Thumb reminds children of their own situations, prompting them to self-awareness, to the cognitive activities that mark them as individuals.

According to Stewart, the miniature furnishes "a diminutive, and thereby manipulatable, version of experience" (69). Displaying objects of the world as subject to human machinations, miniatures reflect and ratify "the individual perceiving subject" (44). Scaled down to manageability by remarkable feats of craft, miniatures improve upon their originals, thus furnishing a version of experience "which is domesticated and protected from contamination" (69). The miniature perfects the experience it so carefully reproduces. The idealized form of the miniature then articulates as it exemplifies a sense of individual interiority as separate from and superior to the world. Certainly the dollhouses and model railways described by Stewart present perfected selections of the domestic and technological worlds. No messes or accidents occur in these artifactual environments.

Not all minute forms, however, appear perfect. While eighteenth-century constructions of the miniature, such as Swift's island of Lilliput, do afford visions of orderliness and proportion, they also often include anxieties and disorder. Tom Thumb is vulnerable precisely because he is such a tiny being and his experience appears an intensification of the dangers and difficulties of the known, imperfect world. Even Tom's success suggests less an idealization of experience than the frank fantasy stories can provide. The miniature of personhood that Tom embodies, and that all the tiny books titled as Tom Thumb items represent, does not insulate the development of the child's interiority from the world. Instead, Tom Thumb narratives, however improbable, display a constant acknowledgment of the external world with which individuals engage. Interiority depends upon and develops through such engagements; the fact that it is a representational process, one that often relies on representational forms such as stories, pictures, or toys (and, as Locke stresses, conceptual representations such as reputation and example), does not signify what Stewart calls the "transcendence" (69) of interiority. Stories like *Tom Thumb* may depict the overcoming of circumstances, but they do not simply offer a fantasy of accomplishment. The Tom Thumb story contributes to children some practical tools for living their lives, for negotiating the dynamics of inside and outside, self and others that compose the individual. In acknowledging and addressing the considerable cognitive capacities of children, the pedagogy of childhood initiated by Locke and implemented through eighteenth-century children's literature puts children to work in the world into which they are born.

In the less fantastic (though perhaps equally improbable) new children's stories invented by eighteenth-century writers, poor children such as Goody Two-Shoes and Giles Gingerbread display an industriousness that makes them successful and respected adults. The victimized—or underprivileged—child often becomes, like Goody and other virtuous heroines and heroes of children's literature, the capable child who skillfully negotiates the circumstances of life. Exemplars of good students, Goody and Giles achieve wealth and position because they diligently pursue their lessons in reading.[14] The translation of Tom Thumb's ingenuity in remarkable circumstances to the child's diligence in more mundane fields pervades eighteenth-century pedagogy. The 1755 edition of *Fenning's Universal Speller,* the most widely used speller in colonial schools, along with Dilworth's (discussed in Chapter 3), includes the story of "Virtuous Tommy" who unlike his counterpart Naughty Harry is "good-natured, pleasant and mannerly." Tommy accordingly becomes a rich and revered man while Harry falls into a life of crime and misery.[15] In a similar moral tale in a 1771 edition of the *New England Primer,* "Master Tommy Fido not only loved his book because it made him wiser, but because it made him better too."[16] Good boys and girls work for their prosperity; this success story would find its archetypal American form in Franklin's *Autobiography* and then, in the nineteenth-century, the Horatio Alger stories.

By the end of the eighteenth century, the Tom Thumb story itself incorporates the pedagogical values of Giles Gingerbread and Tommy Fido. In a 1780 version published in Boston, Tom ultimately settles in a kingdom where his greatest contribution to the people is teaching them reading and writing. The lessons that follow this narrative of Tom's life echo this conclusion, as one rhyme proclaims "He who ne'er learns his A, B, and C / Forever will a Blockhead be / But he who to his Book's inclin'd / Will soon a golden treasure find." The last entry in the book is a poem about the exemplary "Tommy Toy" who "listn'd and learn'd, when his friends did advise / And so became wealthy, and happy, and wise."[17] Tom Thumb in this book, likewise "a dutiful child," consults "both his mother and father" before undertaking his travels. When his parents object, he holds his own, eventually convincing them to approve his plans and then "receiving their blessing."[18] So as much as the book promotes the child's dutifulness, it also respects the child's reasoning and capacities, and honors the fact that a child's judgment might be better than that of his parents. As Tom Thumb turns into a scholarly paragon like Giles Gingerbread, he retains his independence.

It is Tom Thumb's combination of independence and industry that makes him successful and thus a good example for children. The virtues demonstrated and recommended by the tiny hero in the later-eighteenth-century versions of the tale apply to adults as well as children, and particularly to adults in positions of leadership. In teaching children how to be adult, the Tom Thumb story also provides adults with a primer for remodeling conduct. When Tom confronts the giant—named Grumbo in these versions—he does not do so in self-defense but for purposes of reformation. Tom does not worry about being eaten by this giant; he is more concerned to alter Grumbo's bad conduct toward his subjects. Noting that Grumbo "was proud, selfish, and so tyrannical and cruel, that his subjects were afraid to come near him," Tom determines to reform him through behavior modification. So whenever Grumbo began to sleep, Tom "pricked him with his little sword [a needle]." After continual sleep deprivation, Grumbo becomes so weak he cannot walk. Tom keeps the giant in this state until he has learned the language of the country and can communicate further with Grumbo. He then issues the tyrannical giant an ultimatum:

> "Are you inclined, O Grumbo, to live or to die? If you would live, you must take my advice, and behave with humanity and kindness to all your subjects and to me; but if you would rather die than be good, do so, for nobody will be sorry for you." (16)

Terrified by being menaced by such a tiny being, the giant begs to be permitted to amend his behavior.

> So from this time Tom left off goading him with his little sword, and he soon recovered. After this, he was very fond of Mr. Thumb, and would do nothing without him, so that, Tom had, in a manner, the whole direction of the kingdom, and made all the people happy, by a fair and equal distribution of justice; and for that purpose he rode in pomp, in a coach drawn by ten squirrels, all around the kingdom. (17)

Tom, however, takes care not to tax the people for his leadership. "To avoid putting the inhabitants to an expence on his journey, he carried his provisions with him . . . and ordered his squirrels to draw him every night up a tree, where they all lodged safely, without either trouble or expence" (17).

In overcoming and transforming the giant, Tom clearly takes on a supervisory role; his speech to Grumbo sounds like a parent's or teacher's reprimand of a wayward child. Under Tom's discipline, Grumbo learns to reconsider and reform his conduct, the primary lesson of Lockean child pedagogy. As in Locke's thought, this education fosters liberal political principles. The most important effect of Grumbo's self-improvement is his recognition and respect for his subjects. Tom's assumption of adult practices and authority demonstrates the aptitude, if not superior talent, of the subordinate classes, children and subjects, for managing their society. Gaining "the whole direction of the king-dom," Tom proves to be not only a kinder, gentler ruler, but also a much more economical one. Even though reformed in disposition, Grumbo in effect also reforms the structure of government, ceding his royal power to Tom who exercises it far more democratically. The antimonarchical tale unfolded in this story of Tom Thumb makes clear that more than an alteration of the king's behavior is necessary for the good of the people: the people need representatives of themselves as their leaders.

Casting Tom as a spokesperson and activist for democratic reforms, the story grants significance to the hitherto politically insignificant—to powerless subjects. Tom's tininess makes him a fitting emblem of the unentitled.[19] Tom's diminutive stature, however, operates to stress his adultlike attributes rather than his childlike qualities. The story is not advancing an argument for children's rights or a case for children rul-ing the world, or even the belief dear to nineteenth-century American reformers that children are natural democrats. Rather, Tom Thumb, in all his smallness, displays the fact that children can and do grow up. His inferior size—even though it does not change—never actually disad-vantages him in his encounters with the world because Tom develops cognitive and linguistic skills. He becomes adult in the ways that Locke identified as crucial for citizens: he learns to exercise his judgment, much to Grumbo's initial discomfort. The story underscores Tom's own self-improvements by beginning with accounts of Tom's mischie-vous acts, the acts of a naughty boy. Before Tom begins his moral and political reform of Grumbo, he amuses himself by stealing the giant's food and by soiling Grumbo's pockets. These childish behaviors then disappear as Tom devotes himself to learning the language and affairs of the kingdom and to changing Grumbo.

The limits of Tom's body are overcome by the growth and agility of his mind. Most people's bodies grow bigger along with the develop-ment of their minds. The fact that Tom remains tiny dramatizes the mental potentiality of every body, the potentiality that Locke defined as the basis for the political rights of every individual (albeit the indi-vidual understood as white, male, and British). Tom's successes despite his stunted size elaborate in a fantastic mode the Lockean premise of the entitled child. Far from limiting a child's possibilities in the world, the initial frailty of his body guarantees that a place be furnished for

him in the world prior to his finding one for himself. Locke clearly subordinated body to mind, taking the primary task of childhood education to be teaching the child to control his body's desires and frailties.[20]
In minimizing Tom's size, the eighteenth-century narrative of Tom's
experiences follows Locke's hierarchy of mind over body—especially as
the Tom Thumb books evolve into pedagogical texts during the latter
half of the century.

The Tom Thumb story thus becomes less a record of the remarkable
feats of an especially little boy than an account of the features of a very
little person who is an exemplary individual. It is finally not about as-
tounding or prodigious capacities of children but about what right-
minded persons can accomplish over time. A chronicle of childhood's
evolution into adulthood, this story follows Tom into fatherhood:
Grumbo bestows his daughter on Tom and this giant wife bears him
giant twin sons. While the Arthurian legends of Tom Thumb also trace
Tom into his maturity, he remains subject to his king, and ultimately
suffers his death for offending his king. His offense, significantly, stems
from uncontrolled adult bodily impulses: he attempts to rape the
queen. Within a monarchical ethos, Tom comes to an ignominious end
because he violates the king's trust. The later variant of the story of
Tom's sexual maturity brings Tom into kinship with the king as Tom
both transforms the government and produces his own family. Tom
here directs the desires of his adult body in an acceptable fashion,
which results in the founding of a new social order. While it is unclear
whether monarchy disappears from Grumbo's land, Tom's connection
with it has certainly checked the tyrannical tendencies of Grumbo.
Tom provides Grumbo with more than a family connection. On the
occasion of the birth of Tom's children, Grumbo's grandchildren,
Grumbo learns to understand the value of written language. Far away
from Grumbo's court, Tom communicates the news of the twins' birth
by writing to a court member to whom he has taught reading and writing. Seeing that persons can represent themselves over the distances
and time that constrain bodily contacts, Grumbo receives with his
grandchildren his final and most important lesson from Tom: the value
of representation in and for society.

In this final episode, the tale encapsulates the significance of representational practices. Before Tom Thumb's reforms, Grumbo used terror and superior force to express and implement his will. Tom's learn-

ing of Grumbo's language and later introduction of writing and reading (the language appears to be an unwritten one) temper Grumbo's rule and suggest alternative modes of conducting sociopolitical relations. In this story, the acquisition of language techniques displays how even those out of sight and those who are speechless—the babies—can make their presence known. Grumbo's own connection to the future, the continuance of the royal family, depends upon imagining his descendants in his place, somehow perpetuating his identity. Pairing the arrival of the grandchildren with the advent of literary communication, the tale links posterity with representation. The connection between Grumbo and his royal heirs, the fact of Grumbo having heirs, becomes known through the public circulation of words; this connection also depends on the (physical and cognitive) mediations of Tom. Continuity thereby becomes a function of operations independent of the monarch, operations that enable transcendence of corporeal limits. Whereas the hereditary power held by monarchs traditionally relies on the reproduction of the royal family, Grumbo's posterity and their claims to power stem from Tom and his ways even more than from Grumbo. The means of self-perpetuity thus also mark the succession and replaceability of individuals like Grumbo or Tom. Children, like the language that communicates their arrival, may or may not resemble their progenitors; in representing the families into which they are born they inevitably introduce other or new characteristics. Tom Thumb's children significantly appear simultaneously with the introduction of reading and writing in the kingdom, signaling the rise of representational political principles during the eighteenth century.[21]

By learning and disseminating the uses of language, Tom exhibits the crucial role of language in supplementing the body. Fittingly, the 1780 Boston *Tom Thumb's Folio* relates that Tom, during his travels and many civic activities, "wrote a particular account of the country and their inhabitants, their laws, customs, and manners; which, we are told, will soon be revised and published" (17). More than a puff for future editions of *Tom Thumb*, this announcement also identifies Tom as a writer. As the narrative associates literary, pedagogical, and political projects, it reiterates Locke's emphasis on the importance of reflection, the mental consideration of acts performed or projected. The time and space of reflection, in which the past can be repeated or various futures enacted, extends beyond the space and time inhabited by the body, providing intervals in which individuals can read themselves.

Locke situates individual freedom, the basis of consent, in the human capacity to see human acts, past and future, as narratives subject to judgment and revision.[22] The representational practice of self-reflection, like the reading and writing of letters or books, allows persons to gain perspectives not immediately available to them: to see themselves in the manner they have conducted themselves as well as in manners they might have or still might conduct themselves. Seen in light of Locke's portrait of the features and habits of the consensual individual, the eighteenth-century Tom Thumb story most often circulated under the title *Tom Thumb's Folio* celebrates the processes of narrative revision by which persons can improve themselves and their society. Tom Thumb, we are told, is revising his account of Grumbo's kingdom even as he is revising the rule of the kingdom. Tom Thumb teaches that political customs, like children, evolve and change.

At the beginning of the Revolution, when Paine was writing *Common Sense*, the individual force manifest in Tom Thumb's marvelous mastery of ogres and giants was evident also in the less extensive proficiencies of Goody, Giles, and the exemplary Tommies. Though these children do not change the world, they manage to transform the circumstances of their own lives. At the heart of the appeal for suffering children thus stands a confidence in the ability of children to make it on their own.

The Wrongs of Children

Paine urges Americans to apply the contemporary faith in children's endeavors to the case of their own independence. But he first projects the vulnerability of the American situation. The task of Paine's address is to establish a common feeling of long suffering among the colonists that will issue in a collective rebellion against England. To make the Revolutionary cause common sense, Paine appeals to what he conceives as universal feelings about injury and redress, which he calls "those feelings and affections which nature justifies" (89). Paine allows that the "thousands already ruined by British barbarity" may "have other feelings than us who have nothing suffered" (94). "Having noth-

ing more to lose," they quite naturally "disdain submission" to England. He needs to convince those who have not yet suffered to align
themselves with those already committed to revolution. Paine thus argues that everyone, because "sensible of injuries," can imagine what it
feels like to be driven from house and home, to have property destroyed and circumstances ruined. Everyone can and should make the
sufferers' case his own. As Paine reasons, "the social compact would
dissolve, and justice be extirpated [from] the earth, or have only a ca-
sual existence were we callous to the touches of affection. The robber
and the murderer, would often escape unpunished, did not the injuries
which our tempers sustain, provoke us into justice" (100).

In Paine's conjectural portrait of the formation of societies and governments, vice "unavoidably" intrudes on and interferes with the basic
social affections that unite persons. Government is a "necessary evil"
that people establish "to supply the moral defect of virtue," to restrain
"our vices" (65). Social organization is thus fundamentally compensa-
tory, and redress of injury is the standard operating procedure by which
both social affiliations and disaffiliations occur.

Making his case for the injured colonial subjects, Paine developed
the Lockean figure of the child-citizen into the figure of crime victim.
Vice, according to Paine, "unavoidably" arises from a "remissness" in
persons' "duty and attachment to each other" (66). To restore a sense of
"common cause," Paine urges his readers to recall their social affections, the common concern epitomized by parental sentiment for children. In an essay published six months before *Common Sense*, Paine
censured the "unprincipled" British for having forgotten social affections: "They have lost sight of the limits of humanity." Americans must
defend themselves and their children against the British because "the
portrait of a parent red with the blood of her children is a picture fit
only for the galleries of the infernals."[23] Paine's repeated exhortations
in *Common Sense* to remember the children and their future children
expand the population of sufferers under England's rule and thereby
widen the sympathy required to relieve such suffering. Breaking from
the abusive British parent, therefore, "'Tis not the concern of a day, a
year, or an age; posterity are virtually involved in the contest, and will
be more or less affected, even to the end of time, by the proceedings
now" (82). To avoid the break, Paine stresses, would only defer revolution to the next generation, and therefore would burden them with suf-

ferings that could be prevented. "Wherefore since nothing but blows will do, for God's sake, let us come to a final separation, and not leave the next generation to be cutting throats, under the violated unmeaning names of parent and child" (90).

Paine figures England as not only an abusive parent but also an illegitimate one. "Europe, and not England, is the parent country of America" because "this new world hath been the asylum for the persecuted lovers of civil and religious liberty from *every part* of Europe" (84). The "phrase of parent or mother country as applied to England only" accordingly seems to Paine "false, selfish, narrow and ungenerous" (85). After "the fatal nineteenth of April 1775" when the English troops massacred Americans at Lexington, King George can only be disdained as "the wretch, that with the pretended title of FATHER OF HIS PEOPLE can unfeelingly hear of their slaughter, and composedly sleep with their blood upon his soul" (92). Because such illegitimate and abusive authority "sooner or later must have an end . . . as parents, we [Americans] can have no joy, knowing that *this government* is not sufficiently lasting to ensure any thing which we may bequeath to posterity" (87). So "the precariousness with which all American property is possessed" threatens present and future persons. The effects of Britain's injuries against Americans appear permanent and perpetual. Marked and forever altered by these injuries, Americans must halt any continued affiliation with England. Indeed, "the last cord now is broken" for "as well as the lover can forgive the ravisher of his mistress" can "the continent forgive the murders of Britain" (99).

"There are injuries which nature cannot forgive," Paine declares; the injuries that the American colonists have suffered from the British government appear to be assaults on persons that amount to robberies of their former conditions. Because violence invades and irrevocably alters bodies, it interrupts the natural courses of persons—it robs them of time as they have known it. Thus Paine puts the American complaint in the form of a lament: "Can ye restore to us the time that is past? Can ye give to prostitution its former innocence?" (99). In the image of the ravished mistress, as well as in the image of the prostitute whose "former innocence" can never be restored, Paine represents colonial Americans as permeable bodies, bodies now altered beyond the innocent state of childhood and that must be protected by separating them from their former relations. The offspring who represent the future of these bodies—their generative, affective, and economic capacities—will also be protected by the break from Britain. Paine thus envisions the reformation of the North American colonies into an independent nation as the establishment of an "asylum for mankind" (100), that is, no less than a protective act for the future of humanity.

Futurity and Debt

In Paine's vindication of the wrongs of children, sympathy for the suffering child redirects Americans from a sense of obligations to the past, embodied in monarchy, to a sense of obligation to the future. Against monarchical power and custom, Paine asserts the rights of men, present and future. Rather than deferring to tradition, Paine urges Americans to look forward. This redirection of obligation toward children instead of parents identifies the rights and interests of present persons with posterity.[24] The unborn appear as potential victims whom present persons must act to protect; they are doubles of those already suffering under British rule. Paine thus multiplies the number of injured persons, and in invoking bodies not yet existent, summons as well the image of bodies exempt from the present circumstances of the colonists. The appeal to the future thereby both intensifies and allays the threat of suffering. The apparition of future children suffering not only justifies rebellion from England as a defense of humanity, but also displays the possibility of relief from present distress. To establish materially (and immediately) a connection to the future and to obtain the alleviation of present difficulties that the future offers, Paine proposes that American colonists should contract their own national debt.

Whereas late-twentieth-century rhetoric sets up an antinomy between children and national debt, Paine strikingly conceives national debt as the "national bond" (102) that will sustain affective relations between present and future. As the sign of Americans' obligation to their children, debt will remind future generations of what their Revolutionary ancestors have done for them. Not to establish independence from Britain, according to Paine, "is using posterity with the utmost cruelty; because it is leaving them with the great work to do, and a debt upon their backs from which they derive no advantage" (101). As a British colony, America at that time had to contribute to the payment of Britain's considerable national debts. By allowing this situation to continue, "we [Americans] are running the next generation into debt" (87). If future Americans are to be obligated to a debt, it should be a debt made by Americans: "We ought to do the work of it, otherwise we use [posterity] meanly and pitifully" (87). The work of eighteenth-century Americans in contracting a national debt—the work of revolution and nation-building—therefore will serve and save future Americans. "Whatever we may contract on this account will serve as a glorious memento of our virtue. Can we but leave posterity with a settled form of government, an independent constitution of its own, the purchase at any price will be cheap" (101).

In Paine's view, contracting a national debt enables and benefits the generations who inherit it.[25] An American debt will stand as a testament to a new social compact in which present Americans bequeath their descendants with their own nation. As documentation of a commitment to the future, debt conveys to future generations their own right to manage their relation to the past and to the future. These future peoples, of course, might choose to relinquish or reconceive their relation to the past. Paine sees debt as beneficial to posterity because in presenting this choice, debt confirms the sovereignty of the people. Even though debt may commit future generations to repayment, it does so only if those generations choose to continue the political system into which they are born. As Noah Webster put it in 1787, people "have no right to make laws for those who are not yet in existence."[26] Making debts confers responsibility on those not yet alive only if they accept the authority of their government and therefore authorize that government to assume debts, old or new.

For the sake of the Revolutionary cause that affects the fate of posterity "even to the end of time" (82), Paine turns Americans from their ties to the past to their duties to the future. In one of the most memorable of the many striking images in *Common Sense*, Paine envisions how the Revolution will inhabit the landscape of distant generations to come: "The least fracture now will be like a name engraved with the point of a pin on the tender rind of a young oak; the wound will enlarge with the tree, and posterity read it in full grown letters" (81). Enacting revolution and contracting a new national debt with a new nation will transform the world. The event will leave its mark, significantly in the process of natural growth, to be seen, traced, and appreciated. Time will enhance the magnitude of the message that present acts convey as these acts accrue in the age and girth of the oak.

Just a few months previous to writing *Common Sense*, Paine had sym-
bolized the American cause in the image of a tree in his poem *The Liberty Tree*.[27] In the poem, subtitled "A Song, Written Early in the American Revolution," the "Goddess of Liberty" brings to America "the
plant she named the Liberty Tree." Once rooted in America, the tree
makes its locale synonymous with liberty:

> The celestial exotic stuck deep in the ground,
> Like a native it flourished and bore;
> The fame of its fruit drew the nations around
> To seek out this peaceable shore.
> Unmindful of names or distinctions they came,
> For freemen like brothers agree;
> With one spirit endued, they one friendship pursued,
> And their temple was the Liberty Tree.

The regularity of the rhymes and lines match the portrait of uniformity
that Paine describes here. Within the vicinity of the Liberty Tree, distinctions among persons disappear and social harmony ensues. Obviously a wholly idealized account of the diverse and divided interests
and individuals in colonial America, Paine's poem imagines what does
not yet exist: a unified American society. The poem furnishes mythic
origins for this society, the divinity's gift of the tree, which far from introducing human problems as the tree of the knowledge of good and
evil did in Eden, confers and encourages the human virtues of brother-
hood, equality, amity, and peace. Thus life beneath the tree appears
paradisiacal:

> Beneath this fair tree, like the patriarchs of old,
> Their bread in contentment they ate,
> Unvexed with the troubles of silver or gold,
> The cares of the grand and the great.

Exempt from economic concerns, untroubled by desires, the American
colonists seem to live at ease in a state of nature. But Paine quickly alters this idyllic portrait by noting in the next line that the American
colonists do labor, for "with timber and tar they Old England supplied." Besides passing on the resources of America to England, Ameri-

cans also "supported her power on the sea / Her battles they fought." Though living under the Liberty Tree, Americans serve England's imperial power as they perform these efforts "without getting a groat / For the honour of Liberty Tree." American subjection to England contradicts the ideal of America as a land of liberty. Paine accordingly characterizes the pre-Revolutionary situation of the colonies as England's assault on the Liberty Tree:

> But hear, O ye swains ('tis a tale most profane),
> How all the tyrannical powers,
> Kings, Commons, and lords, are uniting amain
> To cut down this guardian of ours.

Paine then calls Americans to arms "in defence of our Liberty Tree." In the rather crude allegory here, Paine makes what would become his standard identification of the cause of America with the cause of universal liberty.[28]

In *Common Sense*, however, Paine sets out a less abstract and more immediate threat to Americans by focusing on bodily harm. Thus his descriptions of American Revolutionary acts as lasting effects upon the landscape welds Americans to their land, to the locale in which they reside. In the image of the oak tree engraven with the American Revolution, Paine abandons the theoretical symbology of the Liberty Tree for a more intimate metaphor, the almost personified oak that stands witness to history. More long-lived than persons, the tree both suffers and survives human acts. Casting the American Revolutionary moment in the experience of the oak tree, Paine intensifies and magnifies the significance of present suffering and actions. If the American experience belongs to the larger enterprise of universal liberty, it begins with the experiences of American bodies and their effects on the world they inhabit. *Common Sense* claims that the cause of liberty undertaken by Americans eventually will become a global phenomenon, the project of all humanity. Paine thus characterizes Americans as the initiators of discourses about liberty, as composing a new narrative of liberty rising from the American case rather than fitting the American case into an older narrative like that of the "patriarchs of old" under the Liberty Tree. References to the past never accompany the description of America in *Common Sense*; America appears only in tandem with the present and future. "Now is the seed time of continental union," Paine proclaims, announcing the originary acts by which Americans will generate their nation. The urgency of action that Paine repeatedly stresses involves not only reaction to England but also foundational acts for America: Americans must plant as well as defend their own trees.

In using tree imagery, Paine was employing a long-standing emblem of British history, a sign linked to monarchy. During the eighteenth century the oak still popularly figured the king, as in the alphabet rhyme "The royal Oak, it was the tree / That sav'd his royal majesty," which commemorated the survival of Charles II.[29] Aligning America with a "young oak," Paine deliberately reclaims the associations of the tree with liberty and severs the tree's connection with monarchy and England. Instead of sending their timber to England and relying on the ancient English symbology of trees, Americans should use and develop their own trees and genealogies of meaning.

Paine himself assumed the pen name "The Forester" during the spring of 1776 when he was writing replies to attacks on *Common Sense*, continuing the tree imagery that the poem and pamphlet promoted.[30] Paine finds in and takes from the tree symbol not just a natural image for liberty but also, more importantly, materials for writing. Trees provide both the physical materials and symbolic possibilities of rewriting the identity of colonial Americans. Thus, in *Common Sense*, Paine employs the oak tree to herald the reparative and revisionary possibilities available to the colonists. Through the scarred and inscribed oak, Paine offers a representational strategy for relieving the harmful situation so powerfully described in his own rhetoric of imperiled children.

Relief and Representation

To counter and repair the image of Americans as wounded children, an image sustained in the description of the impressionable "tender rind of a young oak," Paine imagines their Revolution as a healing incision. The Revolutionary "fracture" operates not to injure or destroy but to furnish the future with a record of commitment to it. Paine describes this wounding as a form of writing, a process that succeeds and memorializes the present. The pain and suffering ascribed to the injured colonists are thus relieved and replaced by the activities of working, rebelling, fighting, contracting, and building. It is not enough for Americans to think of themselves as injured children. They have to become rescuers and guardians of themselves and those children yet to come. The prosthetics of revolution, debt, manufacture, and trade that Paine prescribes thus also invoke the figures of heroic children who accompany the eighteenth-century figures of suffering children. Significantly, as Paine envisions the future in *Common Sense*, the image of abused children gives way to lists and enumerations of potential American prosperity, to representations of possibilities awaiting incorporation rather than reports of unalterable bodies. Moving from scarred bodies to numerical projections, from the detailing of injuries to the counting of compensations, *Common Sense* follows the same chronology as the late-eighteenth-century narratives of Tom Thumb's life. Like the Tom Thumb stories, Paine's narrative proceeds from vulnerability to strength, from subjection to self-government. As in Tom Thumb's experience, representational techniques make this progress possible. Words and numbers extend beyond the limits of the body, beyond its frailties or incapacities due to size or power, supplying a way of imagining better conditions for the body.

To the third edition of the pamphlet, Paine appended a list of calculations of the cost of building an American navy for national defense and commerce. The numbers by which Paine tallies the expense of this enterprise, for which he recommends contracting a national debt, promise security and comfort. Rather than concluding with the imagery of permanently altered bodies—such as the ravished mistress, ruined prostitute, or hurt child—Paine supplements the all too vulnerable and evanescent location of the body with written figures that measure (or at least predict) the accumulation of resources that will sustain bodies. The continued safety and welfare of bodies requires the metaphysical operations that numerical and linguistic figures perform. Thus for Paine, the measures of statistics and future history (itself a statistical conjecture) record and convey what persons have done and can do.[31] The scarred, no-longer-young oak survives; its marks of injury become both the sign of its healing and the register of something more. The surviving oak exhibits the growth that the future can bring. Paine's imagery of pain gives way to an imagery of the gains that can succeed pain.

It is by virtue of growth that the tree outstrips the past that has marred it, a growth that from an immediate standpoint can be grasped only imaginatively. Providing the prospect of better conditions, Paine proffers the advantages of colonists' identifying themselves with (a healthy) posterity. He thus substitutes the imagined bodies of progeny for the present injured bodies. Present bodies may be more perceptible, but they are no less subject to Paine's exhortation to see them imaginatively, as wounded children. Paine continually urges Americans to regard themselves as entities that could be otherwise. If the reader "will divest himself of prejudice and prepossession," Paine enjoins, "he will put *on*, or rather he will not put *off*, the true character of a man, and generously enlarge his views beyond the present day" (81–82). In a pamphlet written several years later, he famously proclaims the success of the changed perspective he sought to achieve with *Common Sense* and the Revolution: "We see with other eyes; we hear with other ears; and think with other thoughts, than those we formerly used. We can look back on our own prejudices, as if they had been the prejudices of other people."[32] The possibility of present persons becoming "other people"—different and better people than their former selves—begins in the present. Urging Americans to act now ("now is the seed time of continental union") and to look forward, Paine initiates the project of becoming other people through reflection and projection. Children furnish the best model of how people change. Children's bodies grow and overcome their initial frailties and limitations; along with the passage of time that brings this growth, children mature through the development and exercise of their cognitive skills. The latter avenue of growth can continue beyond the culmination of bodily growth so that even adults can still become other people.

At least as dramatic as Tom Thumb's attainments of poise and power is the giant Grumbo's reformation. The transformations by which children become adults and continue to mature show how far the initial state of bodies can be surpassed. As Tom Thumb demonstrates, this progress can occur even when bodily growth does not ensue. The body, as Paine uses it in *Common Sense*, is an object to be acted upon, an occasion for something better. From the spectre of suffering children, Paine therefore summons both the feeling of a situation demanding immediate response and the confidence that present inequities and difficulties will be overcome. For Paine and other early Americans, the idea of the empowered child depends crucially on the ephemerality of childhood, on the courses of natural and cultural history that inevitably change bodies. Following Locke's recognition of children's malleability (within limits), Paine pictures Americans as children only to imagine them as otherwise. His association of children with change assures Americans that their condition can and will be improved. Improvement, though, will not come simply and naturally with time. To be otherwise in any significant way—which is to say, to be subject no longer to British rule—requires effort and determination in the present. "Youth is the seed time of good habits, as well in nations as in individuals" (107–108). The immediate enterprise of American colonists will have lasting effects on themselves and their progeny. Thus the wounding of the tender rind of a young oak refers not just to British injuries of American bodies but to the revolutionary acts of Americans. Only Americans themselves can mend fully the wrongs stemming from their subjected condition. The mixture of metaphors that Paine's rhetoric generates and exploits operates on a principle of change; objects possess the capacity to become agents and minds can surpass bodies.

Because of the capacity for change that plants and persons manifest, Paine can see alternative possibilities in all present circumstances. He describes the revolutionary actions of colonists in the same terms as the repressive acts of Britain. Both leave permanent marks on Americans. Yet Americans act upon themselves to different effect; their acts of self-determination will stamp a distinctive message on the American landscape that future generations will receive with gratitude. Because actions carry long-term representational effects, touching even the unborn, there is an urgency to present deeds—the urgency pervading *Common Sense* to perform "our duty to mankind at large, as well as to ourselves" (86)—because of their imagined scope. This imagined import, for Paine, is no less real for being abstract. More than bodily pain, which after all usually passes, the prospect of lasting effects, whether harmful or beneficial, demands immediate attention. Bodies and actions, the specific loci of history, from the start signify beyond their spatial and temporal limits. Thus Paine's spotlight on the vulnerable bodies of children illuminates what he takes to be most compelling about the sight of children suffering. More than the atrocity of weak creatures in distress, the possibility of this peril reaching into the future appalls Paine.[33] In showing how far suffering can go, Paine suggests that individual bodily pain is not an isolated experience but an event that, once described, touches on all humans. When he characterizes an independent American nation as an "asylum for mankind" (100), he is making his universalist point about the effects of every human experience and thence the "necessity" of the American Revolution.

The first edition of *Common Sense* ends with the word necessity. The urgency of the current situation is also, Paine emphasizes in the appendix to subsequent editions, an opportunity: "We have it in our power to begin the world again" (120). Paine likens the momentousness of the present occasion to the Biblical event of destroying and rebuilding creation. "A situation, similar to the present, hath not happened since the days of Noah until now" (120).[34] By this imaginative leap, Paine identifies Americans with a violent but ultimately productive and beneficial event for humanity. If imagination multiplies and intensifies human suffering, it also can supply relief. Hence the value of representational schema for Paine lies in the improvements and progress that narratives, statistics, predictions, tables, lists, and graphs allow us to envision. While the narrative arc of *Common Sense* begins with the body and ends with words and numbers by which the body is to be augmented, Paine's rhetoric of the body from the start depends upon understanding corporeality as a function of mental operations, including fantasy, sympathy, analogy, revision, and calculation. These operations can take the literary forms of fiction, metaphor, and simile, or the mathematical forms of formulae, graphs, and statistics. To improve upon the body, to alter either its given natural state or historical condition, Paine looks to the imaginative faculties of bodies by which they overcome their limitations.

By supplementing representational processes, bodies can be bettered. Representative government, the plan Paine recommends to the colonists, provides this supplementation, materially securing Americans with the means of protecting and improving themselves.[35] Consenting to be governed by a "select number chosen from the whole body" of people, Americans will be able to trust their representatives "to have the same concerns at stake which those have who appointed them" and to "act in the same manner as the whole body would act were they present" (69). Through representation, their situations and requirements can be made known and addressed by the government. Elected representatives supplement the bodies of the electors, who are subject to exigencies of time, space, work, and other obligations. The great advantage of representation, according to Paine, is that it is an

entity different from and better than a body—it is beyond the vulnera-
bilities of the body. Thus, in *The Rights of Man*, where he again ac-
claimed the advantages of the representative form of government, he
abandoned altogether the corporeal characterization of a nation. "A
nation is not a body, the figure of which is to be represented by the human body; but is like a body contained within a circle, having a common centre, in which every radius meets, and that centre is formed by
representation."[36] In the geometric figure of a body within a circle,
Paine presents a nation as an entity composed of many individual lines
that intersect at one point, the locus of the representative government
upon which the members of the nation have agreed. The body in this
paradigm for nation recalls the natural order through which civic systems assert their propriety. Beyond this abstract claim for the organi-
cism of nations, the body matters very little in this portrait of nation,
which has as its focal point the center of the circle. The center stands as
the common point of reference for all the points forming the circle;
unlike a body, the figure of the center encompasses equally many individual entities.

In picturing the representative system of government as the center
of a circle, Paine claims for this system the perfect unity of the circle.
The even greater advantage of representative government, for Paine, is
that "it places government in a state of constant maturity. It is . . . never
young, never old. It is subject neither to nonage, nor dotage. It is never
in the cradle, nor on crutches."[37] Paine's language here echoes Locke's
description of "the imperfect state of Childhood" as "ignorant Nonage" (*Second Treatise* VII, 58, 3–4; Laslett, 324). In time, once the child
has acquired reason and knowledge of the law, he can manage without
any governors. For Paine, the imperfection of childhood necessitating
temporary guardianship by adults makes childhood an inadequate figure for self-government. He likewise banishes second childhood, the
frailties of old age, from his portrait of self-government.

Leaving behind the image of nation as a body that includes the weak
features of infancy and senility, Paine chooses a more stable, imperme-
able image from mathematical patterns. While the body offers an example of potential growth, it also bears the uncertainties and inadequacies of both early and late age, vicissitudes that all the powers of
imagination and representation may not allay. Because "government always ought to be superior . . . to all the accidents of individual

man," Paine envisions it in terms more stable than the corporeal can comprise.[38]

Sixteen years earlier in *Common Sense*, Paine had described the prospective citizens of the United States of America (in the first printed usage of this name for the new country) as bodies notable for both their potential and vulnerability: "we are young, and we have been distressed" (108). After unfolding his narrative of distressed children who turn out to be quite capable of taking care of themselves, Paine can consider the adult aftermath of that story. This aftermath, like Tom Thumb's civic career, presents future Americans with the means of bettering themselves through public and political forms of representation. That Americans over two hundred years later conduct discussions of their rights and needs to such a great degree in public venues suggests the enduring success of the eighteenth-century narrative of children's rights, which has thoroughly accustomed citizens to think of themselves as children with complaints to air. For Paine, however, the crucial point to be taken from the paradigm of the child's progress from frailty to empowerment is that childhood ends. As the physical condition of childhood passes, it leaves a powerful legacy. Childhood supplies the pattern, remembered or imagined, of the potential for transformation. This combination of memory and imagination is the common sense that Paine summoned and spurred in the American colonists.

II

*Consent and the
Early American Novel*

Introduction:
The Feminization of Consent

The confidence in children's capacities advocated by Paine's Revolutionary rhetoric carried the Lockean principle of self-determination into political practice. Late-eighteenth-century Americans rebelled from the British government and instituted their own nation by claiming their birthrights. The Lockean legacy to early Americans, however, also included a sense of the difficulties of self-government.

Even though Locke soldered consent to the faculty of reasoning, he worried that "there is nothing more restive and ungovernable than our own thoughts."[1] To get full mastery over our own thoughts is a continual task, one crucial to the exercise of consent. By arranging and regulating our thoughts, we settle upon decisions. Locke readily acknowledged the difficulty of this task, noting "that there is scarce anything harder in the whole conduct of the understanding . . . than for a man to be able to dispose of his own thoughts" (*Conduct*, 96). The difficulty in ordering and settling thoughts stems from the mind's susceptibility to influences that impede the individual's mental movements. Besides custom and prejudice, which both Paine and Locke decry as limitations upon mental mobility, certain psychological phenomena persistently threaten the "liberty of mind" (102). Just as habit ties an individual to a set of ideas, other conditions can make it difficult "to transfer our minds from one subject to another." Like "corporal liberty," liberty of mind is a freedom of movement. The man who is "fully master of his own thoughts" is "able to transfer them from one subject to another with the same ease that he can lay by anything he has in his hand and take something else that he has a mind to" (102).

Locke carefully attends to factors that interfere with the ready transfer of thoughts, the movement of mind necessary to inform and execute judgment. The "most obvious and general . . . cause that binds up the understanding," he finds, is passion (*Conduct*, 99). Romantic love or maternal grief can completely absorb an individual. Such a passion can "take possession of" and rule the mind, as if it were "the sheriff of the place" (97). No one is exempt from subjection to passion:

> There is scarce anybody, I think, of so calm a temper who has not sometimes found this tyranny on his understanding, and suffered under the inconvenience of it. Who is there almost whose mind, at some time or other, love or anger, fear or grief, has not so fastened to some clog, that it could not turn itself to any other object? I call it a clog, for it hangs upon the mind so as to hinder its vigor and activity in the pursuit of other contemplations, and advances itself little or not at all in the knowledge of the thing which it so closely hugs and constantly pores upon. (*Conduct*, 97)

Passion tyrannizes the individual by taking away mental liberty. A mind clogged by passion cannot move beyond its attachment to one object. "Men thus possessed are sometimes as if they were so in the worse sense, and lay under the power of an enchantment" (*Conduct*, 98). In this clogged state of mind, the individual appears invaded by an external force. The mind is no longer "free and ready to turn itself to the variety of objects that occur." Sometimes the intense engagement in just "one object" arises not from passion but by chance (98). Though not caused by any emotional attachment, this obsessiveness nonetheless "works itself into a warmth" so that it resembles a passionate mania (99).

Passionate and accidental clogs hinder mental movements by inhabiting the mind and inhibiting its usual activities. In order to avoid such forms of tyranny, the individual must be aware of the possible intrusions that can occur. Locke accordingly notes another phenomenon that can "importune the understanding": "Some trivial sentence, or a scrap of poetry, will sometimes get into men's heads, and make such a chiming there, that there is no stalling of it; no peace to be obtained, no attention to anything else, but this impertinent guest will take up the mind and possess the thoughts in spite of all endeavors to get rid of it" (*Conduct*, 100).

Odder cases of "this fantastical phenomenon" involve "a sort of visions." Persons lying awake in the dark or with their eyes shut see a train of peculiar, unknown faces. Whatever the form of the "troublesome intrusion," it operates independently of the intruded mind (*Conduct*, 100). A woman acquaintance of Locke reported witnessing a train of faces, "all strangers and intruders" who "as they came of themselves they went too; none of them stayed a moment, nor could be detained by all the endeavors she could use" (101).

"To have the mind captivated" by hallucinations, inner voices, or any other "impertinent guest" strikes Locke as "a sort of childishness of the understanding," a playing "to no end" (*Conduct*, 102, 100). Throughout Locke's taxonomy of impediments to understanding, he foregrounds the permeability of the mind through which an individual can lose the liberty of choosing and moving his thoughts. In his liberal psychology, consent to being governed does not immunize the individual from other nonconsensual experiences. The consensual individual appears to face perpetual threats of intrusion and subjection. Habit, prejudice, passion, obsession, and hallucination often usurp liberty of mind. Like tyrants, intruders in the mind exercise an illegitimate authority, returning the individual to the incapacities of childhood.

But if intrusions introduce tyranny, as they reduce understanding to "a sort of childishness" (*Conduct*, 100), this very subjection rouses the mind to activity, and hence to liberty of movement. Children, according to Locke, regularly resist subjection to anyone or anything that interferes with "their Liberty" for "'tis that Liberty alone which gives the true Relish and Delight to their ordinary Play-games."[2] Children do not yet know how to "set the mind right, that on all occasions it may be disposed to consent to nothing but what may be suitable to the dignity and excellency of a rational creature."[3] But they desire and deserve to operate their own minds. Even though childhood is a condition of insufficient understanding, in Locke's view it is nevertheless a safe haven for individual liberty. The very incapacities of children that warrant temporary dependence upon adults also entitle them to the eventual independent exercise of authority.

Thus the problem of the invaded mind contains its own solution. In conceiving of children's relation to parental authority as consensual, Locke not only establishes political rights as birthrights, but also safeguards these rights from the propensities of individuals to be precipitated back into childish conditions. Instead of undermining individual authority, the recurrence of childhood subjection strengthens it by recapitulating the foundation of that authority in a state of incapacity. Though the very cognitive facility that entitles humans to self-determination in Locke's political philosophy exposes them to various kinds of subjection, this fact does not undercut the importance of cognition for consent. A remedy for mental intrusions is "always at hand"; "the rousing of mind, and setting the understanding on work with some degrees of vigor" can "set it free" from intruders (*Conduct*, 103). The mind itself, in Locke's view, wants to attain liberty. "Children love liberty," Locke asserts, but "they love something more; and that is *Dominion*."[4] By positing the mental instinct to overturn mental subjection, Locke accords authority to individuals even in their most helpless, most childish states. The education that children require to direct themselves never ends. The Lockean individual must work continuously to keep intruders and tyrants at bay, to keep the mind freely and purposively moving from object to object.

By the end of the eighteenth century, discourses on the permeabilities of minds were staples of medicine, psychology, aesthetic theory, and literary criticism. Locke's concerns with mental susceptibility persisted as a rider on liberal individualism, becoming after the Revolution a dominant motif in American culture. Like Locke's figures of the mourning mother and the hallucinating woman, the susceptible individual is usually female: a seduced girl, a deluded female reader, a hysterical woman. The oft-noted late-eighteenth-century feminization of sensibility worked to contain spectres of consent in female bodies. Representations of anxieties about, and hopes for, the nation founded upon consent accordingly took the form of narratives about women in trouble. The situation of a woman beseiged encapsulated nicely Locke's typology of the childishness to which the adult mind can always be reduced. Unenfranchised and sparingly educated, women remained children in status until the twentieth century, when they finally obtained the rights with which Locke entitled all children. For the early United States, then, women perfectly embodied the permeability of the

Lockean individual, whose subjection can be either consensual or non-consensual.

One of the most vivid examples of individual permeability, and of female permeability, appeared in the phenomenon of mesmerism, prevalent in France, and especially Paris, during the 1770s and 1780s. Thomas Jefferson, the American ambassador to France, thought mesmerism "an imputation of so grave a nature as would bear an action at law in America."[5] The French government shared Jefferson's concern as the popular pseudoscience gained adherents among academics and politicians. In 1784, the king of France appointed two commissions, one from the Royal Academy of Medicine and the other from the Royal Academy of Science, to investigate mesmerism.

Franz Mesmer, the Austrian physician who introduced the system named after himself, believed in what he called animal magnetism, a universal fluid existing in and passing among human bodies. Sickness arose from a disequilibrium in the distribution of this fluid within a body, and could be relieved by the restoration of a balanced relation to this fluid. To restore the balance, Mesmer would "magnetize" patients, inciting them to crises from which a healthy ebb and flow supposedly would follow.[6] Magnetizing, or mesmerizing as it came to be called, involved passing iron rods over the patient's body, pressing the regions of the lower belly, and directing the patient by look and word. Often this treatment was performed on a group of patients, who were linked together by hands and ropes around tubs of water designed to facilitate the movement of magnetism.

The mesmerist's manual, ocular, and verbal directions put patients in states of extreme receptivity. Persons under mesmeric treatment became mediums for the will or expression of other persons—sometimes other patients, but more often the mesmerist-physicians. Because of its display of the permeability of persons, mesmerism immediately became associated with women, who were already conventional figures of impressionability.[7] The mesmeric appeared to demonstrate anew the qualities of individual susceptibility that the eighteenth century generally identified as feminine.[8] Like Locke's portrayal of the intruded mind, mesmerism projects a portrait of individuals beseiged by and impinged upon by external forces. This image of the invaded individual suffuses the 1785 report by the Royal Academy of Sciences commission, which investigated and repudiated Mesmer's claims about animal magnetism. The commission's report, written by Benjamin Franklin, pronounced the existence of the animal magnetic fluid "chimerical" (97).[9] "Too subtle to be subjected to observation, . . . it surrounds you or penetrates your frame, without your being informed of its presence. If it therefore exists in us, and around us, it is after a manner perfectly insensible," Franklin wryly concluded (30–31).

The commission came to this conclusion after several weeks of weekly two-and-a-half hour experiments in which they both observed magnetized persons and were themselves magnetized. When a number of (female) subjects exhibited crises independent of the magnetized objects in Franklin's house and garden that were supposedly exerting influence on them, the commissioners came to doubt animal magnetism but maintained an interest in exploring mesmeric states. Though the fluid's existence remained invisible, evidence of individual impressionability appeared too prominent to ignore. The commission observed persons quite dramatically affected by mesmeric treatment, some in quite violent convulsions "characterized by precipitate and involuntary motion of all the limbs" and "by distraction and wildness in the eyes" as well as "shrieks, tears, hiccuppings, and immoderate laughter" (*Report*, 26). "Nothing can be more astonishing than the sight of these convulsions," Franklin reported (27). "It is impossible not to recognize in these regular effects an extraordinary influence, acting upon the patients, making itself master of them, and of which he who superintends the process appears to be the depository" (28).

After witnessing these dramatic effects of mesmerism, the investigators found their own encounters with mesmerization far less notable. Following their resolution "to personally experience the action of the magnetism," they became "acquainted by their own sensations with the effects ascribed to this agent" (*Report*, 39). Their experience was not very gratifying to their curiosity; they seemed as insensible as the agent they were investigating. Even when they increased the experiments to three days of successive treatments, the commissioners found that "their insensibility was the same" (43). Comparing their own relative insensibility to the remarkable effects that mesmerism produced on others, the commissioners noted the peculiar power of "the public process" (43). In the private experiment made upon themselves, "the stupendous influence, which creates such an astonishment in the public process, appears no longer; the magnetism stripped of its energy seems perfectly supine and inactive" (43). The investigating scientists accordingly connected susceptibility with the public and imaginative setting in which mesmerism usually operated. In these proceedings, patients were assembled in a narrow space in a heated apartment "more or less impregnated with mephitic gas, which has the property of acting immediately upon the head and nervous system . . . When the introduction of music is added, it affords another means of acting upon and exciting the nerves" (90).

Mesmerism thus employed specific material techniques to affect groups of persons. As a group activity, mesmerism appealed to and exploited principles of mass influence. The commissioners also were struck by the fact that "in the number of patients in the state of crisis" at the public sessions, "there were always many women and few men" (*Report*, 28). Franklin suggests that the theatrical atmosphere of the mesmeric salons especially affected women because they are already subject to "the empire and extensive influence of the uterus." Just as discourses on womanhood—from etiquette guides to educational treatises to sentimental and Gothic novels to feminist tracts—routinely expressed concerns about the dangers to which women's sensitivity and receptivity exposed them, mesmerism projected the frightening extent to which the sympathetic proclivities of women could go. Already subject to their biology, women under mesmerism readily become sympathetic, if not subject, to other persons. Extending the function of human sympathy, itself an ideal of social consciousness and connection, to emphasize a radical affinity between individual bodies, mesmerism powerfully connects persons to one another.

Mesmer himself stressed the resemblance of his theory to sympathy, which, he wrote, also "consists of reciprocal and mutual attractions."[10] The investigators of mesmerism found too much reciprocity in mesmeric productions. Franklin and his fellow scientists discovered that mesmerized women so identify with one another that they imitate each other's mesmerization. They are, in a sense, mesmerized by each other.

In the public process several women are magnetized at the same time. They begin, after about two hours, to experience crises. By little and little, the impressions are communicated from one to another, and reinforced, in the same manner as the impressions which are made by theatrical representation, where the impressions are greater in proportion to the number of spectators, and the liberty they enjoy of expressing their sensations. The applause by which the emotions of individuals are announced, occasions general emotion, in which every one partakes to the degree in which he is susceptible. (*Report*, 91)

Mesmerism works not just because "the individuals in a numerous assembly are more subjected to their senses, and less capable of submitting to the dictates of reason," but also because individuals in this state identify with one another and reproduce each other's subjection (*Report*, 92). The communicability of mesmerized women reminds Franklin of other cases of mysterious mass female behavior, such as the tremblers of Cevennes. All the women of this town "appeared to be possessed by the devil. They trembled and prophesised publicly in the streets" (92). During this time M. Mandagers, the lord of the local manor, impregnated one of the prophesying women, claiming he did so by command of God to produce a savior. Officials investigating the bizarre events in Cevennes noted that except for "the folly of believing God has commanded him to have carnal knowledge with this young woman," Mandagers's "conversation is as full of reason and good sense, as that of Don Quixote upon all other subjects but that of knight-errantry" (94). Finding Mandagers eccentric but basically sane, the authorities leave him under the supervision of his children in one of his chateaux and send the pregnant prophesying woman to prison. A testament to the strange power of collective mania, this incident also suggests how a collective mania may attract and justify all sorts of participation.

Continuing to liken mesmerism to other instances of mass female experience, Franklin also cites the 1780 phenomenon of the young ladies of Saint Roch, where "in the space of half an hour 50 or 60 girls from 12 to 19 years of age were seized with the same convulsions as a young girl who fell ill during a first communion ceremony" (*Report*, 95). In order "to dissipate entirely this epidemical convulsive affection," the Saint Roch authorities separated the girls. After three weeks, the girls appeared restored to health (95). These stories about the strange occurrences at Cevennes and Saint Roch raise the spectre of collective and contagious femininity. For Franklin, the women of Cevennes and Saint Roch exemplify the noxiousness of identification, the same mimetic consequences that he finds in the mesmeric experience, where "sensations are continually communicated and recommunicated" (96). The production of a mass identity may unmoor the usual gender markers of individual identity. Mesmerized women especially seem to instigate this process.

> The woman of most sensibility in the company gives the signal. Immediately the cords [connecting them], everywhere stretched to the same degree and in perfect union, respond to each other; the crises are multiplied; they naturally reinforce each other, and are rendered violent. In the meantime the men, who are witnesses of these emotions, partake of them in proportion to their nervous sensibility; and those with whom this sensibility is greatest and most easily excited become themselves the subjects of a crisis. (*Report*, 96)

In the mutuality of subjects, the individuality of subjectivity can become submerged into a kind of reflexive suggestibility. In the wake of mass femininity, the masculine form of subjectivity recedes, leaving all individuals in the state of feminine sensibility and hence penetrability. Franklin worries that men as well as women will lose the faculty of choice in their mesmeric subjection. "Who will assure us that this state of crisis, at first voluntarily induced, shall not become habitual?" (104). Observing that "man is incessantly enslaved by custom" (104), Franklin thinks it all too likely that "the propensity to irritation" manifest in mesmeric crises will become "in each sex habitual" (96).

Individual will can disappear in mesmerism and other forms of feminine mass subjection because of a force resident in the mind, "that active and terrible power" known as the imagination (*Report*, 98). Concluding that "the imagination is the true cause of all the effects attributed to the magnetism" (81), Franklin's report places mesmerism alongside other mass experiences that play on the imagination. The effects produced by mesmerism thus "are equally discoverable at the theatre, in the camp, and in all numerous assemblies" (95). In the mass experience of crowds, individuals appear submerged. This image magnifies the crowded nature of individuality itself, a procession of mergers formed by the individual's imitative, identificatory tendencies.[11] Mesmerism does not discover any new natural substance or physical operation, the report asserts, but it does epitomize how human subjectivity works.

From a woman's point of view, the mass psychology that Franklin discerned in mesmeric experience signified not the potential dissolution of gender and individual boundaries but the tightening of the bonds of female subjection. During the summer of 1784 when Franklin and the other commissioners were conducting their investigations, a Madame Millet in Santo Domingo (now Haiti) wrote her sister this account of mesmerism:

> A magnetizer has been in the colony for a while now, and following Mesmer's enlightened ideas, he causes in us effects that one feels without understanding them. We faint, we suffocate, we enter into truly dangerous frenzies that cause onlookers to worry. At the second trial of the tub a young lady, after having torn off nearly all her clothes, amorously attacked a young man on the scene. The two were so deeply intertwined that we despaired of detaching them, and she could be torn from his arms only after another dose of magnetism. You'll admit that such are ominous effects to which women sooner should not expose themselves. [Mesmerism] produces a conflagration that consumes us, an excess of life that leads us to delirium. We will soon see a maltreated lover using it to his advantage.[12]

Women, as well as other subordinated populations, appear particularly vulnerable to mesmeric subjection because they are already accustomed to other forms of subjection. Millet's fear of the manipulative uses to which mesmerism could be put was strikingly realized in French colonialists' applications of mesmerism to Santo Domingo's slave population. "One plantation owner made a big profit in magnetizing a consignment of cast-off slaves he bought at a low price. Restoring them to good health by means of the tub, he was able to lease them at prices paid for the best slaves."[13] In these profiteering employments of mesmeric subjection, the already enslaved subjects appear easily manipulable.

When nonwhite subjects imitated the master class by conducting their own mesmeric practices, they were punished by colonial authority. In 1787, a mulatto named Jerome was condemned to the galleys for his mesmeric practices.[14] Stories of similar cases, which usually associated mesmerism with slave rebellion plots, circulated in U.S. newspapers during the 1790s. In these stories, the mesmerist-rebel leader is always portrayed as a tyrant over his own people, especially over women. Thus the African Makandal was known for his "barbarity" to "his faithless mistresses, and above all, those who refused to grant him favors."[15]

This paradigm of mesmerism as an uneven operation of power also appeared in Franklin's report, in the recognition that most mesmeric subjects were members of subordinate groups—women, children, or lower classes. But the inequality manifest in mesmeric power does not interest Franklin nearly so much as the potential equality among mesmeric subjects. His report's inclusion of incidents of mass experience stresses mesmeric communicability across horizontal lines, a vast potential commonality of identity. Signifying both the singularity of collectivity and the plurality of individuality, mesmerism is memorialized in the report as a product of the imagination, as another species of sympathy and identification. Mesmerism emerges in this characterization as a disturbing example of mass psychology. When persons only too readily become public and collective, as mesmerized subjects do, they merge with others, behaving as a totality. Women, children, and the lower classes therefore pose manifold dangers. They might act collectively against the ruling norms or authority, creating disruptions such as those at Cevennes or Saint Roch. By the end of the century, collective action by lower and enslaved classes resulted in the French Revolution and the Santo Domingo slave rebellion. These revolutionary actions demonstrated the tremendous political force that mergers of individuals could attain. Besides exhibiting people's propensity either to act or to be acted upon as a mass, such group movements exhibit in extreme form the susceptibility to influence residing in every individual.

In the racist horror stories of mesmerism, subaltern persons such as Jerome or Makandal attain power over others, showing how anyone might make use of the individual propensity to be influenced. Thus mesmerism raises the two predominant spectres that regularly figure in debates about the effects of cultural technologies on individuals: a vision of persons as potential automatons and an image of external influence as illegitimate. From this perspective, individuals appear in perpetual danger from both their own tendencies and their external world.

Bringing to the fore the ways in which individuals can be menaced, mesmerism helps compose the psychology of persons in the modern liberal state. A precursor to and prototype of psychoanalysis, mesmerism furnishes a portrait of the individual as a site inhabited by other individuals, in a condition that Freud a century later would call uncanny.[16]

Franklin's report on mesmerism offers a psychology of the liberal subject by examining a particular intrusion into the mind and explaining how this phenomenon exploits the permeability to which everyone is subject. Writing about mesmerism as a variant of the mental intrusions that Locke noted, Franklin recognizes how readily such individual experiences translate into social behavior. More precisely, Franklin perceives how the already social composition of the individual fits into larger social entities, such as the salon, the theater audience, the military camp, the female populace, or the lower classes. The report on mesmerism, which tracks some of the stranger behavioral paths that permeability allows, opens inquiry into all acts of mutual accord.

Mesmeric influence, like one of Locke's tyrannical intruders, interferes with the exercise of individual understanding. Franklin's analysis of mesmeric subjection thus raises issues about the influencing of individuals—issues that are pertinent to the American social contract formed by consent. Techniques other than mesmerism routinely act upon or direct the individual, for good or for evil. Because consent indeed develops under influences, the individual must distinguish between good and bad influences. Franklin himself famously respected and advocated the use of rhetoric in order "to persuade those whose concurrence you desire."[17] Besides this classic, respected mode of influence and mesmerism's disreputable stagecraft, eighteenth-century Americans could be influenced by newspapers, revivalist preaching, propaganda, and novels.

The power of these media becomes clear in Olaudah Equiano's description of his first encounter with reading. On the voyage from Africa to the West Indies, the enslaved Equiano sees the ship's officers reading and immediately believes that their books are spirits talking to them. Men who can converse with spirits must be superior beings, Equiano thinks.[18] Equiano quite rightly recognizes literacy as a power, and determines that he too will be empowered when books—or divinity— speak to him. His life goal then becomes not just obtaining his freedom but becoming a communicant with God, an enlightened reader within a privileged circle of communication. Like reading, rhetoric and mesmerism establish the individual within a certain community or state of mind. Whether communications to the human mind are characterized as magic, animal magnetism, or moving speech, they clearly exert a powerful force over persons, uniting them with other persons or principles. Thus Franklin's investigation of mesmerism sets the stage for subsequent exploration of technologies of influence. As Americans in the late eighteenth century debated the proper roles of education and literature in the new nation, they articulated their concerns about consent in the same paradigms of gender, age, class, and racial subordination that predominate in the mesmerism discourse.

In the wake of the American Revolution and French Revolution, the encounters between self and world through which the consensual individual makes judgments attracted much interest and critical commentary. As early Americans repeatedly wrote about education, seduction, literary influence, conversion, and captivity, they scanned the external agencies informing consent. In these writings, the prototypical individual appears not in the hopeful image of the Lockean entitled child, equipped to eventually sort and choose among assorted influences, but in the more pessimistic image of the *femme couverte*, the unentitled woman always under the influence and laws of others.[19] This turn to women as figures of consent might seem to contradict if not repudiate Locke's political philosophy, but in fact it is consistent with Locke's location of consent in conditions of inadequacy. Like childhood, the situation of women, who pass from childhood into adulthood, should change. Though women do not receive the entitlements conferred upon children, the very fact of their continued subjection constitutes in Lockean logic their right to self-determination.

Seen in this light, women and other subordinated populations represent perfectly the political claims that Locke aligned with children. Thus the movement from the child to the woman in the representational narrative of consent does not necessarily signify a repudiation of consent. For example, an abolitionist agenda could develop from the Lockean consent narrative as in the case of Olaudah Equiano's autobiography. Equiano aligns his right to freedom with his literacy and business competence. By proving himself capable of navigating most circumstances of the white world, he feels entitled to the rights of self-determination that white men possess. Though white standards rule Equiano's logic of manumission, this logic nevertheless eventually gains him his freedom. Whereas Equiano set out to prove himself a capable individual, other slaves discovered a different way to locate themselves in the Lockean consent narrative. Many slaves and abolitionists exploited the racist classification of blacks as children to claim the entitlements due them.[20]

The second part of this book follows the Lockean consent narrative and its feminization into the 1790s. In the following chapters, I examine the portraits of consent in two early American novels, Hannah Foster's *The Coquette* and Tabitha Tenney's *Female Quixotism*. These books present heroines whose eccentricities make them particularly problematic, and therefore illustrative, types of consent. The figures of the coquette and the quixote—a woman who chooses not to choose and a woman who chooses to live in disregard of common reality—bring new considerations to the discussion of consent. The coquette raises questions about consent as self-representation, while the quixote points to the relation between consent and local standards. These heroines try to exercise consent on their own terms, through coquettish equivocation or quixotic fantasy. Their unconventional practices of consent reveal the conventional pressures operating upon consent. As the coquette and quixote fail in their personal quests for self-determination, they underscore the force of customary agreements about gender and class operating in consent. Their stories also suggest that individuals can revise such social agreements, thereby creating new opinions with which to inform consent.

That the eighteenth-century American narrative of consent extends from primers to novels, from triumphant child heroes to unsuccessful adult heroines, attests to the crucial role of the disenfranchised in signifying the limitations of human experience. For eighteenth-century America, the child and woman stand as reminders of natural as well as contrived boundaries—the conditions of age, gender, or race. These conditions require that consent continually be compounded with better and more humane standards of opinion. Consent discourse thus continues to focus on what comes into the permeable individual from prevailing modes of influence. In early American novels' preoccupation with female subjection to sexual and literary influences, adult reformation replaces childhood formation as the traditional drama of consent. The Lockean sense of consent as an ever-present task persists.

5

Coquetry and Its Consequences

When Eliza Wharton, the heroine of Hannah Foster's popular novel *The Coquette*, frankly describes her engagement as the sacrifice of her own "fancy in this affair," she is voicing a standard criticism about the constraints on female and filial consent.[1] In "obedience to the will and desires of my parents," Eliza discloses, she had accepted "their choice" of a husband for her, the "esteemed" Reverend Mr. Haley (5). Her consent to this "alliance" signified no "passion of love for Mr. Haley," only her compliance to her parents' will. Eliza's consent represents not her own desire, but the subordination of personal desire to parental plans.

Eliza's situation appears to be the typical predicament of eighteenth-century novelistic heroines since Clarissa. Women are continually subjected to parental, which is to say patriarchal, authority. This scenario of a daughter compelled to follow her parents' will evokes as well the republican rhetoric of violated filial rights that figured so urgently and effectively in American Revolutionary politics.[2] Stories of compelled consent pervade late-eighteenth-century America, conveying an uncertain—if not antithetical—relation between consent and individual freedom.

In Foster's novel, the image of female and filial subjection is both preceded and succeeded by a display of self-determination. At the opening of *The Coquette*, Eliza announces her "pleasure . . . on leaving my paternal roof," a pleasure won by successfully gambling her con-

sent. As Eliza explains, she has strategically exercised her personal interests even as she followed her parents' wishes. When she "determined that my reason should concur with theirs," she calculated that
her agreement would pose a low "risk" to her "future happiness" (5).
Seeing, from their "first acquaintance, his declining health," Eliza "was
the more encouraged" to chance the engagement to Haley. Her speculation proves successful when both her father and fiancé die before the
marriage can take place.

Foster thus complicates the conventional portrait of consent as a
form of female subjection with evidence of the operation of a woman's
design. The room for individual maneuvering that Eliza finds in her
exercise of consent demonstrates what a woman can do for herself
within the limits of her historical condition, a condition defined by
gender, class, race, nationality, and geography. Presenting consent in a
light potentially more favorable than unfavorable to women's self-determination, Foster underscores agency in consent, even when the consenting agent dislikes the situation to which she agrees.

For those without access to full social, economic, and political self-
determination, the idea that they are agents in consent may under-
standably seem a mockery of freedom. But Foster delineates in Eliza's
practice of consent the limits within which consent always operates.
Locating agency in consent, and more significantly, locating agency
in the consent of the disenfranchised, Foster demonstrates that freedom exists even within the restrictions upon the scope and experience
of freedom. Dramatizing the possibilities as well as the limits of wom-
en's freedom, the portrait of consent in *The Coquette* recapitulates the
meaning of consent developed in liberal political theory and psychology.[3]

Eliza's situation reprises the paradoxical condition of consent as citizens' choosing to be bound to their own determinations. In the act of
consenting to government, individuals choose and accept constraints
upon themselves. Individuals in the act of consent freely determine
their lives, forming states, contracts, and alliances; by these practices,
they also simultaneously exemplify their subjection to cultural authority.[4] Locke's political and pedagogical theory accordingly foregrounds
the individual's response and relation to authority, delineating the psychology of subjects living in liberal societies. In the *Education*, he describes individual authority as developing by the internalization of pa-

rental strictures. Lockean psychology thus anticipates the Freudian conception of the superego; the liberal formulation of self presents the self as always under rule.[5] Thus the sense in consent of the compulsory, which is customarily identified with parents, can never be eliminated. Because Locke defines consent as a relation to authority, and more specifically as an affirmation of one's relation to authority, consent always includes the acknowledgment, however happy or unhappy, of one's subjection. Put another way, consent is a kind of self-dictation: it is the subjection that we acknowledge to our circumstances when we are not objecting to or rebelling from them.

That cultural authority clearly inhabits and inspirits individuals has always provoked doubts about and objections to liberal consent doctrine.[6] More obviously, the fact that some individuals, because of gender or race, do not even get to embody and manifest any cultural authority exposes the partiality in the operation of consent. The limited citizenship of women in liberal societies, for example, would seem to preclude their consent from denoting any form of self-determination whatsoever. Yet this apparent deficiency in consent that the subjection of women and disenfranchised persons exposes lies not in the structure of consent per se, but in the culture that consent affirms. In the case of subordinated populations such as women, American Indians, and slaves, consent marks the limits (as well as the possibilities) of self-determination because it expresses the individual's relation to authority, and therefore the different relations of different individuals to authority.

Far from being a contradiction in terms, then, female consent epitomizes individual subjection in a liberal society. Eliza's manipulation of the terms of her subjection—her plot to elude the marital expectations placed upon her—causes her friends to call her "coquettish" (7), a characterization already ascribed to Eliza by the novel's title. Labeling Eliza "the coquette," Foster draws attention to the guile, the conscious machinations, in Eliza's practice of consent.[7] Eliza's artful use of consent suggests that individuals can appropriate consent for their own purposes. Once released from "those shackles, which parental authority had imposed on [her] mind," Eliza is determined to suit herself and "gratify [her] natural disposition in a participation of those pleasures which youth and innocence afford" (13). Her enjoyment of freedom from marital commitment, however, proves short-lived, as she soon finds herself urged into another engagement to another unappealing minister. Her evasion of this alliance leads to another unsuccessful implementation of consent. Eliza allows herself to be seduced, which results in the pregnancy that ultimately kills her.

Through the limited effectiveness of Eliza's coquetry, Foster examines the failure of coquetry as both a critique and an appropriation of consent. Though coquetry exhibits as it exploits the potential agency of women in consent, Foster's narrative of the coquette's difficulties in pursuing her desires reveals that having agency is not enough. Women as well as men are agents, Foster emphasizes, but their agency operates in different spheres, according to gender definitions. It is in the failure of Eliza's coquetry that the inequality in the compasses of agency becomes most glaring. Featuring agency as a bounded activity, *The Coquette* depicts the perimeter in which female consent in eighteenth-century America operated. Until that perimeter changes, Foster intimates, consent cannot effectively serve women. To make consent a constructive instrument for women, Foster recommends that women eschew coquetry because it sustains only the limited sphere of their self-determinations.

Consent and Coquetry

Coquetry is a dubious tactic for women's self-determination because it entails a disparity between a woman and her word, or between different self-representations. Eliza's calculated act of consent differentiates her public word from her private words and desires, creating at least two versions of herself. In doing so, she exhibits the potential discrepancy between self-representation and self that consent always encompasses. Unfortunately for Eliza, too, a woman's exercise of representational vagaries signifies for her culture not an act of self-determination but a show of deceit, and moreover, an example of the deceitful feminine constitution.

Characterizing Eliza as a coquette, Foster invokes a long-standing identification of women with deception. The imagery and vocabulary of coquetry in late-eighteenth-century America drew on the Enlightenment paradigm of femininity most vividly delineated by Rousseau and most vigorously denounced by women's rights advocates such as Catharine Macaulay, Mary Wollstonecraft, and Judith Sargeant Murray, as well as, I suggest, by novelists such as Foster and Susanna Rowson. Writing the story of a coquette's failure at self-determination, Foster joins in the eighteenth-century feminist project of validating female consent by distancing it from coquetry.[8]

To disassociate female consent from coquetry, feminists sought to revise the characterization of women and consent popularized by Rousseau's writings.[9] While Rousseau's *Julie* furnished a manifesto for filial choice in marriage and self-determination, his equally influential *Emile* provided a portrait of female consent as coquetry. According to Rousseau, "To be a woman means to be coquettish" (365). Coquettishness derives from a law of nature, "that woman is made specially to please man" (358). Pleasing man, according to Rousseau, means sexually provoking him. Sexually provoking a man entails not just attracting him but inciting him to actively, if not forcefully, pursue his sexual desire. The woman "ought to constrain him to find his strength and make use of it. The surest art for animating that strength is to make it necessary by resistance" (358). The woman thus feigns resistance, holding the man at bay with "the modesty and shame with which nature armed the weak in order to enslave the strong" (358). Besides somewhat restraining the man, modesty operates also to "constrain" the "unlimited desires" that Rousseau attributes to women (359).[10] But modesty is only a cover for unlimited female desire, a tactic for manipulating men. Rousseau characterizes women as always desiring and, thus, as always feigning resistance. By this account, female resistance is always provocative. For Rousseau, the truth about a woman can be determined but the woman herself never tells that truth.

Or rather, though she does not *tell* the truth about herself, the truth is nonetheless always apparent. "According to the true inclinations of their sex, even when [women] are lying they are not false" (385). For women's words, by definition dissimulations, are invariably belied by bodily signs. "Why do you consult their mouth when it is not the mouth which ought to speak?" Rousseau asks. Instead, "Consult their eyes, their color, their breathing, their fearful manner, and above all, their soft resistance. This is the language nature gives them for answering you. The mouth always says no and ought to say so. But the accent it adds to this answer is not always the same, and this accent does not know how to lie" (385). The female body and its operations thus convey a different message, modifying and even contradicting a woman's verbal articulations. The meaning of a woman's body language is of course preordained, and so a woman's fear and resistance can signify affirmative responses. Rousseau imagines every woman as a completely legible text, her speech a coquettish denial of—and therefore affirmation of—the truth available to a man beholding her.[11]

Hence arises Rousseau's skepticism about women's accounts of rape. "Whether or not the human female shares man's desires and wants to satisfy them, she repulses him and always defends herself—but not always with the same force or, consequently, with the same success. For the attacker to be victorious, the one who is attacked must permit or arrange it; for does she not have adroit means to force the aggressor to use force?" (359). By this account, women's adroitness compels even violence against themselves. Rousseau locates in woman's natural constitution—that is, in her given coquettishness—the ontological state of not just a false accuser but also a provocateur. In this imagination, rape can scarcely be said ever to occur. Indeed, Rousseau then avers that "rapes are hardly ever spoken of anymore, since they are so little necessary and men no longer believe in them" (360). The existence of rape must be ratified by the word of men, by their declarations of belief. "If fewer acts of rape are cited in our day," Rousseau elaborates, "this is surely not because men are more temperate but because they are less credulous, and such a complaint, which previously would have persuaded simple peoples, in our day would succeed only in attracting the laughter of mockers" (360). Rape depends upon the credulity of the men who hear a woman's "complaint." In this now familiar, frighteningly androcentric construction, rape is an encounter between female speech and male speech, judged and determined by the man. Small wonder that women may find it, as Rousseau says, "more advantageous to keep quiet" (360).

The point of Rousseau's portrait of women as coquettish (which is to say mendacious) is not simply to discredit women's testimonies but to subordinate female consent to other forms of evidence, namely the testimonies of witnesses. His discourse on rape accordingly concludes with his approving citation of a scenario in which the mere possibility of external evidence discounts the woman's word:

In Deuteronomy there is a law by which a girl who had been abused was punished along with her seducer if the offense had been committed in the city. But if it had been committed in the country or in an isolated place, the man alone was punished: "For," the law says, "the girl cried out and was not heard." This benign interpretation taught girls not to let themselves be surprised in well-frequented places. (360)

By this law, rape occurs only in the country, or in isolated places—where no one else is present to witness the attack or contradict the girl's account. Indeed, the implication is that any witnessed sexual encounter must be consensual, for everyone knows women desire and incite sexual advances. If a girl were attacked in the city, where her cries could be heard, the law assumes that such cries actually signify consent and punishes the victim "along with her seducer." The law exempts the victim from culpability only when she has no witnesses.

Rousseau's reading of this convoluted law as benign to women makes sense from the standpoint of a partisan of witnesses. If the external evidence of witnesses defines female consent, the absence of witnesses means that the crime (the man's crime of rape or the woman's crime of seduction and falsity) cannot be determined. The city victim is punished as a false accuser on the premise that her cries of resistance would have been heard in a populous area. Witnesses within earshot of a woman's cries, according to the misogynist logic of the law, would understand those cries not as resistance to rape but as signs of consensual participation in sex. If the girl's cries are heard, they should be understood as feigned resistance. Thus an attack within the range of witnesses can never appear against the woman's will. The lesson of the law, Rousseau concludes, is that if a woman wants to cry rape, she should do so only if her attack was unwitnessed. For Rousseau, we have seen, the role of witnesses is to corroborate the falsity of women's expressions of resistance. The victim out of the range of witnesses is accorded credibility only because no external testimonies can gainsay her.

Given Rousseau's characterization of women as always desirous, always feigning resistance, and always consenting, we might expect him to convict the country victim along with her city sister as a false accuser. But the distinction between country and city experiences is crucial to Rousseau's reading of women and coquetry. To consolidate the determining role of witnesses, and of the physical evidence of the senses upon which they rely, Rousseau must allow for cases in which the absence of witnesses means his interpretation of woman cannot be imposed. When no one can hear the victim's cries, no one can testify to her falsity. Conversely, any evidence of rape is evidence against the woman's claim.

The Deuteronomy story furnishes Rousseau with a parable of the witness's definitive role in female consent. Whatever evidence enters the witness's sensory orbit only confirms the consensuality of all female behavior. The witness is thus endowed with an evidentiary authority based on the fact of physical presence—which is to say, based on the fact of his visibility and the vision he reports. Even though the Deuteronomy tale concerns aural evidence and thus the witness's account of what he heard, this evidence carries the positive weight generally accorded to eyewitness testimony. The weight given to the victim's proximity to witnesses accords not just credibility but absolute veracity to the witness. By the bare fact of hearing, the witness corroborates what custom and law say about women. His mere presence operates as if he were an eyewitness, as if he sees and thus confirms the coquetry of women.[12]

The role of visibility—of the witness as well as of the woman—in verification underscores what is at stake in Rousseau's formulation of femininity: clarity in representation. Feminizing Locke's portrait of consent, Rousseau both acknowledges and simplifies the complexity of self-representation. He makes woman a model of transparency in order to narrow the representational range of consent so that its representational function can be absolutely certain. The incoherence, not to mention injustice, of this fantasy lies in the fact that such transparency expunges the very purpose of consent as self-representation.

Making woman's voice tell against her, Rousseau's formulation of female consent not surprisingly generated a feminist rhetoric of anti-coquetry, which attempted to align woman with her words. For eighteenth-century advocates of women's rights, coquetry is a historical aberration, a negative form of womanhood arising from the inequity of the female situation. "Woman has everything against her," Catharine Macaulay explains in her *Letters on Education* (1790), and therefore "she has nothing in her favor but her subtlety and her beauty" (406). The employment of these "to enthral the man . . . act in a peculiar manner to corrupting the female mind."[13] A woman thus engaged is a coquette, "whose aim is to subject the whole world to her own humour; but in this vain attempt she commonly sacrifices both her decency and her virtue" (407). Macaulay believes that the harmful effects of the co-quette's behavior extend beyond herself. "By the intrigues of women, and their rage for personal power and importance, the whole world has been filled with violence and injury; and their levity and influence have proved so hostile to the existence or permanence of rational manners, that it fully justifies the keeness of Mr. Pope's satire on the sex" (407). Macaulay invokes not just Pope here; her attribution of power to fe-male coquetry closely follows Rousseau. But whereas Rousseau thinks coquetry is the natural condition of woman, Macaulay believes that co-quettes are generated by convention. Because the problem of coquetry derives from social arrangements and inequalities, Macaulay seeks to eliminate this problem through a Lockean treatment, by new edu-cational and political practices. Macaulay accordingly proposes that "when the sex have been taught wisdom by education, they will be glad to give up indirect influence for rational privileges; and the precarious sovereignty of an hour enjoyed with the meanest and most infamous of the species, for those established rights which, independent of acciden-tal circumstances, may afford protection to the whole sex" (407).

Once educated to know and desire their rights, and once endowed with those privileges and rights, women will be protected from the in-direction and precariousness of coquetry. With the proper social condi-tions, women will attain a clarity of representation—one distinct from the manufactured clarity that Rousseau accords them by relying on witnesses whose account of women echoes an a priori definition of women as deceitful. In calling for new forms of education for women, Macaulay and other late-eighteenth-century Anglo-American femi-nists sought to equip women with the means of representing them-selves in the economic and political spheres, and thus to institute a parity between male and female voices. For this goal, the coquette's "sovereignty" had to be overthrown.

Mary Wollstonecraft identified this sovereignty with the immorality of monarchical power that she saw embodied in Marie Antoinette, whom she described as "an adept in all the arts of coquetry that debauch the mind."[14] From this association of coquetry with the corrupt econo-mic and sexual practices of monarchy, the coquette emerged in the late eighteenth century as the antitype of republican virtue. Like Marie An-toinette, "a profound dissembler," the coquette seeks not alliance but tyranny. The young American man in a 1792 moral tale can therefore congratulate "himself that he has escaped from the smiles of a coquette," from social and sexual wiles that would have subordinated him.[15] These "insidious and deluding wiles of the coquette" also come under censure in the advice book for "the Young Ladies of America" that Hannah Foster published the year after *The Coquette*. "How disgusting must this character appear to persons of sentiment and integrity," Foster writes (98). What most bothers Foster and feminist contemporaries about the coquette is her use of deceit—her pretense of consent—to realize her ambition to rule. She dallies with suitors, alternately intimating and revoking her consent to a series of men. In effect, the coquette takes on the role of the seducer, engineering courtships to suit her pleasure. Ambiguous in her language and her acts, the coquette obfuscates the self-representational mission of consent. She thereby undermines consent's purpose as a vehicle of self-representation by detaching it from consequentiality. The consequentiality or importance of individual determinations signified by consent recedes in the coquette's practice of not keeping her word; her word is not a warranty of what can be expected from her. Coquetry takes the consequentiality out of courtship and consent, leaving uncertain the aftermath of a woman's acts.

It is as a figure of faulty self-representation that the coquette comes to epitomize for Foster, Wollstonecraft, Macaulay, and other women in the eighteenth century not female defiance but female debility. The coquette's evasion of consequences exhibits the state of nonconsensuality in which persons exercise no authority for their acts, and therefore have no accountability. From this feminist standpoint, Rousseau's pronouncement that "to be a woman means to be coquettish" might stand as an accurate account of woman's nonconsensual condition. Finding nonconsensuality at the heart of what seems women's most independent activity in social relations, the feminist critique of coquetry casts doubt on all seemingly independent exercises of choice. As the coquette's calculated deployments of consent merely confirm the nonconsensual status of women, she exemplifies not just the weakness of women in androcentric society, but also the potential weakness of all citizens. Self-representation may not accurately or effectively represent the individual. The situation of women thus serves as a parable of the impediments encountered by all citizens in the employment of consent. The stories about female consent that pervade early American fiction register prevailing anxieties about consent by adapting Rousseau's portrait of women and consent into a paradigm for exploring the difficulties within consent.

Consent and the Seduction Story

If Rousseau, in characterizing women as transparent coquettes, provoked feminist anticoquetry, he also, in the contradictory quality of individuality that he imaged (and sought to eliminate) in the coquette, suggested a novelistic model of female character and consent. Taking a cue from Rousseau, eighteenth-century feminists like Foster and Wollstonecraft found the novel a useful format in which to analyze and reformulate androcentric accounts of femininity. In the novel, the very complications in consent and self-representation that Rousseau tried to eliminate through his elevation of the witness can work to credit rather than invalidate an individual.[16] Since women's words conspicuously circulated and mattered in the novel, female consent in the novel could just as readily appear to bear and retain consequentiality as it appeared to defy and deny consequentiality in Rousseau's narrative. This is why women in eighteenth-century novels often suffer so much: they bear the consequences of consent. In these novels' almost obsessive preoccupation with female responses to courtship and seduction, they register both the disadvantages and advantages of representational acts that female consent so vividly typifies.[17]

During the eighteenth century, the law of coverture defined a woman as the property of her father or husband.[18] The circumstances of female consent, in which men choose for women or instruct women in their choices, typify the numerous external interests operating in self-representation. A woman's own interest, such as Eliza's desire to be unattached, gets expressed only through the often unpredictable directions that self-representation can take. Subject to the state (in which they have no voice) and family (to which they must consent), women in the eighteenth century especially rely on the variable paths of representation, on the agility and ingenuity of literary representation. From the early American literature of women's attempts at self-determination emerge narratives of anxiety about consent as an adequate expression of the individual.

The novel of seduction in particular portrayed both the inadequacy of female representation and the measures by which one could enforce, contain, or overcome that inadequacy. The seduction novels popular in early America employ the fate of seduced heroines to signify a variety of views on female consent, which in turn disclose different views on consent. Like Locke's conception of the consenting child, the paradoxical notion of female consent emerges as a prototype of consent. Kept by law in a childlike status, women never arrive at the point of self-determination destined for male children. Yet women continually face choices in courtships and seductions. Their decisions, and the effects of those decisions, come under repeated review in eighteenth-century novels. Women's consent, forever under guardianship, shows even more dramatically than children's consent Locke's alignment of consent with dependent conditions. In associating consent with children, Locke claimed the right to self-determination for all individuals, whatever their present biological or social state. At the same time, by locating consent in states of insufficiency, Locke signaled an uncertainty about when consent will operate and about what will issue from consent. Women's continual state of dependence and disenfranchisement especially exemplifies this uncertainty about consent.

One way to quell such uncertainty is to imagine consent as a regular causal sequence. Generally, in seduction tales, consent is depicted as an act leading to specific consequences. Seduction stories operate on the premise that agency inevitably leaves traces; the stories supply narrative equivalents for the progress of female agency in their formulaic plots and predictable conclusions. The sense of conviction about consequentiality established by the seduction story makes it a perfect vehicle for conveying the ideal of self-determination. Foster accordingly finds the seduction tale an effective medium for her project of translating coquetry into consequentiality.

At the center of the seduction scenario is a woman who comes to a destined end. In her predictably sad story, the seduction heroine demonstrates consent as efficiently initiating a chain of events.[19] Her exercise of consent, her affirmation or denial, can be seen as consequential. In their generative capacity—and all sexually active women in seduction stories seem to conceive immediately—women exemplify an inevitable sequential process of consent that consent theory itself can only fantasize. They produce evidence of consent, and by that evidence consent becomes a truly generative act. Even as the political status of women suggests the imaginary—or at least imaginative—character of consent, women's reproductive capacity furnishes a seemingly irrefutable proof of consent (whether voluntary or involuntary). Compressing the series of events that consent (theoretically) represents, the seduction scenario keeps effects closely connected to causes. The consequences of female desire stay within the compass of the female body. The seduction story's focus on a specific female biological destiny affords a view of consent as the immediate embodiment of personal desire—a spatial and temporal proximity between cause and effect. Generating children thus retells, as it results from, consent. Each generation is a chronicle of previous generations, all testifying to prior acts of consent. Everybody is imagined to be the evidence of somebody else's consent. In this definitive portrait of consent, consent perfectly expresses and matches the individual. Not only does consent adequately represent persons, but persons also represent consent. A society formed on such an ideal standard of consent would be harmonious, composed of persons in complete accord with one another. Like Rousseau's fantasy of a constant consent embodied in women, the seduction story clarifies consent, presenting it as a consistent natural sequence. By the seduction story formula in which desire leads to sex, which results in pregnancy and usually death in childbirth, consent creates and destroys bodies. The babies and corpses produced in the wake of consent become the proofs that consent has occurred.

The feminization of consent that the novel of seduction reflects thus advances the evidentiary role women play in consent. In this gendered arrangement of the liberal imagination, the reproductive labor of women makes consent material. Yet women also produce testimonies and therefore can complicate the reading of physical evidence. Seduction stories from a feminist point of view could question, rearrange, redefine, or even throw out evidence. A novelist like Susanna Rowson challenged whether the conditions for choice and consent really existed in seduction scenarios when she made her fallen heroine Charlotte Temple a fifteen-year-old girl who faints before either consenting to or rejecting her lover, and who then wakes to find herself with him on a boat bound for America. Foster also questions the conditions of consent by casting the coquette, a figure of sovereignty, in the same hapless position as Charlotte Temple. Coquettes were by definition false and (often by act) fallen women, and by syllogism, fallen heroines occupied the same position as coquettes. This syllogism seems more concretely realized in the fact that all women lack authority in consent. The fallen woman says "yes" at the wrong time, violating the proper sense of yes by failing to say and mean the prescribed "no." She enacts in tragic form the game of the Rousseauvian coquette who says no all the time, meaning yes. Both exercise inadequate sovereignty over their self-representations; their obligatory end as abandoned women serves as an objective correlative for the lost—indeed, always already lost—value of their words and hence their characters.

Different novelistic treatments invite different evaluations of these lost characters. Foster's narrative of Eliza Wharton's history restages the question of female character as a debate about consent in the early years of American nationhood. Dedicated to choosing her way and her partners, Eliza appears something of a republican heroine. Her plea, "Let me then enjoy that freedom which I so highly prize" (13), certainly invites this identification, which has become a standard premise of readings of *The Coquette*.[20] Eliza's insistence on following her "natural propensity" for enjoyment invokes the natural rights basis for self-determination prevalent in eighteenth-century republican theory. Her characterization of the change in her situation as a movement from subordination to freedom conspicuously echoes the rhetoric of filialism that figured so urgently in American Revolutionary polemics. Rather than submit to paternal authority, Eliza asserts her right to please herself. Her quest for personal pleasure emblematizes the republican effort to establish the independence of each new generation from hereditary authority.

Yet in her unwise exercise and enjoyment of her freedom—she becomes impregnated by a notorious rake—Eliza can also appear more of a cautionary case than an exemplar of freedom. To her friends Eliza's desire for freedom signifies an unseemly desire for "fashionable dissipation," and she seems to have "the wrong ideas of freedom and matrimony" (30), making them worry that she is as "seducible" (38) as she turns out to be. Whether we take Eliza to typify the desirability or undesirability of the independent exercise of consent, both characterizations regard consent as an act producing some form of certainty. Consent in the radical republican ideal ratifies self-determination by representing it; that is, consent expresses and realizes individual desire.

In the reactionary view, consent appears self-destructive. From this perspective, the seduction story formula, in which desire leads to sex, pregnancy, and usually death in childbirth, only confirms that consent inevitably leads to bad consequences. Indeed, the formulaic vision of female experience usually invoked by reactionary accounts of fallen women epitomizes the clarity and efficacy of individual authority to which the republican ideal of self-determination aspires.

The sheer familiarity and predictability of the seduction story make it the perfect vehicle for conveying the concepts of—indeed, commitments to—causality and generation embedded in the idea of consent, whatever attitude toward consent a writer may wish to promulgate. Eliza's story is not simply a seduction tale, but also a retelling of a well-known story, as Foster's subtitle acknowledged: *The History of Eliza Wharton, a Novel; Founded on Fact.* The fact in this case was the 1788 incident of an unmarried woman named Elizabeth Whitman dying at a Massachusetts inn after giving birth to a stillborn child. Before Foster wrote her version of the story, numerous accounts of it circulated in newspapers, sermons, and other novels, notably in what most literary historians identify as the first American novel, William Hill Brown's *The Power of Sympathy; or, The Triumph of Nature, Founded in Truth* (1789). Long after the publication of *The Coquette*, the Elizabeth Whitman story continued to be retold. The continual retelling of the story by successive generations demonstrates the way in which seduction stories are freighted with particular visions of consent. Between 1875 and 1912, Caroline Dall, William Bolton, and Mary Crawford published rebuttals of what they took to be Foster's distortion of Elizabeth Whitman's character. They argued that the young woman was, in fact, secretly married. She was thus telling the truth when she told the innkeeper that she was waiting for her husband to join her. As Dall insisted, there was no "evidence of that coquetry which [Foster's] novel has attached to her name."[21] Instead of a cautionary tale of a seduced and abandoned woman, the Elizabeth Whitman story in these retellings becomes an exemplum of faithful, enduring love. In keeping with this legend, the tombstone of Whitman in Peabody, Massachusetts, became in the nineteenth century a celebrated tourist attraction for lovers.[22]

These rehabilitations of Whitman's character attempt to legitimate her consent. They adhere to all the details of the original affair but imagine that a morally acceptable exercise of consent propelled Whitman's experience. These attempts to purify the seduction tale, however, do not alter the inevitable chain of events following from female consent. The same consequences—pregnancy and death—follow for the heroine whether she is married or unmarried.

In the various narratives written about Whitman, her life always proceeds according to the inevitable sequence of the seduction story. Foster uses this well-known story to examine the commitment to consequentiality that both republican and reactionary conceptions of consent assert. Since there is no suspense or mystery in the unfolding of Eliza's history, she can appear at once absolutely self-determining and utterly subject to her fate. Thus to celebrate or censure Eliza is to imagine that individual liberty can be uncoupled from the limitations upon that liberty (limitations that in fact define that liberty).[23] The very terms in which the seduction protagonist gets didactically cast—whether as victim of insufficient liberty or victim of excessive freedom, whether as honorable heroine of filial rights or cautionary figure of filial wrong—register the entanglement of freedom with constraint. The political interpretations that the novel has provoked rearrange the coupled terms, freedom and constraint, in a sequential relation. Either freedom becomes constraining, or even dangerous, as in the reactionary view; or constraint necessitates freedom, as in the republican view. Converting the liberal conjuction of freedom and determinism into a causal sequence, both narratives aim to identify an accountable agent, to reduce the number of actors or agencies active in consent to one authorizing agent or source. In this fashion, both republican and antirepublican readings of Eliza foreground and extract the lines of causality that they assume to be performative in consent.

The story of consent that *The Coquette* tells tracks the competing authorizing agents of consent in Eliza's exercise of consent. Everyone in the novel, from Eliza's family to her friends to her suitors to her seducer to Eliza herself, wants Eliza to consent. They differ only in the consequences to which they wish her to consent. The novel entertains all these interests as it includes alongside Eliza's claims for her "freedom" the omnipresent fears of her "prudish" friends about where the liberty to indulge her own "pleasures" might lead (13). The world of *The Coquette* is thus one of constant scrutiny, by oneself and one's relations, even by comparative strangers—such as Selby, the friend of

Eliza's suitor the Reverend Boyer, who takes it upon himself to be "alike interested" in Eliza, going to social events expressly to observe her (45). Tracking the variety of perspectives on Eliza, Foster's novel displays the populousness of consent and the prominent role of witnesses in defining consent. The goal of the parties competing to define Eliza's consent is to reduce this crowded state. Each interested spectator wants to make consent represent the voice that he or she endorses, one direct line of cause and effect. The difficulty of people wanting to achieve this univocality is underscored by Foster's choice of the epistolary style for telling the Elizabeth Whitman story. Foster thus amplifies the various voices speaking, as well as the differences among and within those voices. The congregation of witnesses with which Foster surrounds Eliza ultimately comes under as much scrutiny as does Eliza. As Eliza's coquetry denotes the variability of meaning within consent, the consequences of her coquetry point to the unreliable role of other persons in consent. In Foster's reformulation of the seduction tale, new questions about character emerge: questions about the credibility of the witnesses who corroborate consent.

Coquetry and Consequences

When Foster calls Eliza "the coquette," then, she is drawing attention to the indeterminacy and ineffectuality that coquetry typified in the feminist republican narrative of consent. In keeping with this view of coquetry as nonconsensuality, Foster portrays Eliza as never quite saying yes or no. Eliza initially declares to her friends and her suitor Boyer her "wish for no other connection than that of friendship" (6), and her distaste for matrimony's "consequences, care, and confinement" (66). Nevertheless, almost immediately after her first fiancé's death Eliza is entangled in another courtship. She allows Boyer to write her, visit her mother, and "expatiate on the subject" of marriage, "provided he will let me take my own time for the consummation." Assuring her friends that she will be a wife "after awhile, when I have sowed all my wild oats" (53), Eliza is "loath to give up either" this marital prospect or the decidedly nonmatrimonial interest of the rake Peter Sanford. Eliza's deferral of her consent, "her loathing to bring [Boyer's] courtship to a period" (78) while she continues to enjoy Sanford's company, finally makes Boyer withdraw his suit and, as he puts it, triumph "over the arts of a finished coquette" (77). Having "repelled the infatuating wiles of a deceitful girl" (78), he celebrates his passage from subjection to this "charmer" to subjection to the "empire" of reason (77). After Boyer's renunciation, Eliza eventually becomes mistress to the recently married Sanford. Pregnant by Sanford, Eliza leaves her home, and like Elizabeth Whitman, delivers a stillborn child in an inn and shortly thereafter dies. Thus the uncertain fate introduced by her procrastination of consent is counteracted by the predictable end to which seduction brings her.

In the seduction that replaces courtship, the coquette comes to suffer the consequences of consent that she initially evades through her protraction of courtship. The punishment of coquetry is exactly what Sanford plots when he judges "this young lady is a coquette" and accordingly avows to "avenge my sex, by retaliating the mischiefs, she meditates against us" and to "let her beware of the consequences" (18). His self-appointed mission against coquettes will bring the courtship of Eliza to a period, and ultimately bring Eliza to an end. Sanford's campaign against Eliza is novelistically destined to succeed from the moment her name is linked to the term coquette. The point of anti-coquetry rhetoric, in either a feminist or patriarchalist agenda, is to bring women to account—to bring the coquette to consequences. Besides fulfilling his own desire, Sanford's mission thus serves to bring to conclusion the unfinished courtship of Eliza. By seducing Eliza, Sanford finally obtains her consent and subjects her to its fatal effects. In Foster's portrayal, seduction succeeds courtship in order to establish the chronology of consent and consequentiality to which courtship directs women. Eliza's sin, therefore, appears to be not her illicit relations with Sanford but her coquettish relation with Boyer.[24]

In telling the Elizabeth Whitman story as a rake's crusade against a coquette, Foster includes in her novel a feminist indictment of patriarchal determinism. That is, the novel invites us to consider Eliza's fate as fully determined and sealed by the rake who plots her destruction. Even as eighteenth-century feminists vilified the figure of the coquette, they regarded her male counterpart as more vicious and dangerous. "There are quite as many male coquets as female," Wollstonecraft noted, "and they are far more pernicious pests to society, as their sphere of action is larger, and they are less exposed to the censure of the world."[25] In the world of Eliza Wharton, rakes do receive their full due of censure. The moral that Eliza's friends draw from her history is to beware of rakes:

> From the melancholy story of Eliza Wharton, let the American fair learn to reject with disdain every insinuation derogatory to their true dignity and honor. Let them despise, and for ever banish the man, who can glory in the seduction of innocence and the ruin of a reputation. (168)

Yet if Foster's treatment of the career of the coquette indicts the rake, the novel does not hold the rake wholly and solely accountable. Eliza accords blame to herself as well as Sanford. In her last conversation with him, she condemns coquetry in both its female and male forms.

> May my unhappy story serve as a beacon to warn the American fair of the dangerous tendency and destructive consequences of associating with men of your character, of destroying their time, and risking their reputation by the practice of coquetry and its attendant follies! But for these, I might have been honorably connected; and capable, at this moment, of diffusing and receiving happiness! But for your arts, I might have remained a blessing to society, as well as the delight and comfort of my friends! (159)

It is her own "practice of coquetry" as well as Sanford's arts that ruin Eliza. Eliza furthermore acknowledges her own fault "for disregarding the counsels, warnings, and admonitions of my best friends" (159).

Censuring all practices of coquetry, however gendered, the novel dramatizes an enmity between society and coquetry. Eliza feels torn between her friends on the one hand and male and female coquetry on the other. Sanford clearly recognizes and underscores this polarity between society and coquetry when he decides to pursue Eliza in "revenge for [Eliza's friends'] dislike and coldness" (158). Though he desires Eliza, he seduces her not just for his own satisfaction but also for the satisfaction of offending her society. Rakes and coquettes both set themselves against social conventions by seeking to evade the consequences of courtship. In Foster's novel, both come to suffer the repercussions of their behavior. Uttering the standard words of the seduced woman—"I am undone!"—Sanford finds himself in the very poverty that he had schemed to avoid by marrying an heiress instead of Eliza. Just as Eliza's friends wish that Sanford "ought forever to be banished from human society" (163), he recognizes that he "must become a vagabond in the earth" (165). As long as he lives, Sanford attests, "I must feel the disgraceful, and torturing effects of my guilt in seducing [Eliza]! . . . Her friends, could they know the pangs of contrition, and the horror of conscience which attend me, would be amply revenged!" (165).

With the biologically determined exits of coquettes and the socially decreed evictions of rakes, Foster's novel would appear to be making coquetry consequential with a vengeance. Yet as Eliza and Sanford come to their fates, their histories no longer appear narratives of coquetry. Lovelace-like, Sanford reconstructs his rakish actions into those of a lover toward his beloved. After ruining Eliza, he wishes he could legitimate their relation. For her part, Eliza does attain a form of legitimation through her friends. They rehabilitate, if not sanctify, her character in their memorial inscription on her tombstone:

> This humble stone, in memory of ELIZA WHARTON, is inscribed by her weeping friends, to whom she endeared herself by uncommon tenderness and affection. Endowed with superior acquirements, she was still more distinguished by humility and benevolence. Let candor throw a veil over her frailties, for great was her charity to others. She sustained the last painful scene, far from every friend; and exhibited an example of calm resignation. Her departure was on the 25th day of July, A.D.—, in the 37th year of her age, and the tears of strangers watered her grave. (169)

The epitaph converts the story of coquetry into the biography of a moral paragon. This posthumous transformation of Eliza, moreover, aligns consent with an image of virtuous and civic-minded women. With the end of the coquette, the character of consent as an expression of community affiliation prevails. Thus the words on the tombstone recall less the history of Eliza Wharton than the "truly republican" creed of female consent espoused early in the novel by her friend Mrs. Richman (44). Women, Mrs. Richman asserts, have a voice in politics because they, like all citizens, are affected by politics. As members of the community, subject to its "happy effects" as well as its "evil," women must be "interested in the welfare and prosperity of our country." They therefore "claim the right of inquiring into those affairs, which may conduce to, or interfere with the common weal" (44). Mrs. Richman stops short of claiming political equality for women, accepting that "we shall not be called to the senate or the field to assert its privileges." Tracing women's role in the state, her argument relies on the cause-and-effect consent narrative in which effects signify, or are taken to signify, the intentions of persons. By this logic, the present state of subjection to the state marks prior consent; the continued existence of a government manifests the authorization of its subjects. If women are subject to the state's authority, Mrs. Richman reasons, women are not just subjects but also, hence, interested agents of the state. Thus the present state of American women in the eighteenth century can be conceived as the effect of women's participation in a social compact. Republican womanhood retroactively gains authority as Mrs. Richman invokes a consensual origin for communal subjection.

To fortify this vision of consent, *The Coquette* undertakes the eighteenth-century feminist goal of disengaging coquetry from female consent. Yet the novel's reconfiguration of consent to signify women's membership in the social contract remarkably refuses to celebrate Eliza's republican-minded friends.[26] Mrs. Richman, Lucy, and Julia, all well-to-do and socially prominent, appear most often as annoying exponents of gender and class proprieties rather than as advocates of the rights of individual women. The disparity between Eliza's desires and her friends' recommendations (a disparity sometimes internalized in her as her own conflicting desires), and between her life and her friends' posthumous account of it, abides at the novel's close. Women's participation in the social compact does not necessarily serve the rights of women, particularly if female members of society espouse only long-standing androcentric views of class, courtship, marriage, and family.

In Foster's writing of the seduction tale, the men as well as the women, the virtuous as well as the nonvirtuous, speak and behave in contradictory or confusing manners. Macaulay's and Wollstonecraft's feminist expectation that women clarify themselves to society proves unreasonable for either sex. Rather than obligating women to earn consent, Foster's novel shows the inequity of holding women to an impossible standard of clarity. She accordingly assigns the task of establishing a substantial form of female consent not to women but to society. Foster goes further than proscribing and eradicating coquetry to undo the Rousseauvian paradigm of female consent. After getting rid of coquetry, she invalidates the witnesses, who in Rousseau's view constitute consent. Witnesses come and go in *The Coquette* as Foster presents Eliza's history through a succession of observers and correspondents: Lucy, Selby, Boyer, Sanford, Julia. The novel's cast of observers typifies the preeminence of witnesses in identifying consent.

If Foster gives these witnesses the final word on Eliza, she clearly undermines both their credibility and the validity of their word. Not only do the last words on Eliza revise her character as they reinforce the logic of consent articulated by Mrs. Richman, but they also reiterate, word for word (except for the change in name from Elizabeth Whitman to Eliza Wharton), the inscription on the Whitman gravestone in Peabody, Massachusetts.[27] In their misrepresentation of Eliza's life, her friends basically plagiarize another's epitaph. If one epitaph can serve any or all fallen women, testimonials to character can simply be generally stipulated. Such stipulation requires the witnessing of readers who will attest to and perpetuate given accounts of persons or events. In Foster's novel, however, what the reader witnesses in the reappearing epitaph is the inconstancy of Eliza's witnesses, who rewrite her character as easily as they successively pair her with various suitors. They vary as much as Eliza does in dallying with Boyer. Worse than inconsistent, the testimony of these witnesses is prefabricated. Their account of Eliza merely recapitulates the public record and popular lore concerning another woman.

By recycling the already known testimonial from the Whitman grave, Foster demonstrates how a witness's testimony, instead of shedding light on a case, may reflect and replicate social customs and biases—in this case, a standard practice of renouncing female vice by expurgating it. While the feminist repudiation and reformation of coquetry certainly improve upon Rousseau's dictum that all women are by nature coquettes, Foster extends that feminist critique to an examination of the terms upholding conventional views of femininity. The Rousseauvian account of woman obviously relies on external perspectives, on witnesses to female behavior. In calling for women to behave reasonably, eighteenth-century feminists continue to define woman from an external perspective. Presenting a seduction story in which all perspectives appear unreliable, *The Coquette* calls into question the validity of the witnesses and testimonies that serve as evidence in accounts of women.

As a well-known narrative of female experience, the seduction story carries an aura of authority. By its sheer familiarity, the seduction tale appears a valid account, substantial because proverbial. Replaying a scenario customarily associated with women, seduction stories confirm a long-recognized pattern of female behavior. The sense of recognition upon which the stories depend stems from a common perspective, which seems valid because pervasive. External perspectives gain evidentiary weight by virtue of their numerousness and congruence. Foster employs the seduction story in order to examine the status of what passes for evidence in accounts of women. Reprinting the actual Whitman memorial, Foster exposes how formulaic narratives such as seduction tales gain evidentiary significance through circulation and repetition. In applying words written for a real woman to a fictional woman, Foster displays the arbitrary application of a preexistent characterization that persistently operates in formulations of women. Marking Eliza's end by remarking the words commemorating another fallen woman, Foster illuminates how the seduction story, and the structure of consent it exemplifies, perpetuates specific androcentric definitions of gender. It is Foster's revisionary achievement in *The Coquette* to use the seduction formula not only to show the different points of view that can be introduced in and through it, but also to scrutinize the formal operation of all views. Under such scrutiny, Eliza's witnesses appear disqualified from any corroborative role in seduction and consent.

Along with witnesses, *The Coquette* accordingly calls into question the standing of offspring as evidence of consent. No epitaph witnesses Eliza's stillborn infant. Indeed, all children disappear in Foster's treatment of consent. All progeny in the book, even the legitimate babies of Sanford and his wife and of the exemplary Mrs. Richman, die. The ubiquitousness of infant mortality assigns to everyone the same consequences that the coquette and her infant warrant.[28] Terminating the generative capacity of consent, Foster places all visions and uses of consent under the aegis of mortality. In Foster's treatment of seduction and consent, the body and its destiny become an inadequate because indiscriminate measure of individual agency.[29]

The effect of this reminder of common subjection to mortality is not to level the competing claims for consent—whether the misogynistic blanket attribution of consensuality to women or the feminist republican claim for women's civic virtue—but to foreground the permeable and impermanent bodies from which consent putatively emanates. Because these bodies, like Eliza's, may internalize or channel the interests of others, consent can never be reduced to one strain of consciousness. It never solely represents the individual or the society, Eliza or her friends. A confluence of voices and interests, consent as Foster delineates it is the ontological state of the liberal individual and the ontological burden of women in the liberal imagination. Thus the life of Elizabeth Whitman has passed from newsprint to novel to ever more commentary, testifying to the materiality of consent that women (still) customarily convey.

For women, this ontological burden includes—indeed demands— their reproductive labors: their production of the evidence of consent. By the liberal logic of seduction stories that I have been unfolding here, pregnancy proves the operation of consent, recognizing it even in its extralegal, extramarital, or premarital exercise. Indeed, as in Rousseau's portrait of consent, nonconsensuality barely seems an option for women when all their pregnancies, whatever the circumstances of insemination, signify consent to sexual relations. Hence the seductions ascribed to rakes and coquettes, and so often recounted in late-eighteenth-century American literature, seem to suggest an extending franchise of consent. If women thus gain entitlements in a liberal society, they do so at the price of the suppression of their nonconsensuality. But Foster strikingly refuses to give generation the evidentiary function it usually has in seduction stories. If all offspring, legitimate or illegitimate, die, no one substantiates female consent. Without children, the Lockean tradition of measuring consent by self-projection and self-retrospection halts.

In drawing attention to the mortality of the body, Foster dramatizes the fragility of this form of evidence for female consent. Eliza's removal from Foster's narrative, coincident with her impregnation and the progression of the pregnancy, thus signifies not only Foster's expulsion of coquetry but also her refusal to yoke consent merely to physical evidence. Without the standard physical evidence of consent, the witnesses who confirm consent can present only anecdotal evidence: the final testimonial that they offer to Eliza's mother is quite literally anecdotal, the words borrowed from Elizabeth Whitman's epitaph. What the end of *The Coquette* underscores, then, is not the consequences of Eliza's consent—"Let candor throw a veil over her frailties," the epitaph counsels (169)—but the task of redefining the testimonials of consent.

6

The Quixotic Fallacy

When a four-year-old asks his mother upon her return from a trip to Paris if she saw Madeline and the old house covered with vines there, he is expressing an ancient, enduring conception about fiction: its continuity if not identity with life. Reading, both the activity of reading and the content read, continually describes and explores various relations between fiction and reality. A range of possible relations exists. The matter of fiction may or may not coexist with actual objects; it may improve upon or depreciate, invert or exaggerate, underscore or obscure, invent or ignore reality. As even this partial list indicates, fiction may just as often complement and elaborate reality as contradict it. We are accustomed to the matches as well as mismatches between fiction and actuality. If Madeline could not be seen in Paris, my son would readily understand that she exists only in the stories. Some things do exist solely in the imagination and its literary instantiations. But he was also gratified to learn that I had seen the Eiffel Tower, which also appears in the Madeline books.[1]

The fact that sometimes a story is just a story heightens the reader's satisfaction when reality actually accords with fiction—which is to say, when fiction has so successfully represented reality that reality appears to verify fiction. One's sight of the Eiffel Tower confirms one's sense of it from literary or pictorial representations; in this case, another person's sight of the monument performs the same confirmation. An identity between reader's and viewer's experiences affirms that the objects encountered by the reader exist and that they can be made present in many forms: as story, picture, Parisian landmark, or souvenir statue. By bringing unseen objects or events into view, fiction routinely performs a testimonial function that can be amplified by the presence (or testimony to the presence) of appropriate objective correlatives.[2] Thus readers with mimetic expectations signify not so much a naïvete about fiction as the perspicacity with which readers habitually understand the representational and representative properties of fiction.

The figure of the reader with mimetic expectations, who expects life to conform to literature, has long been a subject of fascination and entertainment. Most memorably typified by Cervantes's Don Quixote, whose confusion of fiction with actuality introduced the term "quixotism," the quixotic reader would believe that Madeline lives or lived in Paris just as the book says (and might go looking for her there). In an even stronger mimetic experience, the quixotic reader might become the heroine, as in the American poet and painter John Trumbull's 1773 description of the quixotic reader: "Harriet reads, and reading really / Believes herself a young Pamela."[3] By the end of the eighteenth century, the case of the impressionable or deluded reader was a common theme in literary criticism as well as in the novel itself.[4] The quixotic fallacy, in which life is confused with fiction, attests both to the power of fiction to represent reality (or what can be taken to be reality) and to the susceptibility, whether reasonable or unreasonable, of readers in accepting fictional representations.

In this portrait of reading, the successful mimetic operations of fiction proceed at the risk of misleading readers who might take literary representations as real. The quixotic fallacy, an extreme version of what Wimsatt and Beardsley call "the affective fallacy," leads readers not only to confuse literature with its effects—to take the literary artifact as a personal mirror—but also to forget altogether the artifactual status of a literary representation.[5] Readers unable to differentiate fiction from actuality might act not just oddly but also destructively, like Updike Underhill, the unsophisticated hero of Royall Tyler's 1797 novel *The Algernine Captive*. While reading *Pilgrim's Progress*, Underhill "stuck a skewer through Apollyon's eye in the picture, to help Christian beat him."[6] I want to suggest that the quixotic fallacy, in its appearances with the rise of American culture, points less to concerns about a noxious power in fiction than to worries about the behavior of readers. Quixotic readers like Underhill who often appear in early American novels epitomize the misjudgments that the susceptible Lockean consensual individual can make. The foolishness of the reader who mistakes fiction for reality illustrates not any determinate harmful effect of mimesis but error in choice of the objects she imitates or credits. Thus while criticism of the quixotic fallacy always involves concern with the objects in literature that may be imitated, overcoming the fallacy requires the re-education of the reader. In other words, concerns about the quixotic fallacy do not indict literature but register the unreliability of readers in their relations to what they read. For a democratic society, where the perennial problem is agreement upon the fundamental general rules to which individuals should conform, the quixotic fallacy furnishes a vivid narrative of the difficulties that occur when individuals follow standards other than the established general rules of their society.

Novel-Reading and the New Nation

The problem, or at least one problem, with really believing you are Pamela or Clarissa—which was an issue much discussed in early national literary commentaries—is that you forget the circumstances of life in America. As Tabitha Tenney remarked in the most extensive early American novelistic treatment of quixotism, *Female Quixotism: Exhibited in the Romantic Opinions and Extravagant Adventures of Dorcasina Sheldon* (1801), novels impart "false ideas of life and manners," and even "airy delusions," especially about marriage.[7] There may be no romance in "the connubial state" (325), or no rich Mr. B's to marry. Noah Webster similarly worried, "The heads of young people of both sexes are often turned by reading descriptions of splendid living, of coaches, of plays, and other amusements. Such descriptions excite a desire to enjoy the same pleasures. A fortune becomes the principal object of pursuit; fortunes are scarce in America, and not easily acquired; disappointment [inevitably] succeeds."[8] By this account, reading can unduly raise the expectations of the reader, presenting her with objects that are not necessarily available. If young Americans are to learn and uphold their own culture, they should not be distracted by desires for unavailable or unfamiliar objects.

Echoing Webster's distrust of novels and commitment to American literary nationalism, Royall Tyler declared, "If the English novel does not inculcate vice, it at least impresses on the young mind an erroneous idea of the world in which she is to live. It paints the manners, customs, and habits of a strange country; excites a fondness for false splendor; and renders the homespun habits of her own country disgusting."[9] In these criticisms of novels for creating improper mimetic expectations, Webster and Tyler argue that the novel should help form national identity by presenting familiar phenomena, the matters and manners characteristic of American experience.

Conversely, the British novel could be seen as providing exactly the right types of manners to emulate. Judith Sargent Murray in 1798 accordingly recommended *The History of Clarissa Harlowe* as "the best model for the sex that I have ever yet seen portrayed." Some eighteenth-century American readers of *Clarissa* found its heroine's conduct not only an exemplary model of female behavior, but also a pattern of rightful rebelliousness against parental tyranny, and thus an excellent archetype for all Americans.[10] Contrary to Benjamin Rush's recommendation to "subdue that passion for reading novels which so generally prevails among the fair sex," Murray believed that novels "may very properly and advantageously constitute" part of female education.[11] And novels may benefit not only women, she thinks, but the entire populace: "Novels, under proper direction, might be made much more extensively subservient to the well-being of society."[12] Novels can and do present admirable patterns of conduct. Such moral claims shaped most defenses of the novel; in order to counter charges of promulgating false ideas and images, many novelists asserted that their books either contained a didactic truth or represented actual events. Hence the claims of so many early American novels to be renditions of "true stories."[13] The oft-expressed anxiety about fiction, an anxiety expressed not only by critics but also by novelists and characters in novels, in fact works to maintain the authority of novelistic representation. Quixotic readers, who so thoroughly grant the truth of fiction, thus typify the common appeal of fictional power. Since novels can significantly affect individuals—as Webster, Tyler, and Murray all believe—they are key media in the shaping of consent, in the forming of agreements under which Americans live.

Late-twentieth-century critical debates about the early American novel continue to address the question of what allegiances novels encourage. One way to view the widely professed antifictional bias of the period is to see novels as a discourse of individuality that contradicts or even threatens the values of civic republicanism upon which the new nation was supposedly established. In an important study of early American culture, Michael Warner has noted the crucial role of print media in the forming of a new republican society in the American colonies. In contrast with early American letters such as essays, manifestos, broadsides, and treatises, the appearance of novels for Warner represents the discovery of a different purpose for printed literature: the formation of a private sphere in which the individual locates herself. Within Warner's schema opposing republicanism and individualism, the anxious discourse surrounding early American novels expresses both "an ideal of republican literature in which publication and the public sphere remain identical" and the "worry that the environment of fictitious identification might no longer entail public knowledge or civic activity." Early American novels, then, "could only narrate their anxieties about the hazard to the republic that they themselves posed."[14]

Alternatively, Cathy Davidson finds an important communicative purpose operating in early American novels. In her feminist reading of these novels, Davidson analyzes the prevalence of women in the novels and their readership, concluding that novels provided women in the new republic with a critical forum. Novels therefore worked to remember "the Ladies in ways that John Adams and his Constitutional cohorts did not."[15] Whereas Warner sees novels as undermining the civic values of the republic, Davidson sees them as supplying a public mode of female participation in the republic. Davidson's account follows Murray's 1798 recognition of the usefulness of novels for circulating constructive information for and about women. Discovering a feminist function in early American novels, Davidson regards novels as extending the republican processes of public discourse.

Though Davidson and Warner differ in their accounts of the novel's relation to the republic, both assume that reading operates within the dichotomy of public versus private interests. Finding novel-reading a public activity for women, Davidson discovers a progressive politics in the rise of the American novel. Regarding novel-reading as a private pursuit, Warner discerns in the novelistic vogue a regressive politics, a retreat from republicanism to individualism. Formalist political interpretations follow from the assumption that reading serves either public or private purposes. For novels uniformly to undermine or uphold (by improving) the republic, they would have to convey the same message to all readers. To imagine that novels undermine republicanism is to imagine that they discernibly remove persons from connections to public life.[16] To imagine that novels uphold, or even extend, republicanism is to imagine that they uniformly operate as liberal political discourse. By claiming a public function for the novel, Davidson places the early American novel in the public realm, beyond the private sphere that Warner deems antirepublican. Yet for both Davidson and Warner, the positive value of novel-reading depends upon novels being a public rather than private medium.

Reading, when pursued in private, can obviously isolate individuals, encouraging and demanding interior experience. Yet public forms of reading do not at all obviate interior experience. Even the more communal reading experiences such as family Bible-reading and storytelling or listening to a public reading of proclamations or laws involve mental activities in which readers (and auditors) register, compare, consider, endorse or dismiss the representations that they encounter. Thus the proliferation of print culture that the rise of the novel exemplifies does not necessarily entail a radically new privatization of reading.[17] Reading always involves a private, interior activity. Conversely, reading is already public because the cognitive acts involved in reading, reading alone no less than in a group, require the individual to relate to external notions, to a sense of the public or general standards in which she lives, beginning with the common meanings ascribed to words.[18] In short, reading is never exclusively public or private; it indeed epitomizes the continual flow between these realms.

Though marked divisions in American life, such as the placement of women's labor in the home and the separation of the home from centers of industry, begin to appear in the late eighteenth century, these rearrangements of spheres of economic and political activities need not, and should not, be understood within the too simple dichotomy of public and private spheres.[19] Children's sense of the continuity between books and life, such as my son's connection between Paris in *Madeline* and Paris in reality, aptly registers the associative and transitive movements that reading both enables and enacts. Reading requires crossing boundaries between public and private, between representation and reality. The activity of reading is such a contested issue—the question of whether reading novels helps or harms Americans perdures—because readers can move to different places, can identify with positions that may be incongruent with the views of their peers. Because novels conceivably can move readers to a majority or minority position (or to confusion or even to no position at all), the significance of what they do depends on both the vagaries of the reader and the particular goals of the critic.

The variety of readers and their interpretations therefore belies the formalist historical accounts of early American fiction developed by Warner and Davidson, who read novels in light of an antinomy between public and private or republican and individualist interests.[20] Such a critical paradigm neatly presupposes the novel's historical performance, furnishing a clarity about both the meaning and effects of novels. This attractive lucidity is precisely what novels, themselves an ongoing experimentation with generic modes (such as romance, history, parables, biography, autobiography, diary, gossip, journalism, advice books, letters, travelogues, and sermons), so often do not provide, and indeed interrogate. Placing is what novels explore: they sometimes encourage or discourage the particular positioning of persons, while always drawing on the reader's capacity to credit the situations made present through novelistic representation. Because novels can and do provide schema of human life, they immediately attract political interests. Novels indeed can be quite specifically political but it is not their fictional character itself, their representational mode, that determines their political functions and messages. Thus the meaning of the antifictional prejudice embodied in quixotic figures will vary depending upon the source of this sentiment.[21]

Both the antirepublican account of early American novels advanced by Warner, and Davidson's alternative reading of this literature as subversive, capture specific features and effects of early American fiction. These accounts attempt to establish the place of this fiction by naming the political and social positions that the novels (seem to) occupy and endorse. Concerns about novel-reading, then and now, bespeak the desire to know and delimit the boundaries of fiction. What novels continually generate, in early as well as in contemporary America, is apprehension about where readers may go and what they might do, an uneasiness about where novels might lead. To attribute a specific political

character to the genre itself is to fix the destination of novelistic peregrinations. In this sense, Warner and Davidson reiterate Tenney, Webster, Tyler, and Murray, sharing the expectation that fiction provide
useful or desirable social models. All these commentators understand
reading as a particular kind of mimetic relation, as what I am calling a
quixotic relation. They therefore find it important that literary objects
be worthy of imitation. Yet the variety within these critical views displays the difficulty of making such judgments: readers can and do develop different identifications with literary objects.[22]

Whereas Rush and Webster fasten on the cultural specificity of British novels—on their depiction of a class system, and certain classes—
Murray is taken with the exemplarity of Clarissa's individual behavior,
identifying with the qualities of her character. These commentators
differ in their prescriptions of what one should read because they differ
in their own readings. Even if critics could agree on the exemplarity of
a given literary work, they could not control the ways readers would relate to any book. If a woman emulated a literary heroine, she could do
so in disreputable as well as admirable ways. Thus novel reading may
harm or improve women readers, or any readers, depending upon what
stories they read, how they interpret them, and what they do in response to their reading.

Female Quixotes and Consent

Because novels can and do inform the consent of women, they became
both the target and engine of late-eighteenth-century consent discourse. This power of books made them standard equipment of seducers such as Belfield in Leanora Sansay's *Laura* (1809).[23] The titular heroine of this novel predictably falls under the influence of the novels
her suitor gives her. Indeed, this novel, through its portrait of Laura,
depicts the female susceptibility to fiction as almost a genetic trait.
Laura's mother, a Portuguese woman named Rosina, after reading the
"story of some beautiful lady delivered from enchantment by a valiant
knight," escapes from a convent, marries, and emigrates to America.
There her husband dies, leaving her with a baby daughter. Rosina then
encounters the realities of being a poor, single mother; as if she had
lived the life of a fallen heroine, she finds herself treated as a seduced
and abandoned woman. Rosina manages to remarry and then dies.

From her mother Laura inherits the tendency to see her life in the fashion of romance. Though Rosina's experience underscores the disparity between romantic notions and the actualities of marriage and motherhood, Laura appears oblivious to the lesson of her mother. Like Rosina, she knows nothing "of the world . . . but what she had learned from books" (44). She accordingly follows the standard of reality furnished by the books Belfield gives her, readily entering into the role of a woman in love:

> She read them with avidity and infinite pleasure, but it would be vain to attempt describing the effect produced on her ardent imagination by Pope's letter of Eloisa to Abelard. In every passage she discovered sentiments of which she felt herself susceptible, and to experience, even during a short interval, the tenderness, the passion, the transports of Eloisa, she thought would be cheaply purchased by a life of torture. Fatal illusion! which was still more fatally augmented when she heard the eloquent, the pathetic voice of Belfield, repeat the tenderest, the most impassioned lines of that dangerous poem. (39)

In this stock scenario, Laura succumbs to Belfield's seduction by putting herself in the place of Eloisa vis-à-vis Abelard. One of the predominant worries about women becoming quixotic readers was that they would then be easily subject to seduction and ruin. Once a woman thought herself Pamela or Eloisa, she became susceptible to anyone willing to play Mr. B or Abelard to her heroine. Quixotism thus could facilitate seducers in doing what they wanted to with women, but interestingly, only if seducers would enter into the literary expectations of women. While quixotic women may become literally more manipulable in tableaux designed to approximate romances already familiar to them, their susceptibility depends upon seducers meeting their literary demands—by conforming to the manners and matter of their sexual imaginations. Even if Belfield initiates Laura's seduction by giving her a guidebook for erotic love, his plan can succeed only if Laura finds "pleasure" in the "transports of Eloisa" (39).

When Dorcasina Sheldon, the heroine of Tabitha Tenney's *Female Quixotism* (1801), cannot find a man to reenact her literary pleasures, she makes her maid Betty dress as a man and deliver romantic speeches to her. It is the common knowledge of Dorcasina's preoccupation with romances that causes both numerous fortune hunters and her friends to enter into the romantic scripts that so please her. Tenney thus cleverly underscores the point that female desire preexists and can even preempt male desires. The quixotic mode of reading exhibits for women their pleasures in themselves and in reflections of themselves, suggesting a narcissism so delightful that others (of both sexes) are moved to join in the enactment of the reader's fantasy. This description might also stand as an account of pornographic reading, especially when we recall the centrality of narration in eighteenth-century pornography. In pornographic novels, a lecturer, storyteller, or witness usually relates not just scenes of erotic content but also the effects of those scenes upon herself or himself.[24] Not surprisingly, the objections to quixotic reading resemble what has become a standard critique of pornography, the concern that it incites readers to copy what they read. So injunctions against quixotic reading often take the form of *Laura*'s warning that reading literally can ruin a woman.

This warning assumes that the literary power to arouse, excite, stimulate, and provoke somehow lessens the agency of the reader. In translating words to deeds, reading to actions, the reader acts as an automaton. Under literary influence, she cannot exercise the judgment of a consensual individual; she becomes subject to the books that most attract her. The quixotic reader thus embodies Locke's portrait of the susceptible individual who loses "liberty of mind," the capacity of freely moving her thoughts.[25] Her subjection suggests how easily consent can be misdirected, or even preempted. A woman under the influence of fiction is malleable to manipulation by those who know her fictional preferences. Laura's literary pleasure fits all too well into Belfield's seductive designs. Fortune hunters pursue Dorcasina by adopting the language and manners of romance novels. In these parables of the effects of fiction upon female consent, women become automatons of literary suggestion, a suggestive power intensified by unscrupulous individuals who exploit the women's pleasure in fiction.

Locke, whose formulations of the imaginative social tasks of individuals in a republican society so pervasively influenced eighteenth-century America, recognized the strong connection between personal pleasure and reading. He accordingly advocated teaching children to read by appealing to their sense of enjoyment. Aiming to make reading a pleasurable process to which children will easily commit themselves, Locke recommended that tutors and parents give children books with attractive pictures and pleasant contents. The exemplary texts in Locke's literary curriculum include fables, some Biblical stories, and *Don Quixote*, the first, or at least best-known, quixotic fable. "Of all the Books of fiction, I know none that equals Servantes his History of Don Quixot in usefulness, pleasantry, and a constant Decorum; And indeed no writings can be pleasant which have not *Nature* at the bottom, and are not drawn after Her Copy."[26] The pleasantness of literature, according to Locke, consists in the fact that it is a copy; it approximates nature. That Locke's exemplary useful and decorous fiction is a story of a man who copies obviously inaccurate representations of life underscores the importance of readers learning to evaluate and use representations appropriately. Don Quixote copies an imaginary chivalric code of conduct, inappropriately applying the rules of romance to life. Cervantes's novel accentuates the impropriety of Quixote's identifications, the absurdity of the behavior stemming from his literary relation. The problem is not that Quixote imitates the chivalric models to which he aspires, but that he fails to recognize the fictional status of these models. Readers of the novel take pleasure in the many comic disparities produced by Quixote's literalism.

Locke's point that literary representation affords pleasure by virtue of copying nature emphasizes reading as the activity of judging literary copies according to accepted standards or rules. When readers lose the liberty of mind to evaluate reasonably what they read, their pleasure signifies not this active intellectual enjoyment but an uncontrolled dependence, the involuntary condition of the mesmerized subject. In basing the individual's relation to reading upon pleasure, Locke aligns that pleasure with perspective, with the reader's function within a frame of reference that enables her to see the discontinuities as well as continuities between life and Quixote's impossible dream. The reader's pleasure inheres in the various relations between nature and copy.

Quixotic women readers like Laura and Dorcasina, whose literary pleasures distract them from all but their imaginary standard of reference, thus perfectly typify Locke's worries about individual susceptibilities to "clogs" in the exercise of judgment.[27] The feminization of the quixotic figure, beginning with Charlotte Lennox's novel *The Female Quixote* (1752), intensifies the sense of the quixote's impressionability by linking it to the permeability and sensibility customarily attributed to women. So female quixotes such as Laura and Dorcasina, or Alicia Lefanu's Lucy Osmond and Sukey Watson's Emily Hamilton, predominate in the early American novelistic discourse of consent.[28] A few male quixotes do surface. Besides the previously mentioned Updike Underhill, the male quixotic figure appears memorably as the hero of Hugh Henry Brackenridge's voluminous *Modern Chivalry* (1793–1815), an extensive treatment of early national social and political manners. The novel's protagonist, Captain Farrago, styles himself "the modern Don Quixote."[29] Farrago's disenchantment with his contemporary society makes him think of himself as a man living in the wrong time and place. He believes in traditions that seem strange and eccentric in his present world. This novel dramatizes this dissociation in the differences between Farrago and his servant-squire Teague O'Regan, a prototype of the immigrant democratic individual. For early American readers, gender differences rather than class differences furnish the most popular paradigm in which to represent the permeability of the consensual individual. Though *Modern Chivalry* continually demonstrates the susceptibility of persons to external influences, the prevalence of cautionary tales about female quixotes suggests that characteristics of sexual difference most effectively dramatize anxieties about individual susceptibility.[30]

The especially exquisite sensibility attributed to women makes it easy for them to wander from the conventional frame of reference and to follow fictional standards that please themselves. A quixotic woman reader thus does not share the sense of reality acknowledged by most members of her society. She seems wayward not because she reads with mimetic expectations and is propelled to mimic what she reads, but because she reads according to an aberrant criterion. Her reading does not square with peer perceptions of literary and real objects precisely because she expects continuity between fiction and reality. Far from being too mimetic, the quixote fails to be mimetic enough—that is, mimetic of what everyone else mimes. She is, we might say, mimetically incorrect. So stories of the quixotic fallacy initially appear to be fables about solipsism.

Yet quixotic identifications clearly do not proceed independently of external coordinates. Quixotes very much depend upon models they find in fiction. Like John Trumbull's Harriet who "really / believes herself a young Pamela," most quixotes in early American fiction take their models from British books or culture. Laura emulates Eloisa, and Dorcasina patterns herself after British and French romantic heroines. They follow the models that cultural nationalists such as Webster and Tyler think inappropriate for Americans. The pervasive stories about quixotic readers in early American fiction and cultural criticism thus serve the nationalist project of advancing a different habit of readerly identification. As female quixotes epitomize subjection to a wrong standard of reference, their allegiances appear aberrant and absurd, well worth discarding.

What is crucial to fables of quixotism, however, is not the elimination but the conversion of the quixotic reader. As the object of conversion—conversion to a model worthy of emulation—the quixote commands both sympathy and respect. A strikingly characteristic feature of quixotic tales, therefore, is the way in which the quixote almost invariably manages to be humored by others.[31] Members of the quixote's community enter into the quixote's delusion, corroborating and sometimes amplifying the details of the delusion. The quixote raises such affective concerns among her family and community that they hasten to make her odd sense of reality commonplace. This sense of reality, however absurd, is always intelligible, available for imitation. Honoring conformity to general rules in her own bizarre fashion, the quixote exemplifies the way that reading customarily works.

Narratives of quixotism further underscore the quixote's respect for conformity by often concluding with her admission of folly and endorsement of reality. Ultimately quixotic mimeticism leads to social mimeticism, with quixotes affirming a common reality. The reformation of the quixote thus illustrates and celebrates the process through which individual citizens concur with their society. So while quixotes epitomize susceptibility to the wrong literary influences, they also exhibit the capability to overcome this subjection and to subject themselves to a different authority. Fables of quixotism do not merely delineate the American from the non-American, then, but recapitulate the process of individual consent so crucial to forming the new nation. In establishing their own nation, Americans had to commit themselves to common standards. To accomplish the complementary task of perpetuating their national consciousness through education and literature, they promoted the processes of social mimesis that consent encapsulates. Once a nation, the United States relied on stories such as the quixotic fables told in fiction and criticism to restate the common grounds of national affiliation.[32]

Mimeticism and Consent

A quixotic relation to reality throws into relief the social mimeticism from which the quixote varies. To take pleasure in the quixote's rambles, readers must refer to their own relations to the common sense from which the quixote deviates or dissents. The quixote herself believes and follows in extremis a different standard of reality, thereby appearing quite eccentric if not mad. Yet like the mad, with whom quixotes were often identified, quixotes very much adhere to an order, displaying a fundamentally social orientation. Quixotes choose to mime well-known characters: heroic and noteworthy figures, or famous personages from history or fiction. Their objects of emulation must be a recognizable part of social currency in order for their emulations to make sense to themselves. Convinced of the plausibility of their identifications, quixotes accordingly assume, to great comic effect, that their viewpoints are perfectly comprehensible to others. Firmly committed to a social order, they strictly observe the etiquettes and practices associated with their models and expect other people to follow suit. Tenney's Dorcasina, for instance, rejects her first suitor, despite her father's desires for the match, because the young man's speech and manner of writing do not meet the style of lovers in romance novels.

The importance of protocols in quixotism shows mimesis to be a fundamentally social phenomenon in which every individual is engaged. Everyone matches personal identity to some standard, thereby testifying to the crucial function of mimesis that Mikkel Borch-Jacobsen calls mimetic efficacity.[33] Identity depends upon the activities of mimesis through which individuals define themselves. In imitative and representational forms—literature, history, art, or the imagination—individuals encounter a panorama of figures. From these encounters, persons compose themselves. The quixotic composition of personal identity exhibits in radical form the comparative and identificatory operations that persons perform in mimetic experience. Quixotes most clearly display the mimetic process of identity in their faithfulness to their fictional models. Their observances of their chosen rules simply exaggerate the congruity between representations and persons that mimesis both enables and entails.

In imitating what they read, quixotes signify their commitment to similitude between reality and fiction. However eccentric Dorcasina seems, she adheres to the rules of her favorite romance novels, wanting her life to resemble them. Laura likewise seeks resemblance between romance and life, wanting a love like that of Abelard and Eloisa. The interest and comedy or tragedy of these women's stories obviously depend upon the discrepancy between their real and imagined situations. The quixotic investment in resemblances thus works to uphold standing principles of differentiation, such as the distinction between books and life. The more Don Quixote identifies his life with medieval romances, the more Cervantes accentuates the disparity between the two.

Characterizing Don Quixote as a hero of modern identity, and *Don Quixote* as "the first modern work of literature," Foucault has stressed how the Knight's insistence upon similitudes (between medieval romances and his present experience) registers "the cruel reason of identities and differences."[34] Reason is cruel, according to Foucault, because it works by maintaining distinctions. Distinctions themselves mark social agreements about what constitutes similarity and what constitutes difference. Out of accord with common reason, the quixote shows how normality is based upon certain agreed upon distinctions, such as that between life and literature. By failing to remain merely mimetic, the quixote reveals the mimetic basis of society. Appearing mad because he adheres to his own conception of likeness between life and literature, Don Quixote reveals the social construction of the categories by which persons develop their conventional or nonconventional allegiances.

Because the quixotic insistence on resemblances between reality and fiction so accentuates the accepted wisdom of a fundamental dissimilitude, quixotes can appear admirable idealists or inspired dreamers as Don Quixote does in *The Man of la Mancha*. Quixotes also can be social critics and rebels. Making her consent contingent upon her preferred set of social mores, Dorcasina manages to exercise her own will in courtship. Thus, after spurning her father's chosen husband for her, she attempts to make her father accept her own choice, the fortune hunting criminal O'Connor who deliberately adopts the romantic manners that

Dorcasina cherishes. Although the eventual exposure of O'Connor's imposture—he pretends to be an exiled nobleman—disappoints Dorcasina, she goes on to imagine a series of other unsuitable objects as her lovers. For Dorcasina, quixotism extends an avenue for self-fulfillment, a means of getting one's way or one's pleasure. Quixotic scenarios allow for rewritings of the marriage plots usually foreordained for women. Consequently, female quixotism has inspired feminist interpretations, which appreciate the scope that quixotism affords individual desires and expressions, however fantastic.[35]

Women quixotes, like all quixotes, certainly make (up) their own worlds. In their inappropriate exercises of sexual and marital consent—they consent according to their own romantic values—eighteenth-century quixotes wield an influence in their lives not then socially and legally accorded to women. At the same time, their adherence to romantic protocols marks the connection between consent and social mimeticism. The quixotic exercise of consent in early American fiction represents women claiming their right to self-determination by declaring their conformity with a set of social rules taken from their reading. Even though the quixote pledges allegiance to an imaginary community, her exercise of consent nevertheless operates in a social context. Thus the feminist employment of quixotism epitomizes how consent works for all those who employ it—as an identification of self-interest with some external codes agreed upon by other individuals, real or fictive.[36]

Tenney's *Female Quixotism* describes precisely the mimeticism upon which quixotism relies and proceeds. Like most quixotic readers, Dorcasina employs an extreme formalist mode of judgment. Because the men in romances are usually disguised aristocrats, she thinks that all men must be noblemen. She similarly assumes that because men in romances are inevitably in love with the heroine, all men who meet a quixotic heroine must be in love with her. Dorcasina's syllogistic thinking involves an additional technique in which factors of actual experience are placed in the extensive logic of romance fiction. In a sort of reverse of personification, or peculiar version of it, she transforms actual agents and persons into literary types. Finding personifications like the romantic hero in bodies at hand, Dorcasina makes persons proxies of characters. For example, her Irish servant John Brown appears in her perspective an exiled nobleman. Having recently read *Roderic Random*, in which the hero, "under the name John Brown, had lived with his be-loved Narcissa (whom he afterwards married) as a servant," Dorcasina "immediately" concludes that "his namesake" in her household "must likewise be a gentleman in disguise" (227).

In reading persons as romantic characters, Dorcasina regularly ele-vates persons in class and financial status. Through her misconstruc-tions, an immigrant servant such as John Brown instantaneously real-izes the democratic ideal that any individual can aspire to and attain any position. She similarly imagines herself as a beneficent agent of so-cial transformation when she fantasizes the prospect of marriage to a Virginia gentleman as her opportunity to free his slaves. Dorcasina's romantic fantasies also inspire the persons around her to alter their class, gender, race, or personal identity as they variously try to trick or help this deluded heiress. For example, the fortune hunter O'Connor poses as an exiled Irish aristocrat; the servant James impersonates his army major master; the family friend Harriot Stanley disguises herself as a military captain; the black gardener Scipio appears to Dorcasina as her Irish lover; the schoolmaster Mr. Smith pretends to be a love-struck young man named Philander as well as Philander's jealous mis-tress. And as previously mentioned, Dorcasina requires her servant Betty to "dress yourself in a suit of my father's clothes, and then come and personate O'Connor" (97).

In the course of serving her mistress's various romantic whims, Betty regularly suffers from Dorcasina's "blindness and credulity" in pur-suing her fantasies (143). When Betty grudgingly complies with Dorcasina's wish to reenact her first meeting with O'Connor, the rest of the household staff mistake her for a thief. After realizing that the "thief" was Betty dressed in men's clothes, they "could not refrain from bursting into an immoderate fit of laughter." Though Betty's fellow servants "were unable to comprehend what Betty or her mistress could mean by such a frolic" (100), the fun-loving local schoolmaster com-prehends exactly what these romantic impersonations mean and is in-spired to engage Dorcasina in further follies. Posing as the lovelorn Philander, he writes letters seeking assignations with Dorcasina in the grove where she used to meet O'Connor. Mindful of proprieties, and still loyal to O'Connor, Dorcasina makes Betty accompany her. Worse than being "the mortified object" of her fellow servants' mirth (99), Betty now undergoes verbal and physical abuse. Rather than appearing as Philander, the schoolmaster shows up as Philander's enraged mistress and attacks Betty. As she complains to her mistress, "I was thump'd, and cuff'd, and bounc'd, and shook, and twirl'd, and had my clothes stripp'd off, and tore to tatters, as if I had been nothing at all. Besides, what I shall not soon forget, in a grum and angry voice, that was no woman's, he call'd me old, and ugly" (116). This is not the end of Betty's pains for Dorcasina's sake. She subsequently finds herself bound, gagged, and carried away with her mistress when Philander stages a kidnapping as a sign of his violent passion for Dorcasina. In these absurd episodes, which mime adventures from Dorcasina's favorite novels, it is Betty who bears the brunt of their reality. Because her mistress believes these events to be part of a familiar and cherished narrative, and because Philander carefully respects Dorcasina's actual status as an upper-class woman throughout his prank, Dorcasina is immune to the emotions and pains that Betty suffers.

As the unwilling participant in Dorcasina's quixotism, Betty personally feels the real effects of Dorcasina's imaginary narratives. Thus Tenney shows how imaginative activities, far from being merely frivolous or inconsequential, require quite real exertions and produce material effects. Dorcasina's pleasure proceeds at the cost of Betty's pains. The invective addressed to Betty, the characterization of her as old and ugly, also applies to Dorcasina, who in Tenney's unsparing presentation goes from "a middling kind" of appearance to an unattractive, toothless, wrinkled, ultimately bald, old age in the course of the novel (5, 234). Dorcasina's delusions protect her from recognizing what her household and neighborhood, as well as the reader, readily sees. While treating Betty and everyone around her as fictional characters, Dorcasina remains strangely unsympathetic to them. Her own readiness to see fictional characters as real does not translate into sympathy for them. She thus fails to follow the conventional novelistic invitation to sympathize with fictional bodies.[37] In this uncharacteristic insensibility, Dorcasina ignores Betty as both a real person and a fictional character. Betty, of course, does not experience her body as made up, as a fictional entity. Betty serves as a surrogate for the sufferings to which Dorcasina could be subjected; precisely because Dorcasina resides in a privileged class position, she need not suffer from either her own dislocation or the mobility of persons about her. Those who adopt different identities to indulge Dorcasina eventually have to return to their true statuses, which in the case of a servant like Betty means having to accept some unusual work-related injuries or in the case of the impostors O'Connor and Philander means leaving town to avoid prosecution.

The serial narrative of masquerades inspired by Dorcasina ends only when her quixotic activities threaten her community's social hierarchy by actually settling one of her imagined lovers in a new social position. When Dorcasina plans to marry a servant in whom she sees a disguised nobleman and to make him master of her household and fortune, the community acts to restore the socioeconomic order threatened by all of these identity changes. To prevent Dorcasina from making an unsuitable marriage, her friends resort to entering into one of her romantic plots. They kidnap her and hold her prisoner in a secluded country-house. There she eventually learns the error of her judgments. She comes to understand how her friends have duped her, and she realizes how she has persistently misread persons and events. Dorcasina learns to attach her associations to different objects, to the same objects that her friends value. She accordingly renounces fictional romance as a standard of behavior. Yet even though at the novel's close she cautions young women against reading this genre, she significantly states that she still enjoys such novels: "I read them with the same relish, the same enthusiasm as ever; but, instead of expecting to realize scenes and situations so charmingly pourtrayed, I only regret that such unallayed felicity is, in this life, unattainable" (325). This is now a suitable declaration since Dorcasina has learned to read appropriately. Once independent of the rule of romance, her pleasure in reading novels is harmless, a personal eccentricity, an individual taste now safely sequestered.

Obviously, this narrative of reformation by abduction and confinement describes a case of forced consent, which could suggest compulsion at the heart of social compact, at the heart of community. I do not think, however, that this novel is making this standard critique of liberal consent theory. Rather, *Female Quixotism* demonstrates how the cultural context in which one lives both shapes and directs the operation of consent. It is fine for Dorcasina to go on loving romance novels so long as that love does not alter the distribution of wealth and the class positions in her community. Once she has renounced her custom of translating novelistic scenarios into social relations, her wealth remains inaccessible to all fortune hunters.

After Dorcasina's rehabilitation, she becomes a philanthropist who

supports "those who, by misfortunes, and without any blameable mis-
conduct of their own, have been reduced from opulent or easy circumstances to indigence" (324). Previously celebrated for her charity to the
poor, Dorcasina now tends particularly to the maintenance of those
who have fallen in class position. She thus serves aristocratic values
rather than the class mobility that so many of her previous actions have
promoted, however unwittingly. If her quixotism initially gave scope to
progressive impulses, her post-quixotic perspective mirrors a conservative reaction to the progress of democratic values.[38]

Consent in *Female Quixotism* affirms a set of affiliations, a form of
community that is finally antirepublican, that is itself an aristocratic romance of arresting democratic movements. Ironically, this quixotic fable uses consent to ratify the social compact of an exclusive group.
Dorcasina ultimately consents to the covenant of a privileged class.
Tenney's novel shows that while quixotism can be a consent story, a
consent story is not necessarily only the story of a democratic society.
The social mimeticism of quixotism can vary in its address: the suitable
objects of identification differ from class to class. In *Female Quixotism*,
it is no more acceptable for Dorcasina's maid to marry a wealthy mer-
chant (who mistakes her for her mistress) than it is acceptable for
Dorcasina to marry a poor Irish immigrant. The social compact reinforced by Dorcasina's quixotism—which is to say, by Dorcasina's consent—requires strict governance and direction of mimeticism.

Post-Quixotic Reading

According to Tenney, the misdirected mimeticism of quixotism stems
from the absence of proper parental direction of children's reading. Mr.
Sheldon, who owned and enjoyed a library full of novels, "unfortunately indulged his daughter in the full latitude of her inclination;
never considering their dangerous tendency to a young inexperienced
female mind; not the false ideas of life and manners, with which they
would inspire a fanciful girl, educated in retirement and totally unac-
quainted with the ways of the world" (6). Thus corrective education
takes the form of an intervention that treats the quixote as a child or in-
competent, under protective authority until capable of independence
in the world. The reformed quixote gains her independence when she
demonstrates her willingness to be directed by social conventions.

Once she has admitted and affirmed the authority of her community, she can enjoy her (albeit limited) freedom in that society.

The redirection of quixotic consent into conventional limits appears equally vividly in another story, Maria Edgeworth's "Angelina; or, L'Amie Inconnue" (1801).[39] Her quixotic heroine Angelina readily understands that romances are imaginary but this comprehension does nothing to lessen her esteem for them. Rather, her delight in fictive romances leads her to revere "Araminta," the author of her favorite romances, and to begin a correspondence with her. In an extreme form of quixotic conflation, Angelina assumes that Araminta is writing autobiographical novels and thus must embody all the qualities of her heroines. Araminta, a hack writer who barely supports her lover and their alcoholic existence, senses a potential patron in Angelina and so encourages the relationship, following Angelina's suit in using—and professing to prize—the romantic terms of her own fiction. Delighted to be confirmed in her sense of Araminta as the living type of romantic heroines, Angelina decides that she must meet this beloved paragon and sets out alone from London to Wales to see her.

Like Dorcasina, who alters her given name Dorcas with "a romantic termination" (*Female Quixotism*, 6), Edgeworth's heroine has changed her name from the simple Anne to the more romantic sounding Angelina. Her literary education also resembles Dorcasina's: "She had passed her childhood with a mother and father, who cultivated her literary taste, but neglected to cultivate her judgement: her reading was confined to works of imagination rather than any knowledge of realities" (14). Lacking parental guidance in reading, Angelina models her life after her favorite romances. "Miss Warwick had an ungovernable propensity to make a display of sensibility, a fine theatrical scene upon every occasion;—a propensity which she had acquired from novel-reading" (24–25). She accordingly thinks of her servant Betty Williams, "she's actually a female Sancho Panza" (95). So immersed in her literary perspective is Angelina that, as Edgeworth points out, "her own more striking resemblance to the female Quixote never occurred to our heroine" (95). Though she dramatizes all her experiences, she cannot help but notice that others do not quite match her literary expectations. Seeing a minstrel at an inn, she disappointedly notes that he is "a mere modern harper—he is not even blind!" (22).

When Angelina, after a set of predictable misadventures, finally meets Araminta, she has to compare what she sees with what she has read and imagined. After seeing the disparity between the actual and fantasized Araminta, she can acknowledge her mistaken manner of perceiving the world. "I am fully sensible of my folly," she now concedes to her old friend Lady Frances. To affirm Angelina's reformation, Lady Frances then recommends that they read Lennox's *The Female Quixote* to learn more about that folly. Edgeworth's narrator enthusiastically reports that this reading about the reformation of another female quixote wholly succeeds: "In short, we have now, in the name of Angelina Warwick, the pleasure to assure all those whom it may concern, that it is possible for a young lady of sixteen, to cure herself of the affectation of sensibility, and the folly of romance" (142).

Edgeworth thus interestingly concludes not by proscribing novels, but by finding them useful for reforming the very excesses that they are thought to promote. The way to cure quixotism is through supervised reading, a common prescription that many contemporary novelists recommended. Judith Sargent Murray, for example, in *Story of Margaretta* (1798), advises active maternal participation in a daughter's novel reading, including "suggestions and observations" on each book, to supply an effective "antidote to the poison, of which the pen of the novelist is too often fraught."[40] The presence of a reading monitor like Edgeworth's Lady Frances or Murray's aptly named Mrs. Vigillius guides the reader's identifications in a desired direction, teaching her "properly to appreciate the heroes and heroines of the novelist."[41]

Tenney suggests that a monitorial function inheres in the very act of reading. "Learn to be wise by others' harm / and you shall do full well" is the antisympathetic motto of this novel, which Tenney addresses "to all Columbian young ladies, who read novels and romance" (*Female Quixotism*, 3). The readerly disposition recommended here for women and for the new nation is distantiation. Reading can be profitable so long as the reader differentiates herself from the characters and events about which she reads. Following the tradition of reformed quixotes, Dorcasina does present an obligatory admonition against novels, as she recommends withholding "the pernicious volumes" from young girls (325). Tenney's motto, however, suggests a way to turn the dangers of fiction to useful account. Readers unsubjected by the quixotic fallacy can learn from the mistakes and misadventures of fictional persons. Edgeworth does not recognize this didactic potential in fiction for she finds individuals far too susceptible to allow them such independence in reading. Only a monitor's supervision of the reading experience can reform Angelina. Yet Angelina's quixotism never was wholly untutored, for Araminta has inspired and encouraged it. Angelina's credulity depends in great part on Araminta's confirmation of the girl's fantasies.

Casting the quixotic relation as one between reader and author, Edgeworth makes explicit the social relations (even though here based on deception) involved in reading or misreading. Lady Frances can successfully replace Araminta as Angelina's reading guide because Angelina is already committed to seeking confirmation of her interpretations. Her journey to meet Araminta enacts the social logic of reader response that she has learned from reading. She expects perfect agreement between writer and reader, a meeting of soul mates. The task of reforming Angelina, then, is simple: to find another authority for her reading once she has discovered that Araminta is unsuitable. Unlike Dorcasina, who has to undergo a long reeducation involving several months of protective custody until she can act as an adult and change her affiliations, Angelina simply switches affiliations in the space of a few sentences.

For Edgeworth, the social nature of reading relations means that readers readily seek reading companions; reading makes one desire company like oneself. Hence a homoerotic danger lurks in her account of reading: Angelina appears wrong both in her assessment of Araminta (thinking the author is like herself) and in her attachment to Araminta, which takes her from the company of her own class and from the business of courtship in that class. In reading, or rather misreading, Angelina pursues her fantasies inspired by another woman. Her devotion to Araminta, built upon the author's public persona, shows the development of reader response into the fan's personal attachment to a public figure. Fan(tastic) relations work on the imaginative insistence that the chosen idol matters in the fan's own life because the fan matters to the idol. In all the labor and ritual of maintaining this fantasy, the fan expresses her hopes and desires, often restricted to fantasy because of the unlikelihood or impermissability of these aspirations. To detach Angelina from her obsession with Araminta, then, Lady Frances cannily becomes Angelina's reading companion and confidant. Lady Frances points Angelina to heterosexual romantic plots. Together they read Charlotte Lennox's *The Female Quixote*, the comic story of the quixotic heroine Arabella who eventually quits her romantic fantasies and accepts the reality of marriage to her cousin.

For Tenney, the reader's pleasure, however eccentric, need not interfere with conventions of sexuality. Even after Dorcasina reforms, she still reads her favorite novels, but now she keeps to herself her pleasure in those books; she no longer tries to enact it in her world. With reading pleasure privatized, the reader can indulge her own desires without interfering with the class and sexual arrangements of her society. Whereas Edgeworth sees a continuity between reading pleasure and social behavior, which requires maintenance by right-minded monitors (to circumvent influence from the wrong sort of mentors), Tenney recognizes and encourages a discontinuity between reading and living. In counseling readers to distance themselves from literary figures, Tenney also implicitly counsels readers to treat themselves, or their behavior—and the harms they have done to themselves—as objects to be outdistanced. Dorcasina learns to alter her conduct by seeing herself as others, as readers, see her. After being abducted in the fashion usually experienced only by heroines in romance novels, Dorcasina can read, criticize, and change herself.

When Dorcasina learns to read herself unsympathetically, as another, from her peers' perspective, she can learn from the example of her own follies. *Female Quixotism* ties Dorcasina's rehabilitation to the fact that she ages in the course of the narrative, growing ever further from the chronology of sexuality and child-bearing that most women in the early nation experienced. By aging her heroine, Tenney furnishes her with a span of time in which she can be viewed by herself as well as by other readers. The reformation of her reading, unlike that of Angelina, entails not just switching attachments but also introducing and instituting a division within herself: a partition between herself as reader and as object of reading. Dorcasina finally learns what all children usually glean quite readily in the course of growing up: to see and think about herself differently.

Dorcasina's education, her attainment of more reading skills, alters her mimetic course so that she now congrues with her community, and more particularly, with her class. Tenney's emphasis on differences between persons—between actual and fictive figures, and among actual or fictive persons—not only reflects class distinctions but also relies on this differentiating system as a means of preserving a border between the realization and the imagination of individual desires. Indeed, it is this border, this mark of differences, that sustains the preferred social affinities, that defines one set of similitudes as better than another. First Dorcasina's peculiarity, and then her self-condemnation, underpin the distinction of her peers.

Miming mimeticism by matching life with fiction, the quixote only differs in degree from her conventional counterparts. Her condition thus represents what Borch-Jacobsen calls a "malady of identity," a disturbance in the standard state of identity. We have seen in Dorcasina that however mad or bizarre a quixote seems, her "malady of identity" exacts from her a sense of propriety even as it exhibits her deviance from the social order that she inhabits.[42] The characteristically communal mimetic activity engaged in to humor and dispel quixotism also displays the recognition of the mimetic nature of identity epitomized by quixotism. Like exorcisms of the mad or possessed, cure of the quixotic requires group affirmation of the quixote's perceptions; that is, a sympathetic engagement first to valorize the quixote's perspective and then to reorient it. Through the rehabilitation process, the quixote finds support for her new identifications. In this reenactment of the social compact, the quixote realigns herself by engaging with new objects of sympathy and identification. As Dorcasina becomes a charitable guardian of her class, she relegates her prior attachments to a secluded space in her personal life, to the harmless leisure of reading for fun. Her new arrangement of the place of reading in her life distinguishes between community and personal interests, allowing for both so long as the individual proclivities remain subordinate. *Female Quixotism* finds a place for Dorcasina's literary pleasure in the reading closet, where by recalling the shame of her foolish affiliations she can most closely monitor her future choices. Embarrassment, which is to say social anxiety about herself, will be her best future guide.

The Politics of Mimeticism

Rectifying quixotism requires redirecting mimeticism from quixotic standards to current or desired social norms, from one interest to another. As the escapades of Dorcasina so candidly exhibit, different (and often conflicting) interests can and do operate in the performance of social mimeticism. *Female Quixotism* depicts a variety of disparate interests, including Dorcasina's own somewhat feminist impulses, her community's hierarchies, and outsiders' ambitions. In this novel, the community and its interest in preserving a hierarchical class structure prosper by the quixote's reformation. Tenney thus portrays the power of a dominant group and how it can use the democratic mechanisms of consent and competition to perpetuate itself.

In affirming a hierarchical class system, Tenney's quixotic tale reiterates some Federalist principles of the party to which her U.S. Senator husband belonged.[43] The most explicit, and perhaps most extreme, early American advocacy of class distinctions emerges in the views of Gouverneur Morris. During debates on the formation of the Constitution, Morris had proposed organizing the national government according to class. Morris's plan envisioned a Senate composed only of the most wealthy, propertied citizens.[44] The House of Representatives would be composed of poorer, but still propertied, men. Morris thought that the visible distribution and division of wealth among the members of Congress would spotlight class interests in such a clear way that such interests could be checked or modified. This strategy of openly acknowledging class differences, which both respected and restrained propertied classes, would make an ever-present spectacle of the hierarchization of society. With such differences in clear public view, Morris thought that the wealthy would be curbed by a sense of public oversight of their activities. Morris's disregard for the representation of the unpropertied not surprisingly offended his more democratic-minded colleagues. Morris's counterparts at the Constitutional conventions also did not share his view of the rich as innately sensitive to social responsibility and appearances, and accordingly did not endorse his plan institutionalizing class differences in the composition of Congress.[45]

The Morris plan conveys the same frankness about class differences that Tenney imparts in *Female Quixotism*, written nearly fifteen years later during her husband's tenure as a Federalist senator in the Democratic-Republican Jefferson administration. As if to underscore her own allegiances, Tenney gives Dorcasina and Betty speeches composed of stock antirepublican rhetoric denouncing the "pernicious sentiments, the growth of other climes" coming to America through the writings of "one Tom Paine." "May heaven prevent the further progress of Jacobinism, atheism, and illuminatism," Dorcasina declares. To which the faithful Betty answers, "Amen, say I" (316).[46] The two women then attribute the deceitful behavior of the con men who have duped Dorcasina to these different cultural movements. Yet Tenney has provided ample reason for all the frauds undertaken in the novel: Dorcasina's wealth motivates everyone. If *Female Quixotism* is a Federalist novel, its identity with Federalist politics lies in its general regard for wealth rather than in any specific policies or proscriptions. In other words, the novel clearly delineates a central Federalist premise about the centrality of wealth and position to society. Rather than simply polemicizing for the Federalists, Tenney's novel contributes to American political culture a manual for democratic public relations. *Female Quixotism* describes the imaginative means by which a particular interest garners the sanction of individuals. The novel's narrative of the reformation of Dorcasina demonstrates how a privileged class can gain endorsement for itself by appealing to the eccentric.

The imaginative work that *Female Quixotism* accomplishes for early American culture is to dramatize the process of social accord. In staging the resolution of contradictory tendencies in a liberal society, Tenney includes in her story numerous interests with which readers can identify. The reader of Dorcasina's misadventures in consent can discover in the novel, either to her pleasure or displeasure, both a feminist case for women's self-determination and a conservative confirmation of class differences. That these contradictory positions coexist in the novel attests to the scope that quixotism affords individual differences even as it affirms social conformity. No such allowance for individual difference figures in Edgeworth's portrait of quixotism, where social conformity proceeds by eliminating differences. Quixotism, in Tenney's treatment, strengthens the force of social mimeticism, demonstrating that the social drive to mimeticism outruns and overtakes even the most erratic mimetic courses that an individual can pursue.

While American novels about quixotism follow an imperative to reorient the quixote, they do not at all disregard individual freedom of choice as they seek to define the horizons of that choice. Tenney's Dorcasina and Sansay's Laura freely make poor choices of men and eventually freely admit their mistakes. The examples of the quixotic fallacy appearing throughout early American fiction often display neither distrust of mimeticism nor disrespect for the errant reader, whose faulty identifications often appear an admirable idealism or a perfectly

comprehensible misunderstanding.[47] This benign or opportunistic attitude toward the quixotic reader expresses another crucial function of
quixotism: it protects and affirms individual consciousness even as it ultimately tends to maintain standards for social harmony among individuals. Reiterating, then, the liberal doctrine of individualism, quixotism in its early American manifestations reflects the difficult endeavor
of respecting individuality while also tethering individual understanding to external standards that imply the consent of many individuals.

The American development of quixotic narratives into a consent discourse reflects how novels change through the ways that readers understand and use them. Bakhtin calls this process "reaccentuation," as
he describes how "great novelistic images [his example is Don Quixote]
continue to grow and develop even after the moment of their cre-
ations" by being inflected differently.[48] Through the perils and possibilities of reader identification, the quixotic fallacy reaccentuates for
early American liberal society the connections between reading and
society.

Tenney's twice-stated prescription for avoiding the fallacy—"Learn
to be wise by others harm / And you shall do full well" (4, 152)—underscores the importance of keeping one's distance from the objects of
identification, of remembering who you are when you read. Reading in
this manner always reminds the individual of herself by appealing to
her difference from the fictive heroine. So avoiding or overcoming the
quixotic fallacy leads to self-recognition of an identity anchored in a simultaneous consent and disavowal. The reader chooses the coordinates by which to locate herself. In this process of sorting through
identifications, a reader may maintain, combine, or alter her set of associations. Within the conventional boundaries of consent, both the
heroine and the reader can move, even toward visions of new or different conventions. Thus as Dorcasina returns to the gentry, her readers
still can prefer, if they like, the peregrinations among class and gender
identifications that her earlier story charts.

William B. Warner recently has characterized the readerly exercise
of preference as "the freedom of readers," a faculty that he studies as a
development within the history of print entertainments.[49] Tenney's entertaining narrative of Dorcasina's romantic opinions and extravagant
adventures sets the freedom of the reader in a particular American context, soliciting the reader's endorsement of the status quo in a certain

community. Even if a novelist harnesses consensual confirmation to nondemocratic projects, as Tenney links Dorcasina's reformation to an aristocratic vision of society, the necessity of solicitation marks the newly institutionalized importance of individuality that Tenney's politics opposes. In the subsequent decades of the early nineteenth century, the American novel continued to provide a forum on literary conversions as it addressed the issue of slavery. For America then and now, the lessons about mimeticism presented in fiction register discordant views about where mimeticism should point each of us.

Epilogue

Through the extravagances of coquettes and quixotes, early American novels explore and express the sundry political significances embedded in the wrongs and reformations of these women. Their misadventures in consent, set in the narrative frameworks of seduction and quixotic fables, dramatize the informing circumstances of consent. These novels highlight the local, prejudiced, manufactured, and contrived conditions of consent, such as its gendered application and interpretation or the select literary relations used to form and elicit it. Consent discourse in the new nation persistently considered the character and utility of the supplements of consent.

For late-eighteenth-century America, the image of women's fates exemplified the anxieties attendant upon consent. The association of consent with women, or more exactly, the association of the insufficiencies of consent with the situation of women, recapitulated Locke's conjunction of consent with children. In the period, both pairings reflect how Lockean consent memorializes the disenfranchised in order to emphasize the continual activity that consent requires. Images of the disenfranchised keep present the state of existence that individuals must always avoid and reject. Forces and influences as various as suggestion, education, literature, social trends, habits, prejudices, passions, obsessions, and hallucinatons commonly impinge upon individuals. A long-standing socioeconomic habit like sexism exemplifies one of the most intractable impediments to individuals in attaining and maintaining a consensual state. In the feminization of consent so markedly rehearsed by early American novels, we see what happens to some former children who never get to realize the benefits due them upon reaching the age of consent. Disenfranchised women suggest that individuals must continue the labor of consent throughout adult life. The civic subordination of women aptly typifies the conventional constraint in which consent operates, even for the privileged. The representational change from children to women in the typology of consent thus reiterates for early Americans the sense that they need to keep redoing the mental and imaginative tasks begun in childhood.

Because novels describe interior experience, revealing what persons feel, think, and sometimes do about their circumstances, they furnish a record of how personality interweaves with convention. The rise of the novel thus helps usher in modern mass culture, not simply because it generates a reading public and a mass market, but because it initiates the custom of continual self-reflection that typifies the modern individual. As the individual habitually measures herself against standards, she considers the forms of information circulating in her culture. She makes her determinations from these forms of information, thereby acting within and against her cultural context.

When twentieth-century commentators ranging from Walter Lippman to Edward Bernays to Noam Chomsky speak of the manufacturing of consent, they register something both new and old.[1] Besides stressing the unprecedented pervasiveness of information in an electronic age, they are reiterating the traditional connection of consent to cultural forms, to external influences. The spectre of manufactured consent implies brainwashing of the populace—in the present-day instance, by news and entertainment media. This threat of automating persons, however much facilitated by recent technological innovations in communications, originates with the initial linking of consent to eighteenth-century educational and literary media. Yet Locke's frankly artifactual definition of consent acknowledges the construction and manipulation of consent while always allowing for and encouraging the individual's own manipulations. If consent is haunted by the shadow of external influences, it also carries the power of exorcising unwelcome presences and impertinent guests who take possession of individual minds. By equipping individuals with the ability to reject and dispel influences, Locke safeguards consent from its own shadow.

American culture commences as a mass culture, one shaped by stories, images, and paradigms that circulated through the colonies over the course of the eighteenth century. The most influential pattern of thoughts for this period, I have argued throughout this book, stems from the Lockean linkage of consent with individual development. By the end of the century, what becomes most prominent in the rhetoric and representations of the self-determining individual is the sense of handicaps (negative and positive) under which individuals do or do not make choices. The feminization of the populace in popular fiction usefully describes both their subjection and their liberty of mind. Even as persons operate within borders, they variously imagine and manage traversals of those borders.

The portrait of persons as shadowed by the conditions in which they are born, even when the conditions of rank and political inheritance are radically changing, attests to the role, rather than the rule, of standards in the life of the individual. This modern coupling of the individual to cultural currents and channels, like Locke's conjunction of the child with the liberal state, immediately brings under scrutiny the predominant modes of influence—whether parents, teachers, governors, textbooks, icons, or novels. The now familiar attacks so regularly brought to bear on the perceived engines of individual formation arose with, not against, the liberal state. At the inauguration of the United States, the habit of worrying about and questioning cultural influences was already in place.

Women as well as other figures of disenfranchisement emblematized worries about the excesses and inadequacies of the influences operating upon consent. While the latter part of this book has focused on some well-known types of female subjection—mesmerized women, seduced heroines, and deluded readers—eighteenth-century consent discourse included others. Victims of religious persecution, Indian violence, racism, or slavery also regularly appear in popular literature. Since the end of the seventeenth century, personal reports and stories of slavery and captivity had related experiences of black enslavement and white abduction. Narratives such as *A True History of the Captivity and Restoration of Mrs. Mary Rowlandson* (1682), the "Panther Captivity" story (1787), and *The Interesting Narrative of the Life of Olaudah Equiano* (1789) describe individuals exercising their consciousness, beliefs, and affiliations under appalling circumstances or within unfamiliar contexts.[2] At the end of the eighteenth century, when Barbary pirates began enslaving American sailors, white slavery became a prominent subject in journalism, drama, and fiction, notably in Susanna Rowson's *Slaves in Algiers* (1795) and Royall Tyler's *The Algernine Captive* (1797).[3]

Both captivity and slavery narratives usually foreground the crucial role of religion in helping the individual through the horrors of abduction, captivity, and enslavement. Popular books about persecuted European Protestants, such as *The French Convert* (1744), likewise stressed the sustaining power of religious faith.[4] Taken from their customary frame of reference, these victims, captives, and slaves maintain themselves by adhering to the compass of their beliefs. Religion is the preferred and paramount influence in all of these narratives; it provides a stable point of reference when all others fail. By mooring individual liberty of mind in a specific religion, such stories uphold the fundamental role of external authority. They thus contribute to the eighteenth-century narrative of consent not only types of subjection but also recommendations for the best influence to which to tie consent. The testimonies to divine providence in the histories of slaves, captives, and martyrs identify individual liberty with God, presenting religious faith as the most effective, or even the only effective, framework of consent.

Eighteenth-century Americans clearly found numerous venues through which to review or reenvision the conditions of consent. How captivity, slave, and persecution narratives take up the representation of consent in American culture is a story still unfolding at the beginning of the twenty-first century in tales of racial memory, recovered memory, addiction, and alien abduction. That these narrative forms epitomize the interests of both privileged and subordinated segments of the population reflects the fact that the spectre of subjection operates for the advantaged as well as the disadvantaged. By its very nature, consent is never enough. But it does represent a much-needed sustenance for those who do not yet have it. For both the enfranchised and disenfranchised, consent authorizes and indeed impels the continual review and reform of its conditions. The Lockean legacy is the reminder to be always alert to the movability of even the most settled circumstances and opinions.

Notes
Acknowledgments
Index

Notes

I. Introduction

1. Preamble to the Constitution of the United States of America.

2. John Locke, "The Second Treatise," in *Two Treatises of Government*, ed. Peter Laslett (Cambridge: Cambridge University Press, 1960), chapter 8, section 95, lines 3–4, page 348. Laslett's edition draws on all the editions of the treatises published during Locke's life and on Locke's notes to them, thus forming a version "which would have satisfied Locke at the time of his death, or something as close to that version as an editor can make it" (Laslett, 146). Because the pagination differs among Laslett's 1960, 1967, and 1988 editions, citations of the *Treatises of Government* will appear throughout this book in this format: chapter, section, and lines of the *Treatise*, followed by the page number in Laslett's 1960 edition.

3. In making hitherto forgotten or peripheral materials—primers, fables, fairy tales—central to the discussion of the emergence of the United States, I am following Jay Fliegelman's lead in exploring the importance of eighteenth-century pedagogical philosophies. See *Prodigals and Pilgrims: The American Revolution against Patriarchal Authority* (Cambridge: Cambridge University Press, 1982).

4. In this book, I will be taking up specific critiques in some detail. Among the best-known arguments on the inequities operating in consent are Michael Walzer, *Obligations: Essays on Disobedience, War, and Citizenship* (Cambridge, Mass.: Harvard University Press, 1970); Catharine MacKinnon, *Toward a Feminist Theory of the State* (Cambridge, Mass.: Harvard University Press, 1989); Patricia Williams, *The Alchemy of Race and Rights* (Cambridge, Mass.: Harvard University Press, 1991); and Clare Dalton, "Deconstructing Contract Doctrine," *Yale Law Journal* 94 (1985): 997–1114. References to other recent important critiques of consent appear in Chapter 1, note 7, and Chapter 5, note 19.

5. Michael Kammen has adopted the term biformity to describe the Ameri-

can transformation of British ideas. See *People of Paradox: An Inquiry Concerning the Origins of American Society* (New York: Alfred A. Knopf, 1972).

6. David Hume, "Of the First Principles of Government," in *Essays, Moral and Political*, ed. Eugene F. Miller (Indianapolis: Liberty Classics, 1985), 32–36. Subsequent references to this essay will appear parenthetically within the Introduction.

7. Historian Edmund Morgan also cites Hume on consent and opinion at the opening of his penetrating study, *Inventing the People: The Rise of Popular Sovereignty in England and America* (New York: Norton, 1988). Morgan takes Hume to be registering the importance of public opinion, which is the subject that both his and my book explore in different ways. For a discussion of the ways in which Hume was attacking Lockean liberalism, see Henry D. Aiken's fine introduction to *Hume's Moral and Political Philosophy* (New York: Hafner Press, 1948), xli–l.

8. John Locke, *An Essay Concerning Human Understanding*, ed. Peter H. Nidditch (Oxford: Clarendon Press, 1979), book 2, chapter xxviii, sections 7–10, pages 352–353. This standard critical edition follows the 1700 fourth edition of the *Essay*, which is an extensive revision of the 1689, 1694, and 1695 editions. Further citations of the *Essay* will appear parenthetically, providing Locke's book, chapter, and section numbers, which are consistent in most editions.

9. Jürgen Habermas, *The Structural Transformation of the Public Sphere: An Inquiry into a Category of Bourgeois Society*, trans. Thomas Burger with Frederick Lawrence (Cambridge, Mass.: MIT Press, 1991), especially 88–99.

10. Thus Habermas supplies the foundation for one of the most important recent reevaluations of eighteenth-century American culture, Michael Warner's *The Letters of the Republic: Publication and the Public Sphere in Eighteenth-Century America* (Cambridge, Mass.: Harvard University Press, 1990). Warner studies specific writings by early Americans within the context of their contemporary ethos of publicity. Other recent Americanist studies conducted within Habermas's framework include Grantland Rice, *The Transformation of Authorship* (Chicago: University of Chicago Press, 1997) and Bruce Burgett, *Sentimental Bodies: Sex, Gender, and Citizenship in the Early Republic* (Princeton: Princeton University Press, 1998).

11. The bulk of Habermas's work accordingly addresses what he perceives as the eroded condition of communication in present modern culture. See, for example, *The Philosophical Discourse of Modernity*, trans. Frederick Lawrence (Cambridge, Mass.: MIT Press, 1987) and *Moral Consciousness and Communicative Action*, trans. Christian Lenhardt and Shierry Weber Nicholsen (Cambridge, Mass.: MIT Press, 1990). For a cogent discussion of the advantages and disadvantages of Habermas's definition of the public sphere, see Seyla Benhabib, "Models of Public Space," in *Situating the Self: Gender, Community, and Postmodernism in Contemporary Ethics* (New York: Routledge, 1992), 89–120. Nancy Fraser raises salient feminist objections to Habermas's theory in "What's Critical about Critical Theory? The Case of Habermas and Gender," in *Feminism as Critique*, ed. Seyla Benhabib and Drucilla Cornell (Minneapolis: University of Minnesota Press, 1987), 31–56. For other responses to Habermas, see *Habermas and the Public Sphere*, ed. Craig Calhoun (Cambridge, Mass.: MIT Press, 1992); Alexander Kluge and Oscar Negt, *Public Experience: Toward an Analysis of the Bourgeois and Proletarian Public Sphere* (Minneapolis: University of Minnesota Press, 1993).

12. Contemporary liberal responses to Habermas, which claim the presence of the public good or public reason in political institutions, therefore miss a crucial point in Locke's liberalism: the importance of not situating the conduct of human understanding, which, in Locke's view, always relates to existent positions. In other words, it makes no sense to render static the people's dynamic relation to circumstances that are both stationary and changeable. Locke wishes to preserve the provisionality of human institutions, beginning with monarchy, while other liberals would institutionalize their ideals. The most forceful contemporary liberal exponent of public reason is John Rawls. See his *Political Liberalism* (New York: Columbia University Press, 1993), which includes the essays "The Idea of Public Reason" and "Reply to Habermas." The exchange between Rawls and Habermas appears in the *Journal of Philosophy* 92, no. 3 (March 1995): 109–180.

13. Chantal Mouffe presents a lucid account of critiques of American liberalism in "American Liberalism and Its Communitarian Critics," in *The Return of the Political* (London and New York: Verso, 1993), 23–40. In her sympathetic summary of these arguments, Mouffe describes the Lockean liberal individual as "an individual endowed with natural rights prior to society," which she takes to be an "ahistorical, asocial, and disembodied conception of the subject" (28). My reading of Locke in this book will demonstrate that such a view completely misunderstands and misrepresents Locke, though it may accurately register problems with the actual operation of liberalism in American history.

14. Louis Hartz, *The Liberal Tradition in America: An Interpretation of American Political Thought since the Revolution* (New York: Harcourt, Brace, and World, 1955).

15. Bernard Bailyn, *The Ideological Origins of the American Revolution* (Cambridge, Mass.: Harvard University Press, 1967; enlarged edition 1992); Gordon Wood, *The Creation of the American Republic, 1776–1787* (New York: Norton, 1969); and J. G. A. Pocock, *The Machiavellian Moment: Florentine Political Thought and the Atlantic Republican Tradition* (Princeton: Princeton University Press, 1975) and *Virtue, Commerce, and History* (Cambridge: Cambridge University Press, 1985). Feminist scholars have extended the republican tradition to include the role of women: see Linda Kerber, *Women of the Republic: Intellect and Ideology in Revolutionary America* (New York: Norton, 1980); and Mary Beth Norton, *Liberty's Daughters: The Revolutionary Experience of American Women, 1750–1800* (New York: Harper Collins, 1980) and *Founding Mothers and Fathers: Gendered Power and the Forming of American Society* (New York: Vintage, 1996). Other important related feminist scholarship is cited in the notes to Chapter 5, which address women's issues in the early republic. The discussion of the republican tradition continues to be extensive. The distinguished list of participants in debates about American republicanism includes Dorothy Ross, "The Liberal Tradition Revisited and the Republican Tradition Addressed," in *New Directions in American Political History*, ed. John Higham and Paul K. Conkin (Baltimore: Johns Hopkins University Press, 1979); Joyce Appleby, *Capitalism and a New Social Order: The Republican Vision of the 1790s* (New York: New York University Press, 1984) and *Liberalism and Republicanism in the Historical Imagination* (Cambridge, Mass.: Harvard University Press, 1992); Isaac Kramnick, "Republican Revisionism Revisited," *American Historical Review* 87 (1982): 629–664; Lance Banning, "Jeffersonian Ideology Revisited: Liberal and Classical Ideas in the American Republic," *William and Mary Quarterly* 43 (1986):

3–19; and Philip Gould, "Virtue, Ideology, and the American Revolution: The Legacy of the Republican Synthesis," *American Literary History* 5, no. 3 (Fall 1993): 564–577.

16. J. G .A. Pocock, "Virtue, Rights, and Manners," in *Virtue, Commerce, and History* (Cambridge: Cambridge University Press, 1985), 40.

17. Pocock offers his own fairly sympathetic reconsideration of Locke in "The Myth of John Locke and the Obsession with Liberalism," in *John Locke*, ed. J. G. A. Pocock and Richard Ashcraft (Los Angeles: Clark Memorial Library, 1980).

18. Numerous studies have traced the connections between literacy and Protestantism. See, for example, David Cressy, *Literacy and the Social Order: Reading and Writing in Tudor and Stuart England* (Cambridge: Cambridge University Press, 1980); and Raymond Williams, *The Long Revolution* (New York: Columbia University Press, 1961). On American Puritanism and literacy, see Kenneth Lockridge, *Literacy in Colonial New England* (New York: Norton, 1974); Philip Greven, *The Protestant Temperament: Patterns of Child-Rearing, Religious Experience, and the Self in Early America* (New York: Knopf, 1978); and Lawrence Cremin, *American Education: The Colonial Experience* (New York: Harper & Row, 1970).

19. Quoted in Henri Petter, *The Early American Novel* (Columbus: Ohio State University Press, 1971), 8. In line with Channing's view, critics have set the nineteenth-century American Renaissance as the starting point for American literary culture. See, for example, F. O. Matthiesson, *American Renaissance: Art and Expression in the Age of Emerson and Whitman* (New York: Oxford University Press, 1941). In the recent revisions of American literary history, early novels are accorded significance for their social or political messages, as in Jane Tompkins's *Sensational Designs: The Cultural Work of American Fiction, 1790–1860* (New York: Oxford University Press, 1985); and Cathy Davidson, *The Revolution and the Word: The Rise of the Novel in America* (New York: Oxford University Press, 1986). For references to other critics, see notes to Chapter 4 and Chapter 5.

20. For a similar characterization, see Lawrence Buell, "American Literary Emergence as a Postcolonial Phenomenon," *American Literary History* 4 (1992): 411–442. To call early American literature postcolonial is to draw attention to both the contextual and formal concerns with which a writer of an emergent people engages. Clearly, emergent peoples differ: the postcolonial British colonial has a vastly different status from the postcolonial colonized American Indians and transported, enslaved African Americans. And postcolonial American white women, unenfranchised and constrained by male property rights, exemplify a still different condition. Thus I think that postcolonial is a useful term to foreground the historical position of persons or peoples, but it is only useful in conjunction with the particulars of a given people's experience. In the case of white male Americans, their postcolonial character operates in tandem with their new national affiliation, their newly acquired character as what Etienne Balibar calls "homo nationalis." See "The Nation Form: History and Ideology," trans. Immanuel Wallerstein and Chris Turner, *Review: A Journal of the Fernand Braudel Center for the Study of Economics, Historical Systems, and Civilizations* 13 (1990): 329–361.

21. An exemplary analysis of this relation from the other direction—from the perspective of American influence on British forms—is Nancy Armstrong and Leonard Tennenhouse, *The Imaginary Puritan: Literature, Intellectual Labor, and the Origins of Personal Life* (Berkeley: University of California Press, 1992).

22. As should be obvious, American Indians only enter the American Lockean narrative of citizenship centuries after their colonization by the British and by the Americans, and then with all the handicaps of their long exclusion from economic opportunities and social benefits that other citizens have enjoyed for generations. My study of the Lockean legacy throws into relief the increasingly explicit practices of racism and sexism after the founding of the nation. Though they had clearly already been long operative, these prejudices gained an institutional force at the end of the eighteenth century, one later augmented by nineteenth-century sciences. In a recent investigation of the early national popular press, Carroll Smith-Rosenberg explicates the formation of a homo Americanus, a figure of the U.S. citizen as male, white, and propertied. This figure replaces the long-standing figure of America as an Indian woman. See her "Dis-covering the Subject of the 'Great Constitutional Discussion,' 1786–1789," *The Journal of American History* (December 1992): 841–873. Concurrently, Smith-Rosenberg argues, the press and novels produced the character of the American woman, imagined as the authorizer of this racially scripted and class-defined homo Americanus. See "Subject Female: Authorizing American Identity," *American Literary History* (Fall 1993): 481–511.

1. The Child's Consent, the Child's Task

1. Alexander Hamilton, *Federalist Papers*, no. 85, ed. Clinton Rossiter (New York: Mentor, 1961), 527.

2. Madison memorably writes in *Federalist Papers*, no. 49 that "the people are the only legitimate fountain of power" (ibid., 313). As Jennifer Nedelsky has demonstrated, self-governance for all members of the population actually "never engaged the attention of the Federalists," whose primary concern was protecting property: "The Constitution of 1787 institutionalized the principle of consent in ways that left open important questions about what to do in a conflict between the rights of people to implement their will through their representatives and the independent rights of property." See *Private Property and the Limits of American Constitutionalism: The Madisonian Framework and Its Legacy* (Chicago: University of Chicago Press, 1990), 7. In addition to economic differences, gender and racial distinctions obviously also restricted the operation of consent; at the same time the ideal of consent has remained potent in motivating and justifying both the extension of the franchise and reform of property rights.

3. Quoted in Mary Beth Norton, *Founding Mother and Fathers: Gendered Power and the Forming of American Society* (New York: Vintage, 1996), 3.

4. I am here following Norton's recent illuminating exposition of early American history in ibid., 3–24. Norton treats mainly seventeenth-century America, focusing on what she identifies as the American colonists' recapitulation of a Filmerian system of unified power in which family, gender roles, and state are closely linked. Norton also discovers nascent Lockean systems emerging in the same period. My treatment of the eighteenth-century American embrace of Lockean consent theory concentrates on childhood (rather than gender) as the medium and set of values through which Americans defined themselves. Consent and monarchy in British history is a well-studied connection. See, for example, Ernest Barker, *Essays on Government* (Oxford: Clarendon Press, 1951), 1–119; J. W. Gough, *John Locke's Political Philosophy* (Oxford: Clarendon Press, 1973), 52–80.

5. *The Declaration of Independence as Originally Reported to Congress*, printed in the "Appendix" to Jay Fliegelman, *Declaring Independence: Jefferson, Natural Language, and the Culture of Performance* (Stanford: Stanford University Press, 1993). Fliegelman's appendix provides an invaluable edition of the Declaration: Jefferson's original text with the additions and deletions made by the Continental Congress before publication. The indictment of the British for their failure to honor familial bonds originated in Jefferson's draft and remained unaltered by Congress. The most thorough account of Revolutionary rhetoric is in Bernard Bailyn, *The Ideological Origins of the American Revolution* (Cambridge, Mass.: Belknap Press of Harvard University Press, 1992).

6. The most influential studies of the history of childhood, and the question of the emergence of what we know as modern childhood, are Philippe Ariès, *L'Enfant et la vie familiale sous l'ancien régime* (Paris: Libraire Plon, 1960), translated by Robert Baldick as *Centuries of Childhood* (London: Jonathan Cape, 1962); Lawrence Stone, *The Family, Sex, and Marriage in England, 1500–1800* (New York: Harper & Row, 1977); and Linda Pollock, *Forgotten Children: Parent-Child Relations from 1500 to 1900* (Cambridge: Cambridge University Press, 1983). For an informative contextualization and comparative analysis of these major theses about the concept of childhood, see David Archard, *Children: Rights and Childhood* (London: Routledge, 1993), 1–41.

7. Criticism of consent theory dates as far back as its emergence. In the seventeenth century, monarchists regularly attacked consent as an incoherent justification of individual rights; for them, the only adequate provision for the rights of men could be found in monarchy. Informative treatments of the varied seventeenth-century critiques and defenses of consent are furnished by Don Herzog, *Happy Slaves: A Critique of Consent Theory* (Chicago: University of Chicago Press, 1989); and Gordon J. Schochet, *Patriarchalism in Political Thought: The Authoritarian Family and Political Speculation and Attitudes Especially in Seventeenth-Century England.* In the eighteenth century, objection to consent theory becomes most succinctly articulated and institutionalized in Hume's dismissal of the notion of an originary social contract. See his "Of the Original Contract," in *Essays: Moral, Political and Literary* (Indianapolis: Liberty Classics, 1985), 465–487.

8. Sir Robert Filmer, *"Patriarcha; or, The Natural Powers of the Kings of England Asserted" and Other Political Works of Sir Robert Filmer,* ed. Peter Laslett (Oxford: Basil Blackwell, 1949).

9. Locke, "The Second Treatise," in *Two Treatises of Government*, ed. Peter Laslett (Cambridge: Cambridge University Press, 1960), IV, section 71, lines 8–15; Laslett, 332. As I stated in note 3 to the Introduction, citations of the *Treatises of Government* will appear throughout this book in this format: chapter, section, and lines of the *Treatise*, followed by the page number in Laslett's 1960 edition.

10. Though Locke uses the idea of children's consent hypothetically here—in the context of explaining how historically children most likely made their fathers political leaders—he is also specifically employing the notion of children's consent here as a dismissal of paternal right as a natural basis for any kind of power. As Gordon Schochet demonstrates in *Patriarchalism and Political Thought*, the connections between family and consensuality so influentially treated by Locke follow from a discussion earlier conducted by Hobbes, Sidney, and Tyrrell, as well as other seventeenth-century thinkers.

11. Elaine Scarry richly elaborates the connections that Locke establishes between tacit consent and residence in "Consent and the Body," *New Literary History* 21 (Autumn 1990): 874–884.

12. See Hanna Fenichel Pitkin, "Obligation and Consent—I," *American Political Science Review* 59 (December 1965): 990–999; especially pages 996–997 and 999; and "Obligation and Consent—II," *American Political Science Review* 60 (March 1966): 39–52.

13. Detaching the right to the child's life from the parent (and vesting it in the state) and making education a private, parental enterprise (rather than the state's), the Lockean project of child-rearing defines the limits of both political and parental authority. Nathan Tarcov stresses this point in his discerning analysis of Locke's pedagogy, *Locke's Education for Liberty* (Chicago: University of Chicago Press, 1984), 72.

14. Locke repeatedly distinguishes between parental and political power in order to repudiate patriarchalist accounts of government. To support the ideal of individuals as distinct from the authority of the state, Locke insists upon the independence of the family sphere. But the privacy of this sphere makes sense only in its relation to politics. In contriving a boundary between the two, Locke sets limits on governmental authority. For example, the parents (or guardians) rather than the state bear the duty of educating children, according to Locke. Yet as the following discussion in this chapter will show, Locke recommends that parents teach their values to their children—values often defined and maintained by the state. Locke makes no simpleminded division between private and political spheres that overlooks their interconnections as he discerns the practical necessity of dividing the two. Lockean liberalism is by no means as myopically individualist as some of its critics assert. The (mis)reading of Lockean liberalism as an absolute division between private and public spheres begins in the eighteenth century with Rousseau's famous observation in "On the Social Contract" that "man is born free and everywhere he is in chains" from social forces.

15. Jay Fliegelman, *Prodigals and Pilgrims: The American Revolution against Patriarchal Authority* (Cambridge: Cambridge University Press, 1982). I am following Fliegelman's lead in studying the significance of Locke's influence on eighteenth-century Americans through his pedagogy and psychology as well as his political philosophy. Locke's own works, though addressed to specific realms, present these concerns as integral with one another.

16. On the importance of childhood in colonial America, see Joseph E. Illick, "Childrearing in Seventeenth-Century England and America" and John F. Walzer, "A Period of Ambivalence: Eighteenth-Century American Childhood" in *The History of Childhood*, ed. Lloyd deMause (New York: The Psychohistory Press, 1974). Seventeenth- and eighteenth-century Americans have left a rich archive of their investments in childhood. See also note 30, this chapter.

17. On the children's stories circulated and read in eighteenth-century America, see Gillian Avery, *Behold the Child: American Children and Their Books* (Baltimore: The Johns Hopkins University Press, 1994), 36–62. I discuss these children's stories in greater detail in Chapter 4.

18. Michael T. Gilmore provides a useful account of Franklin's influence on, as well as frequent appearances in, late-eighteenth-century American literature in "The Literature of the Revolutionary and Early National Periods," in *The Cam-*

bridge History of American Literature, vol. 1: 1590–1820, ed. Sacvan Bercovitch (Cambridge: Cambridge University Press, 1994), 573–574; 622–637.

19. Locke's famous description of the state of nature appears in Chapter 2 of the Second Treatise, and is further developed in Chapter 5, "Of Property." This is the locus of most analyses of Locke's political vision. See, for example, C. B. MacPherson, *The Political Theory of Possessive Individualism: Hobbes to Locke* (Oxford: Clarendon Press, 1962); Andrzej Rapaczynski, *Nature and Politics: Liberalism in the Philosophies of Hobbes, Locke, and Rousseau* (Ithaca: Cornell University Press, 1987), 177–217.

20. In keeping with this understanding of money, Locke took an active interest in contemporary monetary issues. See Patrick Hyde Kelly, ed., *Locke on Money*, 2 vols. (Oxford: Clarendon Press, 1991). Volume 2 contains Locke's published as well as unpublished writings on money. As one of the anonymous readers of this book observed, thinking of money as consent makes particular sense before the rise of national currencies and the introduction of paper money at the end of the eighteenth century.

21. Scarry, "Consent and the Body," 873–881. The emphasis on "active" is Scarry's. For Scarry, the performance of consent invokes and relies upon the body. The body becomes in her account "the grounding of consent," the originary site of consent and individual will (868). But the body, I would point out, is alternatively or contradictorily volitional and nonvolitional, certainly an uncertain source of authority. The body, moreover, is a representational as well as material entity, not a set frame of reference. Founding consent in the body enacts once again the myth of individual control that consent sponsors and exemplifies. In other words, the grounding of consent in the body does not materialize consent; such grounding illustrates even more emphatically the imaginative nature and effectiveness of consent.

22. Locke, *An Essay Concerning Human Understanding*, ed. Peter Nidditch (Oxford: Clarendon Press, 1979), book 2, chapter xxi, section 47, page 263. All subsequent references will be noted parenthetically, citing the book, chapter, and section of the *Essay*. The importance of understanding Locke's *Treatises of Government* in relation to his account of knowledge and judgment in the *Essay*—a relation rejected by such Locke scholars as Peter Laslett—is fully treated in Ruth W. Grant's excellent *John Locke's Liberalism* (Chicago: University of Chicago Press, 1987).

23. Locke, *Of the Conduct of the Human Understanding* (1697), ed. Thomas Fowler (New York: Lenox Hill/Burt Franklin, 1971), 89. Locke originally intended this treatise to be an extra chapter appended to the *Essay*. The treatise first appeared in print in 1706 in a posthumous edition of Locke's writings. Further references to this text, which redacts many of the major points of the *Essay*, will be noted by page number parenthetically in the chapter.

24. Locke, *Some Thoughts Concerning Education* (1693), in *The Educational Writings of John Locke: A Critical Edition*, ed. James L. Axtell (Cambridge: Cambridge University Press, 1968), 152–153, section 56. Axtell's excellent notes to this edition make it the best of the fine editions of Locke's educational writings. Subsequent citations of the *Education*, however, will be to Locke's section numbers, which are available in all editions of the treatise. My reading here of Locke's pedagogy, a reading undertaken in connection with readings of the *Two Treatises of Government*, the *Essay Concerning Human Understanding*, and the closely related essay *Of the Con-*

duct of the Human Understanding, congrues with Tarcov's far more comprehensive treatment of the *Education* in his *Locke's Education for Liberty.* Tarcov compellingly establishes the unmistakable political dimensions of Locken pedagogy, dimensions that, as Grant demonstrates, also are intrinsic to the *Essay.* Tarcov and Grant have produced a very useful classroom edition of Locke's *Some Thoughts Concerning Education* and *Of the Conduct of the Understanding* (Indianapolis: Hackett, 1996).

25. Tarcov similarly takes the desire for esteem to be the fundamental psychological motive upon which Locke builds his pedagogy. See *Locke's Education for Liberty*, 100–176. I am treating Locke's cardinal concept of esteem, or credit, as a representational account of the self; self-development is thus the practice of considering the self in relation to other perspectives of the self, whether these other perspectives come from other persons or the individual. Tarcov observantly links esteem to Locke's emphasis on reason (see 117–118), quoting Locke's observation that children "love to be treated as Rational Creatures" (*Education*, section 81). Locke thus is appealing less to the rationality of children than to their desires for appearing in a favorable light, or in terms of my exposition, to their sense of external standards.

26. The class into which the child is born of course defines many of these individual attributes. Locke directly addresses his *Thoughts Concerning Education* to the gentry, to the sons of gentry. "Yet," as James Axtell observes, "though he was writing for this small class, this does not preclude the possibility that many of the things he said about education, especially its main principles, were equally applicable to *all* children." See "Introduction," *Educational Writings of John Locke*, 52.

27. Locke treats the problem of conceiving knowledge as permanent, especially as it functions through maxims and syllogisms, in the *Essay*, book 4, chapters vii and viii. In the *Education*, he repeatedly emphasizes that knowledge is to be attained through experience. This means that "Nine Parts of Ten [individuals] are what they are, Good or Evil, useful or not, by their Education" (*Education*, 114). As Tarcov notes, education, the experience Locke is here designing, is itself "manmade" and thus "limited," variable, and imperfect (83–84).

28. For example, contemporary attachment theory, an extension of the object relations school of child development, stresses the importance of honoring the child's desire for dependence; see John Bowlby, *Attachment* (New York: Basic Books, 1969). In an attitude strikingly different from Locke's disciplinary regard of children's crying, contemporary childcare expert Penelope Leach advises parents to respect and allow children's crying because self-control, in her view, is impossible for young children—parents should remember that the body and feeling "are totally intermixed" for young children, making self-regulation a wholly inappropriate expectation. See *Your Baby and Child from Birth to Age Five* (New York: Alfred A. Knopf, 1994).

29. Bronson Alcott interestingly extended this concept of physical punishment and shame by devising the disciplinary practice of making the child whip the parent or tutor as a penalty for the child's bad behavior. In this transferral of disciplinary roles, the child's active and aggressive stance toward his own infraction is heightened. At the same time that the child's fault appears external to himself, the child suffers the shame and disorientation of inflicting pain on a revered figure. The child is made to see and reenact the fact that his infractions affect others. In *Record of a School: Exemplifying the General Principles of Spiritual Culture* (Boston, 1835),

Elizabeth Peabody described Alcott's pedagogy and the implementation of it at the Temple School that they ran in Boston from 1834 to 1838. Louisa May Alcott also memorialized her father's practice in *Little Men* (1871), in which Professor Bhaer, who with his wife Jo March runs the experimental school Plumfield, requires a miscreant young boy to whip him.

30. The history of childhood in America is intimately connected with the history of Puritanism in England and America, as scholars have richly documented. See Lawrence A. Cremin, *American Education: The Colonial Experience, 1607–1783* (New York: Harper & Row, 1970); Sandford Fleming, *Children and Puritanism: The Place of Children in the Life and Thought of the New England Churches, 1620–1847* (New Haven: Yale University Press, 1933); C. John Somerville, *The Discovery of Childhood in Puritan England* (Athens: University of Georgia Press, 1992); Peter Gregg Slater, *Children in the New England Mind in Death and Life* (Hamden, Conn.: Archon, 1977); Philip Greven, *The Protestant Temperament: Patterns of Child-Rearing, Religious Experience, and the Self in Early America* (New York: Alfred A. Knopf, 1977); and Edmund S. Morgan, *The Puritan Family: Religion and Domestic Relations in Seventeenth-Century New England*, rev. ed. (Westport, Conn.: Greenwood Press, 1966).

2. The Liberal Lessons of the New England Primer

1. *The History of Goody-Two Shoes; Otherwise Called Mrs. Margery Two-Shoes* (1765) and *The Renowned History of Giles Gingerbread* (1764) were two of the most often reprinted titles of the popular children's books published by John Newbery in London. The development of children's literature, especially during the eighteenth century, is well documented in Gillian Avery, *Behold the Child: American Children and Their Books, 1621–1922* (Baltimore: The Johns Hopkins University Press, 1994); F. J. Harvey Darton, *Children's Books in England* (Cambridge: Cambridge University Press, 1958); Rosalie V. Halsey, *Forgotten Books of the American Nursery* (Boston: Charles E. Goodspeed, 1911); Monica Kiefer, *American Children through Their Books, 1700–1835* (Philadelphia: University of Pennsylvania Press, 1948); Samuel F. Pickering, Jr., *John Locke and Children's Books in Eighteenth-Century England* (Knoxville: University of Tennessee Press, 1981); *Moral Instruction and Fiction for Children, 1749–1820* (Athens: University of Georgia Press, 1993); S. W. Abraham Rosenbach, *Early American Children's Books* (Portland, Maine: The Southworth Press, 1933); William Sloane, *Children's Books in England and America in the Seventeenth Century* (New York: Columbia University Press, 1955); and Geoffrey Summerfield, *Fantasy and Reason: Children's Literature in the Eighteenth Century* (Athens: University of Georgia Press, 1984). In tracing the persistence of the Puritan tradition in American education through the eighteenth century, Robert Middlekauff finds "the impact of Locke's educational views" manifested in New England "largely indirectly." Schoolmasters were more familiar with the texts of Locke's disciple, John Clarke. See *Ancients and Axioms: Secondary Education in Eighteenth-Century New England* (New Haven: Yale University Press, 1963), 75–91. I think Middlekauff underestimates Locke's influence because Clarke's texts, especially his popular *An Essay upon Study* (London: Arthur Bettersworth, 1731), recapitulate almost exactly Locke's points in *Some Thoughts Concerning Education*. Moreover, Locke's ideas become prevalent in the colonies through other forms

overlooked by Middlekauff, namely fiction and primers. Bernard Bailyn, in his excellent bibliographical essay *Education in the Forming of American Society: Needs and Opportunities for Study* (New York: Norton, 1972), rightly emphasizes that eighteenth-century American educational activities need to be studied as a part of the history of denominationalism, a history that can be traced through various popular forms of pedagogical literature as well as through institutional practices. Not only common reading but also commonplace writing furnish an important resource for understanding the relations of persons to cultural values. For an illuminating study of this basic and all too often neglected form of writing, see Susan Miller, *Assuming the Positions: Cultural Pedagogy and the Politics of Commonplace Writing* (Pittsburgh: University of Pittsburgh Press, 1998).

2. This phrase usually appears as the subtitle to the story in both English and American editions of *The History of Giles Gingerbread* (Worcester: Isaiah Thomas, 1773).

3. Throughout the following discussion I will be referring to a 1756 edition of the *New England Primer,* which reproduces the text of the alphabet rhyme most often printed since the 1720s, and then also to a 1767 edition, which is a reprint of 1750s editions. My choice of these editions has been dictated by the conditions of these very fragile books. The chosen editions were among the very few primers suitable for photographing. I am most grateful to Jenna Loosmore at the American Antiquarian Society and Lisa Libbey at the Huntington Library for helping me to locate these editions and acquire photographs of them. Most scholars agree that the first edition of the *Primer* appeared between 1687 and 1690, issued by Benjamin Harris, a Protestant printer who removed to Boston in order to evade British government charges against his illegal printings of radical Protestant texts. For the *New England Primer,* Harris drew on the content of traditional primers and on his own *Protestant Tutor* (1686). The earliest surviving edition of the *New England Primer* is the 1727 copy now held by the New York Public Library. The indispensable histories of the *Primer* remain Paul Leicester Ford, *The New England Primer: A History of Its Origin and Development* (New York: Dodd, Mead, 1897); and Charles F. Heartman, *The New England Primer Issued prior to 1830* (New York: R. R. Bowker, 1934).

4. The woodblocks used in the *Primer* are virtually identical to those appearing in Benjamin Harris's edition of *The Holy Bible in Verse* (1703). These images were standard items in printers' equipment from the late sixteenth century. The most comprehensive discussion of changes in the *New England Primer* is found in Ford, *New England Primer.*

5. In an eloquent discussion of the *Primer,* Elisa New similarly recognizes the *Primer* as providing the child with "a map to a world larger than himself, adult confirmation of children's natural predisposition to awe, and a wider spectrum of understanding and better selection of materials with which to express this awe." But whereas New takes the *Primer*'s introduction of the child to notions of scale as the activity of fostering a Calvinistic "wisdom of regressive expectation," I find a more elastic psychology in the *Primer:* room for the very wayward exercises of will that Calvinism so profoundly understood and attempted to delimit. My reading emphasizes the *Primer*'s relation to and participation in eighteenth-century Lockean pedagogy while New's reading studies the thematics of human insignificance in the *Primer* and Edward Taylor's poetry. See Elisa New, "Both Great and Small: Adult

Proportion and Divine Scale in Edward Taylor's 'Preface' and *The New England Primer*," *Early American Literature* 28 (1993): 120–133.

6. Here Locke is specifically recommending illustrated versions of *Aesop's Fables*. I discuss Locke's own edition of Aesop and the significance of Aesop for the eighteenth century in the next chapter.

7. Locke likewise recommended the importance of learning to draw for approximating more closely the direct experience or description of objects. See *Education*, section 161, and *Essay* 4, iii, 19. His sense of the inadequacy and error of words pervades the *Essay*. See in particular, *Essay*, book 3.

8. In seventeenth-century images, Adam usually appears as the prototype of the monarch, patriarch of a people. The alphabet rhyme's figuration of the sinning Adam initiates the long symbolic tradition of the Adam figure as an American type memorably noted in R. W. B. Lewis, *The American Adam* (Chicago: University of Chicago Press, 1955). See also Ursula Brumm, "Christ and Adam as 'figures' in American Literature," in *The American Puritan Imagination: Essays in Reevaluation*, ed. Sacvan Bercovitch (Cambridge: Cambridge University Press, 1974), 196–212.

9. See, for example, David J. Rothman, *The Discovery of the Asylum: Social Order and Disorder in the New Republic* (Boston: Little, Brown, 1971); and John Bender, *Imagining the Penitentiary: Fiction and the Architecture of Mind in Eighteenth-Century England* (Chicago: University of Chicago Press, 1987).

10. The most infamous of twentieth-century critics of Puritanism is of course D. H. Lawrence; see *Studies in Classic American Literature* (New York: Viking, 1923). The same sense of—and condemnation of—the rigidity of Puritan ideas can be found in more recent feminist readings of Puritanism, such as Wendy Martin, *An American Triptych: Anne Bradstreet, Emily Dickinson, Adrienne Rich* (Chapel Hill: University of North Carolina Press, 1984); and Ann Kibbey, *The Interpretation of Material Shapes in Puritanism: A Study of Rhetoric, Prejudice, and Violence* (Cambridge: Cambridge University Press, 1986). In contrast, the most recent feminist readings of Puritanism tend to focus on the possibilities of individual expression discovered by Puritan women. See, for example, Ivy Schweitzer, *The Work of Self-Representation: Lyric Poetry in Colonial New England* (Chapel Hill: University of North Carolina Press, 1991); and Amanda Porterfield, *Female Piety in Puritan New England: The Emergence of Religious Humanism* (New York: Oxford University Press, 1992).

11. Political theorists Alisdair MacIntyre, Peter Berger, Michael Sandal, Michael Walzer, and Michael Oakeshott challenge what they take to be Locke's premise of individuality as separate from and prior to conventions. See their essays, all in Michael Sandel, *Liberalism and Its Critics* (New York: New York University Press, 1984).

12. The evangelicized rhymes were not published in British editions of the *New England Primer*. It is worth noting that the evangelicism of the rhyme, making substitutions such as "Christ crucify'd / For Sinners dy'd" for "The Cat doth play / And after Slay," could be misdirected, as when printers implemented the changes in the rhymes but neglected to alter the woodblocks. Thus a teacher writing to *The Boston Gazette and Country Journal* in 1759 complains of "The Wicked Primer" in which "the representation of our blessed Saviour's going to the cross, when darkness was over the whole earth, has for its meaning, the destruction of mice by a cat." Quoted in Heartman, *New England Primer*, xxiii–xxv.

13. Sacvan Bercovitch has discussed this injunction to think of oneself in relation to other examples and as a case for exemplarity in the context of Puritan theories of biography; see *The Puritan Origins of the American Self* (Cambridge, Mass.: Harvard University Press, 1975), especially 1–70, 109–135. For children, the capsule biographies of the alphabet rhyme perform the same purpose. Cotton Mather, Bercovitch's great example of the Puritan biographer, notably wrote sermons and books for children as well as adults. See notes 17 and 18, this chapter.

14. This remarkably effective representation of Protestant history turns out to be contrived and inaccurate. John Rogers was put to death because he, a former priest, refused to give up the wife he had taken. His wife and children, by all accounts, did not see him burned as the woodblock depicts. See Ford, *New England Primer*, 32–37.

15. Certain editions of the *Primer* feature changes in the picture to reflect local and contemporary dress, as in the 1762 Boston edition where the British soldiers participating in the 1554 execution appear in eighteenth-century three-cornered hats. See Ford, "Introduction," *New England Primer*, 1. Compare with the 1716 woodblock Ford reproduces on page 89.

16. James Janeway, *A Token for Children: Being an Exact Account of the Conversion, Holy and Exemplary Lives, and Joyful Deaths of Several Young Children* (London, 1671). Another popular seventeenth-century story of child piety was James Fisher's account of his niece Martha Hatfield, titled *The Wise Virgin* and first published in 1656. On Janeway and Fisher, see Gillian Avery, "The Puritans and Their Heirs" and Nigel Smith, "A Child Prophet: Martha Hatfield as the Wise Virgin," both in *Children and Their Books*, ed. Gillian Avery and Julia Briggs (Oxford: Clarendon Press, 1989), 79–93, 95–118.

17. Cotton Mather, *A Token for the Children of New England* (Boston: Timothy Green, 1700). Page references to this text will be cited parenthetically in the chapter.

18. Mather had earlier published his memorial of his brother as *Early Piety Exemplified in the Life and Death of Mr. Nathanael Mather* (London, 1689). Similar narratives appear in Increase Mather, *Memorials of Early Piety, Occurring in the Holy Life and Joyful Death of Mrs. Jerusha Oliver* (Boston, 1711) and *A Course of Sermons on Early Piety* (Boston, 1721).

19. This story appears in the anonymously authored *A Little Book for Little Children* (Boston: Timothy Green, 1702), 72. This collection includes "several directions for Little Children and several remarkable Stories, both Ancient and Modern of Little Children, divers whereof those are Lately deceased."

20. It is likely that the audience for this literature was parents as well as children. Stories of children who died early and went to heaven provided a form of consolation literature in a time of frequent childhood deaths. See Peter Gregg Slater, *Children in the New England Mind in Death and in Life* (Hamden, Conn.: Shoestring Press, 1977), 15–48.

21. Jonathan Edwards, *The Nature of True Virtue* (1765), in *The Works of Jonathan Edwards*, vol. 8, ed. Paul Ramsey (New Haven: Yale University Press, 1989), 620. Subsequent references will be to this edition and will appear parenthetically in the chapter. Ramsey's "Introduction" provides a well-detailed account of the "energetic" character of consent in Edwards's thought (29).

22. For an illuminating, though perhaps overly insistent, study of the influence

of Calvinism on Locke's thought, see John Dunn, *The Political Thought of John Locke* (Cambridge: Cambridge University Press, 1969), especially 203–261. While my study traces Lockean influences in eighteenth-century America, I do not mean to deny the significance of religion in the American history of consent. The definitive study of the role of Jonathan Edwards's thought in the American Revolution is Alan Heimert's *Religion and the American Mind: From the Great Awakening to the Revolution* (Cambridge, Mass.: Harvard University Press, 1966). The ongoing Puritan legacy in American culture is the great subject of Sacvan Bercovitch's work *The Puritan Origins of the American Self* (New Haven: Yale University Press, 1975); *The American Jeremiad* (Madison: University of Wisconsin Press, 1978); and *The Rites of Assent: Transformations in the Symbolic Construction of America* (New York: Routledge, 1993). For Bercovitch, the Puritan legacy is an ideology of consensus, a continuous mode of social order in America. By focusing on Lockean consent, which sometimes coincides with consent in Puritan thought, I mean to suggest a less determinant, more variable dynamic in American culture.

23. In justification of the revivals that Edwards witnessed and promoted in his own congregation, he wrote "A Faithful Narrative of the Surprising Work of God" (1737). The difficulty of knowing and judging the evidence of personal conversion is explored in his "Personal Narrative" (1739) as well as in "A Treatise Concerning Religious Affections" (1746). Unlike the very successful revivalist preacher George Whitefield, Edwards did not elaborate the democratic possibilities suggested by mass conversions. What appeared as the greater accessibility of spiritual experience caused Edwards to question more closely the validity of personal testimonies. Yet even as Edwards himself maintained strict criteria for church membership, rejecting the Halfway Covenant that allowed children partial membership and thus breaking with a few generations of liberalizing tendencies in Puritan practice, he believed in a kind of equal opportunity in the application of these criteria. He accordingly undertook missionary work among American Indians, using the *Primer* to teach them English and religion.

24. Edwards develops his argument about the scope of individual determinations in *Freedom of the Will* (1754), in which he isolated himself from the contemporary trend in American Puritan thought by reiterating the now unpopular doctrine of predestination. Perry Miller astutely recognizes Edwards's exposition of free will and determinism not as a conservative Calvinistic attack on liberalism, but as an incorporation of liberalism into Protestant theology. See his *Jonathan Edwards* (1949; Amherst: University of Massachusetts Press, 1981), 235–263. Miller also demonstrates Locke's influence on Edwards in *Errand into the Wilderness* (Cambridge, Mass.: Belknap Press of Harvard University Press, 1956), 153–183. The importance of Locke for Edwards, noted by many critics, also gets careful attention in Sang Lee, *The Philosophical Theology of Jonathan Edwards* (Princeton: Princeton University Press, 1988). In contrast, another critical tradition emphasizes Edwards's relation to Protestant typology; for a good summary of these arguments, see John F. Watson, "Editor's Introduction," *The Works of Jonathan Edwards*, vol. 9: *A History of the Work of Redemption* (New Haven: Yale University Press, 1989), 1–109. For an excellent account of critical objections to and elaborations of Miller's reading of Edwards, see Janice Knight, "Learning the Language of God: Jonathan Edwards and the Typology of Nature," *William and Mary Quarterly* 48, no. 4 (October 1991): 531–551. While appreciating many critics' objections to

what seems Miller's too ready translation of Edwards's thought into modern liberalism, I nonetheless find Miller's reading to be cogent, particularly if we think of Edwards not in terms of modern liberalism, or in terms of readings of Emerson as a liberal individualist, but in terms of the Lockean liberalism that Edwards absorbed and employed in his theology. The Lockean influence on Edwards can operate consistently with Edwards's own very distinct sense of piety, with the strict and yet extraordinarily sensitive empiricist standard that Edwards applied to defining humanity and divinity. From my perspective, the relation of Edwards to Lockean liberalism distinguishes rather than diminishes Edwards's thought, since consent as Edwards develops it from Locke, comprises a psychology and pedagogy as well as a politics. To link Edwards to Locke is hardly to scant the enormity of aesthetic and interpretive issues in his theology. Edwards's understanding of human piety as a consensual relation is thus the logical starting point for Elisa New's beautiful study of the crucial role of experience in American poetic and philosophical treatments of vision. See *The Line's Eye: Poetic Experience, American Light* (Cambridge, Mass.: Harvard University Press, 1998), especially chapters one, two, and six.

25. "Sinners in the Hands of an Angry God," Edwards's most memorable and most often reprinted sermon, at times directly addresses the young men and women and the children in his congregation. The famously frightening images in this sermon seem less striking, and less brutal, in the context of the then customary exposure of children to images of death and punishment such as those delineated in the alphabet rhymes.

26. Such dialogues and dramatic allegories, popularized by John Bunyan, had been an important part of Dissenters' children's literature since the seventeenth century. See C. John Somerville, *The Discovery of Childhood in Puritan England* (Athens: University of Georgia Press, 1992), 111–132.

27. Quoted in Ford, *New England Primer,* 27–29. On the changes in the later eighteenth-century editions of the *Primer,* see also Mary Lystad, *From Dr. Mather to Dr. Seuss: 200 Years of American Books for Children* (Cambridge, Mass.: Schenkman Publishing, 1980), 40–62; Rosenbach, *Early American Children's Books*, 81; Kiefer, *American Children through Their Books*, 16–21.

28. The breadth of publication sites for the *New England Primer* is documented in Heartman, *New England Primer.* While southern colonies rarely printed the *Primer* (an occasional edition appears in Virginia and even in Catholic Baltimore), the influence of the *Primer*—or more exactly the Lockean pedagogy it exemplifies and circulates—extended through all colonies by their use of it or other primers that followed the same basic format. Printers sometimes published the *Primer* under different titles, such as the *New Yorker Primer* or the *Columbian Primer.* See Ford, *New England Primer,* 18–19. In the last decades of the eighteenth century, more and more American primers begin to appear, all closely modeled after the *New England Primer.* The best known of these primary readers was the *Franklin Primer* (1802), which closely followed the format of alphabet rhymes, Biblical history (in pictures and sentences), moral lessons, hymns, and catechism. See Clifton Johnson, *Old-Time Schools and School-Books* (New York: Dover, 1963), 233–264.

29. *The Columbian Reading Book or Historical Preceptor* (Philadelphia, 1799).

30. The questioning of Phillis Wheatley's literary abilities has become a locus classicus for race issues in American literary history; see William H. Robinson, ed.,

Critical Essays on Phillis Wheatley (Boston: Hall, 1982); John C. Shields, "Phillis Wheatley's Struggle for Freedom in Her Poetry and Prose," in *The Collected Works of Phillis Wheatley*, ed. John C. Shields (New York: Oxford University Press, 1988), 229–270; Henry Louis Gates, *The Signifying Monkey: A Theory of Afro-American Literary Criticism* (New York: Oxford University Press, 1988); David Grimstead, "Anglo-American Racism and Phillis Wheatley's 'Sable Veil,' 'Length'ned Chain,' and 'Knitted Heart,'" in *Women in the Age of the American Revolution*, ed. Ronald Hoffman and Peter J. Albert (Charlottesville: University Press of Virginia, 1989), 338–444; Richard H. Popkin, "Medicine, Racism, Anti-Semitism: A Dimension of Enlightenment Culture," in *The Languages of Psyche: Mind and Body in Enlightenment Thought*, ed. G. S. Rousseau (Berkeley: University of California Press, 1990), 405–442; Houston Baker, *Workings of the Spirit: The Poetics of Afro-American Women's Writing* (Chicago: University of Chicago Press, 1991); Betsy Erkkila, "Phillis Wheatley and the Black American Revolution," in *A Mixed Race: Ethnicity in Early America*, ed. Frank Shuffleton (New York: Oxford University Press, 1993), 225–240; John C. Shields, "Phillis Wheatley's Subversive Pastoral," *Eighteenth-Century Studies* 27, no. 4 (Summer 1994): 631–647; Paula Bennett, "Phillis Wheatley's Vocation and the Paradox of the 'Afric Muse,'" *PMLA* 113, no. 1 (January 1998): 64–76; Nellie Y. McKay, "Naming the Problem That Led to the Question 'Who Shall Teach African American Literature?'; or, Are We Ready to Disband the Wheatley Court?" *PMLA* 113, no. 3 (May 1998): 359–369.

31. To redress the infantilization of races, and the denial of their rights that such infantilization supports, nineteenth-century reform movements such as abolitionism thus regularly assert the resemblances among all children, the universal nature of childhood. Harriet Beecher Stowe, for example, makes her abolitionist appeal in *Uncle Tom's Cabin* by urging white mothers to think of slave children as if they were their own children.

3. Fables and the Forming of Americans

1. A popular variant of the Washington rhyme was "By Washington / Great deeds were done." See Paul Leicester Ford, "Introduction," *The New England Primer: A History of Its Origin and Development* (New York: Dodd, Mead, 1897), 29.

2. Ibid., 27–28.

3. In these updatings and revisions of the *Primer*, printers often simply changed the name under the portrait so that Washington sometimes appeared with the face of George III. See ibid., 48–49.

4. How Americans define and redefine the notion of Americanness and the cultural objects relevant to that notion is the ongoing concern of American literary criticism and history. Insightful accounts of recent aspects of that concern can be found in Sacvan Bercovitch, "Preface," in *Reconstructing American Literary History* (Cambridge, Mass.: Harvard University Press, 1986); Cecilia Tichi, "American Literary Studies to the Civil War," and Philip Fisher, "American Literary and Cultural Studies since the Civil War," both in *Redrawing the Boundaries: The Transformation of English and American Literary Studies*, ed. Stephen Greenblatt and Giles Gunn (New York: MLA, 1992). On the discussion of identity and culture taking place in international and philosophical contexts, see *October* 61, special issue on The Identity in Question (Summer 1992), and *Who Comes after the Subject?* ed.

Eduardo Cadava, Peter Connor, and Jean-Luc Nancy (New York and London: Routledge, 1991).

5. Noah Webster, *An American Selection of Lessons in Reading and Speaking* (Hartford: Hudson & Goodwin, 1789), 3. For an informative treatment of Webster's career as a cultural nationalist, and of his development of American textbooks and American English, see David Simpson, *The Politics of American English, 1776–1850* (New York and Oxford: Oxford University Press, 1986).

6. Benjamin Rush, "On the Mode of Education Proper in a Republic," in *Essays, Literary, Moral, and Philosophical*, facsimile reprint, ed. Michael Moranze (1798; Schenectady, N.Y.: Union College Press, 1988), 5. For further documentation and exposition of early American cultural nationalism, see (in addition to David Simpson, *Politics of American English*) Bernard Bailyn, *Education in the Framing of American Society* (New York: Norton, 1960); Cathy Davidson, *The Revolution and the Word: The Rise of the Novel in America* (New York: Oxford University Press, 1992), esp. chapters 1–3; Sacvan Bercovitch, *The Rites of Assent: Transformations in the Symbolic Construction of America* (New York and London: Routledge, 1993); Jay Fliegelman, *Prodigals and Pilgrims: The American Revolution against Patriarchal Authority* (Cambridge: Cambridge University Press, 1982); and Fliegelman, *Declaring Independence* (Stanford: Stanford University Press, 1993). On gender and American cultural identity, see Linda Kerber, *Women of the Republic: Intellect and Ideology in Revolutionary America* (New York: Norton, 1986) and Mary Beth Norton, *Liberty's Daughters: The Revolutionary Experience of American Women, 1750–1800* (New York: Harper Collins, 1980).

7. For a valuable clarification of the alternate reticence and pragmatism with which eighteenth-century residents of middle North America identified themselves as American, see John Murrin, "A Roof without Walls: The Dilemma of American National Identity," in *Beyond Confederation: Origins of the Constitution and American National Identity* (Chapel Hill: University of North Carolina Press, 1987), 333–348. An important factor in the affiliations and identifications of the colonists was the increase in immigrations from Europe during the pre-Revolutionary decades. See Bernard Bailyn, *Voyagers to the West: A Passage in the Peopling of America on the Eve of the Revolution* (New York: Random House, 1986).

8. John Locke, *An Essay Concerning Human Understanding* (1689), ed. Peter H. Nidditch (Oxford: Clarendon Press, 1979), book 2, chapter xxxiii, section 6. Subsequent references to this work will be cited parenthetically. Locke's view follows an Aristotelian sense of representations as forms of working through ideas. Locke is less interested in Aristotle's perception that representations incite catharsis, an emotional identification and release, than in the intellectual possibilities that such a model of engagement raises.

9. John Locke, *Of the Conduct of the Human Understanding* (1697), ed. Thomas Fowler (New York: Lenox Hill/Burt Franklin, 1971), 89. Subsequent references to this essay will be cited parenthetically.

10. John Locke, *Some Thoughts Concerning Education* (1693), in *The Educational Writings of John Locke: A Critical Edition*, ed. James Axtell (Cambridge: Cambridge University Press, 1968), section 136. Further references to this book will be cited parenthetically by section number.

11. Locke's educational ideas, developed in *Essay Concerning Human Understanding*, *Conduct of the Human Understanding*, and personal letters, as well as in

Some Thoughts Concerning Education, were further popularized in the eighteenth century by John Clarke's pedagogical writings and John Newbery's publications for children (see ibid.). See John Clarke, *An Essay upon the Education of Youth in Grammar Schools* (London: Red Lion, 1720), and *An Essay upon Study* (London: Red Lion, 1731). Newbery's books, such as *A Little Pretty Pocketbook*, a favorite in the American colonies as well as in Britain, appear to be exact implementations of Locke's recommendation that books both please and teach children. In this book, training in making and evaluating correct associations takes the form of specific epistolary addresses to the boy and girl readers. See John Newbery, *A Little Pretty Pocket-Book*, ed. M. F. Thwaite (1767; New York: Harcourt, Brace & World, 1967). The principle of association also could appear purely arbitrary or a printer's whim, as in the first American editions of *Mother Goose's Melodies*, which paired the well-known rhymes with whatever morals or proverbs fit the page. For example, the maxim "the more you think of dying, the better you will live" follows the rhyme "Jack and Gill / Went up the hill," and "Rock a by Baby" is followed by an admonition and a maxim—"this may serve as a warning to the proud and ambitious, who climb so high that they generally fall at last" and "content turns all it touches into gold" (*Mother Goose's Melodies*, 2d American ed. [Worcester: Isaiah Thomas, 1794], 37, 39). The most vivid and best-known of what might be called the arbitrary printing of proverbs was Franklin's *Poor Richard's Almanack*. The account of eighteenth-century children's literature in this chapter has been enriched by the excellent collections of eighteenth-century children's literature held at the British Library, the Oxford Bodleian Library, the American Antiquarian Society, the Pierpont Morgan Library, the Library Company of Philadelphia, the Free Library of Philadelphia, the New York Historical Society, the New York Public Library, and the Columbia University Rare Books Library. This chapter also draws upon the scholarship of Gillian Avery, *Behold the Child: American Children and Their Books, 1621–1922* (Baltimore: The Johns Hopkins University Press, 1994); Clifton Johnson, *Old-Time Schools and School-Books* (1904; New York: Dover, 1963); Mary Lystad, *From Dr. Mather to Dr. Seuss: Two Hundred Years of American Books for Children* (Boston: G. K. Hall, 1980); Robert Middlekauf, *Ancients and Axioms: Secondary Education in Eighteenth-Century New England* (New Haven: Yale University Press, 1963); Samuel Pickering, Jr., *John Locke and Children's Books in Eighteenth-Century England* (Knoxville: The University of Tennessee Press, 1981), and *Moral Instruction and Fiction for Children, 1749–1820* (Athens: University of Georgia Press, 1993); Geoffrey Summerfield, *Fantasy and Reason: Children's Literature in the Eighteenth Century* (Athens: University of Georgia Press, 1985); and Richard L. Venezky, "From Indian Primer to Dick and Jane: An Introduction to the UPA American Primers Collection" (Worcester, Mass.: American Antiquarian Society, 1990).

12. On the history and changing conceptions of the fable, see Thomas Noel's richly detailed study, *Theories of the Fable in the Eighteenth Century* (New York: Columbia University Press, 1975). On the fable's prominent place in the history of printed books, see Lucien Febvre and Henri-Jean Martin, *L'Apparition du Livre* (1958), trans. David Gerard, *The Coming of the Book: The Impact of Printing, 1450–1800* (London: NLB, 1976), 254.

13. As Axtell observes, Locke finds drawings a more precise mode of communication than language, akin to mathematics. See Axtell's informative notes (1 and 2) to his edition of *Some Thoughts Concerning Education* (265).

14. Locke and other Enlightenment thinkers are routinely characterized in poststructuralist accounts as naive believers in the primacy of vision. Lockean empiricism seems to ascribe an absolute validity to sensory perceptions, especially to visual perception. See, for example, Barbara Maria Stafford, *Body Criticism: Imaging the Unseen in Enlightenment Art and Medicine* (Cambridge, Mass.: MIT Press, 1991). It is important to notice that while Locke promotes the importance of visual apprehension and description, he still regards this mode of perception as an approximation, as always subject to testing and evaluation.

15. Fables similarly appealed to Joseph Addison as a polite form of conveying instruction to all ages "without offending." See *The Spectator,* 17 October 1712, vol. 7, no. 512, ed. George A. Aitken (New York: Longmans, Green, & Co., 1908). For another view, in which fables signify ideological closure, see G. W. F. Hegel, *The Philosophy of Fine Art,* vol. 2, trans. F. P. B. Osmaston (London: Bell, 1920), 114–115. More recently, Susan Stewart has treated fables as one of the historicized literary forms—like epic, ballad, fairy tale, proverb, and parody—that "have been pried from a context of function and placed within a context of self-referentiality." Following Hegel, Stewart sees the fable as "a genre revered precisely for stasis, eternity, and closure," one particularly well suited to the "rationalization" of "monopoly capitalism" because it confers it with "timeless wisdom." See "Notes on Distressed Genres," *Crimes of Writing: Problems in the Containment of Representation* (Durham, N.C.: Duke University Press, 1994), 66–101. While fables have accompanied and served the rise of capitalism as well as many other historical developments, I will be arguing in this chapter that it is the plasticity rather than closure of the fable that makes it so effective and so long-lived.

16. Thomas Dilworth, *A New Guide to the English Tongue* (1751; Leeds, Eng.: The Scholar Press Limited, 1967).

17. I develop this account of personification in relation to the contemporary discourse of the personal in criticism in "Critical Personifications," *Confessions of the Critics,* ed. H. Aram Veeser (New York: Routledge, 1996). There as here, my thinking on personification is indebted to Steven Knapp's excellent *Personification and the Sublime: Milton to Coleridge* (Cambridge, Mass.: Harvard University Press, 1985).

18. John Franklin Jones, *Analytical Spelling-Book* (New York: E. Bliss and E. White, 1822).

19. In addition to the sisters-in-law Dorothy and Mary Ann Kilner published by John Marshall, other late-eighteenth-century authors produced a plethora of fictional narratives with nonhuman protagonists, which included hackney coaches, bank notes, peg tops, pennies, guineas, pins, spaniels, lapdogs, bullfinches, flies, bees, and cats. This pervasiveness of personified beings prompted critical arguments about the propriety of representing humans in nonhuman forms as well as about the proper way to describe animals. See Samuel Pickering, Jr., *John Locke and Children's Books in Eighteenth-Century England,* 70–103. In a recent essay on the eighteenth-century popularity of inanimate narrators, Christopher Flint suggests that such object narratives reflect anxieties about the author's position in the new world of print culture. See "Speaking Objects: The Circulation of Stories in Eighteenth-Century Prose Fiction," *PMLA* 113, no. 2 (March 1998): 212–226. Some turn-of-the-century readers, such as William Darton's *Little Truths Better Than Great Fables* (Philadelphia: J. and J. Crukshank, 1800), eschewed animal personi-

fication, presenting instead moral stories about children and separate descriptions
of animal life. This formal distinction between ethics and natural history, humans
and animals, however, could not prevent the reader from analogizing across do-
mains. Most readers continued to rely on animal examples, such as M. Pelham, *The
Rational Brutes; or, Talking Animals* (Philadelphia: B. & J. Johnson, 1801) and the
anonymously authored *Choice Tales* (Philadelphia: Joseph Charles, 1800). One of
these tales, called "The Fortunate Escape, or the Gratitude of Brutes" (pp. 99–
102), depicts the moral and civil superiority of animals for whom "gratitude to
those who have at any time been of service to them is an indispenseable law of
nature."

20. John Ruskin, "Of the Pathetic Fallacy," in *Modern Painters*, vol. 3 (New
York: Alfred A. Knopf, 1987).

21. A narrative of the life of Aesop often accompanied collections of the fables.
The representative surviving Greek and Latin variants of "Vita Aesopi" are reprinted in Ben E. Perry, *Aesopica*, vol. 1 (Urbana: University of Illinois Press, 1952);
a French translation appears in Roger L'Estrange, *Aesop's Fables* (London: A. and J.
Churchil, 1692). On Aesop or his fables as prototypes of slave narratives, see Louis
Marin's fascinating treatment of Aesop himself as a "fabulous animal," a body in the
process of developing the self-preservative power of words ("The Fabulous Animal," *Food for Thought*, trans. Mette Hjort [Baltimore: The Johns Hopkins University Press, 1989]). This sense of fables (and language in general) as a tool for overcoming precarious conditions can be seen also in Joel Chandler Harris's emphasis
on African American dialects in his "plantation fables." Harris considered his rendering of the dialect in which the tales of his collections were originally told and
circulated crucial to the meaning and flavor of the tales. See his introductions to
Nights with Uncle Remus: Myths and Legends of the Old Plantations (Boston: Houghton Mifflin, 1881), and *Uncle Remus and His Friends* (Boston: Houghton Mifflin,
1892). Bakhtin's remarks upon the ways that comic forms rely on mimicry of animals and of different classes of humans suggest that Uncle Remus disseminates an
African American point of view that is critical and perhaps even subversive. But the
role of Harris, his narration, and his sources of the tales (who range from servants
to scholars to relatives to chance acquaintances, and from blacks to whites to Cre-
oles to Native Americans) complicate the question of critical intentions. See *The
Dialogic Imagination*, trans. Caryl Emerson and Michael Holquist (Austin: University of Texas Press, 1981), 57–60.

22. Fable 53, "Evil for Good," *Fables of Aesop*, trans. S. A. Hanford from a
Latin translation of Phaedrus (New York: Penguin, 1954), 55.

23. John Locke, ed., *Aesop's Fables, in English and Latin, Interlineary, for the
Benefit of Those Who Not Having a Master, Would Learn Either of These Tongues* (London: A. and J. Churchill, 1703). Locke edited this collection because he could not
find an interlineary edition of Latin literature or Aesop that suited his sense of how
languages should be taught. See Axtell's commentary in *Educational Writings of John
Locke*, 271, note 2. A Latin instructor named H. Clarke subsequently published a
virtually verbatim edition of Locke's book, and it is Clarke's version that was reprinted in the United States, beginning in 1787. See *Fabulae Aesopi Selectae, Select
Fables of Aesop*, 1st American ed. (Boston: Samuel Hall, 1787). Other popular British editions of Aesop's fables republished in the early decades of the United States
include Samuel Croxall, *Fables of Aesop and Others*, 1st American ed. (Philadelphia:

R. Aitken, 1777), and Robert Dodsley, *Select Fables of Aesop* (Philadelphia: Robert Bell, 1777).

24. Samuel Richardson, *Aesop's Fables* (1740; London: Garland Facsimile Editions, 1975).

25. In his 1777 edition (cited above in note 26), Robert Dodsley appends an "Application" to "The Country-man and the Snake" that makes this point in far stronger and more extensive terms: "It is the nature of Ingrates to return Evil for Good; and the Moralists in all Ages have incessantly declaimed against the Enormity of this Crime: concluding that they who are capable of hurting their benefactors are not fit to live in a Community; being such, as the natural Ties of Parent, Friend, or Country are too weak to restrain within the bounds of Society. Indeed, the Sin of Ingratitude is so detestable, that, as none but the most inhuman Temper can be guilty of it, so, in writing to Men, there is no occasion to use many Words, either in exposing the Vice itself, or dissuading People from Commission of it. Therefore it is not likely that a Person of Aesop's sagacity would have compiled this fable, without having something else in view besides this trite and obvious Subject. He certainly intended to put us in mind, That, as none but a poor silly Clown would go to take up a Snake and cherish it, so, we shall be very negligent and ill-advised, if, in doing good Offices, we do not take care to bestow our Benevolence upon proper Objects. It was not at all unnatural in the Snake to hiss, and brandish his Tongue, and fly at the first that came near him; as soon as the Person that saved his life as any other; indeed, more like, because nobody else had so much to do with him. Nor is strange at any time to see a reprobate Fool throwing his Extravagancies, against those, more especially, who are so inadvertent as to concern themselves with him. The Snake and the Reprobate will not appear extraordinary in their Malevolence: But the sensible part of Mankind cannot help thinking those guilty of great indiscretion who receive either of them into protection" (40–41). Other editors of this fable could choose morals that addressed the evildoer, instead of the unwise benefactor. Thus the moral to this fable by the Reverend Thomas James reads: "Those who return evil for good, may expect their neighbor's pity to be worn out at last" (*Aesop's Fables, A New Version, Chiefly from Original Sources* [New York: Collins & Brother, 1854]).

26. For an illuminating case history of how a particular proverb perdures as its meanings and affiliations change, see George Boas, *Vox Populi: Essays in the History of an Idea* (Baltimore: The Johns Hopkins University Press, 1969). Boas's study usefully historicizes the proverb's authority, demonstrating that authority is not generic although a particular genre might be affiliated with particular systems of authority.

27. Elaine Scarry has similarly described fables as strategies and habits of foresight in a forthcoming essay on thinking about nuclear emergencies, "Thinking in an Emergency."

28. Fiske, *The New England Spelling-Book* (Brookfield, Mass., 1802). Though I am tracing a history of this particular fable, I do not mean to suggest a teleological progress by which Americans realize its representational range. Though it is tempting to see the formation of America as such an enlightened enterprise in extending representation and rights, history unfortunately demonstrates otherwise. The potential to extend consideration and entitlements to all individuals, however, lies in the logic of representation that the United States drew from the liberal phi-

losophy of the self, most forcefully delineated by Locke, which also is the logic of fables, as Locke so shrewdly recognized. I do not want to suggest the superiority of the later version. What should be clear is that the fable might be told at any point this way, but for a confluence of reasons, it gets told this way in the United States in 1802.

29. Jean-Jacques Rousseau, *Emile; or, On Education*, trans. Allan Bloom (New York: Basic Books, 1979), 115.

30. Attending to the vagaries of the child reader, Rousseau misses the changeability of power relations within the fable of the lion and the gnat. As La Fontaine relates the tale, the gnat, exhilarated by its victory over the lion, flies off bragging of his accomplishment, eventually flying into a spider web where it is killed and eaten. See *The Fables of La Fontaine*, trans. Margaret Wise Brown (New York: Harper & Brothers, 1940). On the differences in the ways that Locke and Rousseau view fables, see also Noel, *Theories of the Fable in the Eighteenth Century* (New York: Columbia University Press, 1975); and Frances Ferguson, "Reading Morals: Locke and Rousseau on Education and Property," *Representations* 6 (Spring 1984): 66–84.

31. William J. Bennett, ed., *The Book of Virtues: A Treasury of Great Moral Stories* (New York: Simon and Schuster, 1993).

32. John Adams, *A Defence of the Constitutions of Government of the United States of America* (1787), in *The Political Writings of John Adams*, ed. George A. Peek, Jr. (New York: Bobbs-Merrill, 1954). Adams previously had written a protonationalist account of America, "A Dissertation on the Canon and Feudal Law" (1765), reprinted in *Papers of John Adams*, ed. Robert J. Taylor et al. (Cambridge, Mass.: Harvard University Press, 1977). Michael Warner presents an insightful discussion of this essay and its delineation of the integral role of letters, enlightenment, and self-determination in the narrative of America's formation. See *The Letters of the Republic* (Cambridge, Mass.: Harvard University Press, 1990), 1–33.

4. Paine's Vindication of the Rights of Children

1. The conjunction of childhood with rights is now of course a staple of the Anglo-American political tradition. Movements for civil rights and equality have notably employed this alignment. To mention only a few examples, nineteenth-century abolitionist rhetoric insisted on the identity of blacks with all children of God while Martin Luther King also used this image in his "I Have a Dream" speech. King also put the alignment of children with human rights to dramatic use when he organized the children's march in Birmingham. David Archard informatively tracks the coupling of childhood with issues of rights (especially women's rights) in twentieth-century political philosophy and discourse. See *Children: Rights and Childhood* (London: Routledge, 1993), 178–184. Exploring this coupling in the literary realm, Jacqueline Rose sees children's fiction, which first emerged in written and widely available forms in the eighteenth century, as promoting and maintaining "the sexual and political mystification of the child" through which adults define identity. See *The Case of Peter Pan: The Impossibility of Children's Fiction* (1984; Philadelphia: University of Pennsylvania Press, 1993), 11.

2. Lynn Hunt, "The Many Bodies of Marie Antoinette: Political Pornography and the Problem of the Feminine in the French Revolution," in *Eroticism and the Body Politic* (Baltimore: The Johns Hopkins University Press, 1991), 108–130.

3. Thomas Paine, *Common Sense* (1776; New York: Penguin, 1982). All further references to this edition will be cited parenthetically in the chapter. For another recent reading of *Common Sense* that focuses on Paine's use of filial images, see Elizabeth Barnes, *States of Sympathy: Seduction and Democracy in the American Novel* (New York: Columbia University Press, 1997), 26–31.

4. The eighteenth-century American engagement with narratives of parent-child relations is insightfully documented and explored in Jay Fliegelman, *Prodigals and Pilgrims: The American Revolution against Patriarchal Authority, 1750–1800* (Cambridge: Cambridge University Press, 1982), 9–194. Gordon S. Wood furnishes an excellent exposition of American invocations and implementations of Locke's ideas in *The Creation of the American Republic, 1776–1787* (New York: Norton, 1969), chapters 7, 8, and 13. The British, of course, had already recognized the revolutionary political import of Locke. For a detailed exposition of the influence of Lockean thought on British revolutionary politics, see Richard Ashcraft, *Revolutionary Politics and Locke's Two Treatises of Government* (Princeton: Princeton University Press, 1986). The emergence of modernity in the eighteenth century is a much studied subject; the role of eighteenth-century America in that process is explored in *Colonial British America: Essays in the New History of the Early Modern Era*, ed. Jack P. Greene and J. R. Pole (Baltimore: The Johns Hopkins University Press, 1984). A useful discussion of Thomas Paine's role in introducing modern political ideas appears in Jack P. Greene, "Paine, America, and the 'Modernization' of Political Consciousness," *Political Science Quarterly* 93, no. 1 (Spring 1978): 73–93.

5. Abridged versions of *Clarissa* and *Robinson Crusoe* for children appeared in inexpensive chapbook form throughout the eighteenth century. See Margaret Kinnell, "Publishing for Children, 1700–1780," in *Children's Literature: An Illustrated History*, ed. Peter Hunt (Oxford: Oxford University Press, 1995), 26–45. Jay Fleigelman has demonstrated how American abridgements of *Crusoe* varied in their stress on the virtues of self-determination and filial obedience, and how editions of *Clarissa* emphasized the story as a narrative of parental tyranny. See *Prodigals and Pilgrims*, 67–82, 83–88. The fairy-tale aspects of Robinson Crusoe's story, particularly his status as a heroic individual, are stressed in the titles and subtitles of American children's editions, such as *The Wonderful Life and Surprizing Adventures of the Renowned Hero, Robinson Crusoe* (New York: Hugh Gaine, 1774).

6. Also known as "The Babes in the Wood," this tale sometimes depicted the children as victims of improvident parents who abandon them when they can no longer support them. In some versions, the unfortunate children wander on their own into the woods where they get lost and die. A facsimile of a popular early American verse edition of "The Children in the Wood" (the wicked uncle version) is reprinted in Arnold Arnold, *Pictures and Stories from Forgotten Children's Books* (New York: Dover, 1969), 80–84. A prose rendition of the same plot can be found in *The Affecting History of the Children in the Wood* (Hartford: J. Babcock, 1796).

7. The earliest known edition of *Jack the Giant-Killer* seems to be 1711; inexpensive chapbook editions circulated throughout the century. Copies of those published between 1760 and 1770 can be found in the Dicey Collection in the British Library. On the popularity of *Jack the Giant-Killer* and *Tom Thumb* among eighteenth-century child readers, see Geoffrey Summerfield, *Fantasy and Reason: Children's Literature in the Eighteenth Century* (Athens: University of Georgia Press,

1984), 32, 38, 41–3, 48–49, 54–60, 63, 88, 199, 282. The even longer tradition of reading or hearing narratives of *Tom Thumb* is delineated in William Sloane, *Children's Books in England and America in the Seventeenth Century* (New York: Columbia University King's Brown Press, 1955), 73–74. References to Tom Thumb recur through eighteenth-century literature, for example in Swift's "Tale of a Tub" and Fielding's satiric play *The Tragedy of Tom Thumb*. Swift's Lilliput of course can be seen as an exposition of the issues raised by Tom Thumb's miniature experience of life.

8. Long before stories recorded by Perrault (at the end of the seventeenth century) and the brothers Grimm (in the early nineteenth century), Hop o' My Thumb or Le Petit Poucet was a familiar character in France; Thaumlin or Little Thumb appears in Scandinavian folklore, while German traditions include a similar figure named Däumling. In India, the tiny hero also appears, as Khodra Khan in Islamic folklore and Vamuna in Hindu tales. The Japanese counterpart is Little One Inch or Issun Boshi. The striking characteristic of all these stories is the little hero's subjection to being swallowed. The earliest mention (in English) of Tom Thumb appears in Reginald Scot, "Discoverie of Witchcraft" (1584). Scot lists Tom Thumb along with goblins and changelings as long-standing figures of magic and terror. The earliest published English version of Tom Thumb's story seems to be Richard Johnson, "The History of Tom Thumbe the Little, for His Stature Surnamed King Arthur's Dwarf" (1621). A beautiful (and the only known) copy of this 1621 book is housed in the Pierpont Morgan Library. An informative history of the tale can be found in Iona and Peter Opie, *The Classic Fairy Tales* (Oxford: Oxford University Press, 1974), 36–40.

9. "Little Tom Thumb," *Perrault's Fairy Tales* (New York: Dover, 1969), 115. This edition uses A. E. Johnson's translations of *Histoires ou contes du temps passe, avec des moralitez* (Paris, 1697), which he published as *Old-Time Stories Told by Master Charles Perrault* (New York: Dodd Mead, 1921). The economic and moral features of Tom's exploits suggest a rather different significance than that offered by Marina Warner in her informative and provocative feminist study of fairy tales, *From the Beast to the Blonde: On Fairy Tales and Their Tellers* (New York: Farrar, Strauss and Giroux, 1994); she interprets Tom's adventures as examples of male physical prowess. After Perrault, eighteenth-century versions of the tale also foreground Tom's cognitive skills and his concern for the welfare of others. In the latter part of the eighteenth century, English and American children most likely encountered the story in one of John Newbery's popular editions (1768, 1786, or 1789), which were often reprinted in the colonies.

10. For an account of the literary history of the story of Tom Thumb in England and America, see Harry B. Weiss, "Three Hundred Years of Tom Thumb," *Scientific Monthly* 34 (February 1932): 157–166. Weiss traces variations in the Arthurian Tom Thumb, which consist of Tom's additional afterlife adventures in Fairyland and in later epochs in English history. Tom's story finally comes to an ignominious end after he attempts to rape a queen and, while trying to escape punishment for this crime, falls into a spider's web and is eaten. (I have encountered this version of the tale in *The Famous History of Tom Thumb*, London, 1750, and in a chapbook of the same title published in London, 1775.) Weiss's study does not include the more extensive variants such as Perrault's and those published in eighteenth-century America.

11. *Tom Thumb's Songbook* was the title most often given to collections of what we now (and since the turn of the nineteenth century) call Mother Goose rhymes. Following Mary Cooper's London editions of the 1740s, Isaiah Thomas in 1788 began publishing and regularly reprinting editions of this anthology in Worcester, Massachusetts. Another book produced by Thomas, *The Exhibition of Tom Thumb* (1787), uses the narrative persona of Tom Thumb to introduce a series of geographical, zoological, and moral lessons "for the instruction and amusement of all the pretty masters and misses in America, who are little and good like myself." Narratives of Tom's history often included some lessons. *The Life and Death of Tom Thumb* (Hartford: John Babcock, 1800), for example, begins with alphabet tables before launching into the story. Books entitled *Tom Thumb's Folio* also tended to contain the story of Tom along with some lessons or verses. First advertised by the Newbery publishing firm in 1768, the earliest extant American edition of *Tom Thumb's Folio* appeared in Boston, circa 1780.

Tom Thumb's Playbook (Boston: A. Barclay, 1764), a much reprinted book in the colonies, is essentially a primer that includes alphabet rhymes, lists of letter combinations, catechism, and prayers. This book is subtitled "To Teach Children Their Letters as Soon as They Can Speak, Being a New and Pleasant Method to Allure Little Ones in the First Principles of Learning." Identical editions include *Tom Thumb's Play-Book* (Boston: J. Boyle, 1771) and *Tom Thumb's Play-Book* (Worcester, Mass.: Isaiah Thomas, 1786). Useful bibliographical data on Tom Thumb educational books can be found in Monica Kiefer, *American Children through Their Books, 1700–1835* (Philadelphia: University of Pennsylvania Press, 1948); George Emery Littlefield, *Early Schools and Schoolbooks of New England* (Boston: The Club of Odd Volumes, 1904); A. S. W. Rosenbach, *Early American Children's Books* (Portland, Maine: Southworth Press, 1933); Isaiah Thomas, Jr., *Catalogue of Books* (Boston, 1811). My knowledge of editions and variants of Tom Thumb stories is based on study of the collections at the British Library, Oxford's Bodleian Library, the American Antiquarian Society, the Pierpont Morgan Library, the Free Library of Philadelphia, and the Boston Public Library. On Tom's progressively moral and scholarly character emerging over the course of the eighteenth century, see also Samuel F. Pickering, Jr., *John Locke and Children's Books in Eighteenth-Century England* (Knoxville: University of Tennessee Press, 1981), 61–65.

12. While Locke addressed his *Thoughts Concerning Education* to the sons of gentlemen, Tom Thumb stories seem to have been adapted to better appeal to audiences of different classes. In both the Arthurian and Perrault versions, Tom comes from a very humble background. Following Locke, *Tom Thumb's Folio* and other eighteenth-century narratives make Tom a member of the gentry, the son of "Mr. Theophilus Thumb, of Thumb Hall in Northumberland" (3). Apart from issues of class, Tom Thumb did not strike all seventeenth- and eighteenth-century readers as an appropriate figure to emulate. Gillian Avery discusses Puritan dislike of Tom Thumb and similar adventure heroes in "The Puritans and Their Heirs," in *Children and Their Books*, ed. Gillian Avery and Julia Briggs (Oxford: Clarendon Press, 1989), 98–99.

13. Susan Stewart, *On Longing: Narratives of the Miniature, the Gigantic, the Souvenir, the Collection* (Baltimore: The Johns Hopkins University Press, 1984), 69. For the full breadth of Stewart's argument, see also 37–69, 111–125. Subsequent references to Stewart in this chapter will be cited parenthetically.

14. First published in London by John Newbery, these books circulated widely in the colonies and were often reprinted there. Their subtitles encapsulate the plot and moral that they unfold. See *The History of Little Goody-Two-Shoes. Otherwise Called Mrs. Margery Two-Shoes, with the Means by Which She Acquired Her Learning and Wisdom, and in Consequence Thereof Her Estate* (London: John Newbery, 1765); whose first American edition was published by Isaiah Thomas in Worcester in 1771, and *The Renowned History of Giles Gingerbread, a Little Boy Who Lived upon Learning* (London: John Newbery, 1764), whose first American edition was reprinted by Mein and Fleming in Boston in 1768, followed shortly by Thomas's 1773 edition. On the publication history of *Goody-Two-Shoes* in eighteenth-century America, see Gillian Avery, *Behold the Child: American Children and Their Books, 1621–1922* (Baltimore: The Johns Hopkins University Press, 1994). Samuel Pickering provides an informative discussion of *Giles Gingerbread* in *John Locke and Children's Books in Eighteenth-Century England*, 172–175.

15. *Fenning's Universal Speller*, quoted in Clifton Johnson, *Old-Time Schools and School-Books* (New York: Dover, 1963), 58–59.

16. *The New England Primer*, 1771, quoted in ibid., 88–89.

17. *Tom Thumb's Folio, for Little Giants* (Boston, circa 1780), 26, 32. The same narrative of Tom Thumb's adventures frequently reappears in late-eighteenth-century American editions, such as *Tom Thumb's Folio; or, A New Threepenny Plaything* (Boston: Samuel Hall, 1791), and *The History of Tom Thumb, with His Wonderful Adventures* (Wilmington: James Adams, 1797). It is unlikely that the Boston 1780 edition was an original variant: until after the Revolution most children's literature printed in America was pirated from British publications, and London advertisements for this book had first appeared in 1768. But it is clear that this variant becomes the version most often published in late-eighteenth-century America.

18. *Tom Thumb's Folio* (1780), 13.

19. Commentators on fairy tales have long noted the political resonance of stories featuring such characters as Tom Thumb and Jack the Giant-killer or David and Goliath, in which the small bravely face the gigantic. C. K. Chesterton, for example, takes this drama to signify the universality of the political and moral issues that members of society must confront. His views are quoted and discussed in Summerfield, *Fantasy and Reason*, 32, 301. Interestingly, the narrator of *Tom Thumb's Folio* (Boston, 1780) all too strongly denies the presence of recognizeable political connections in his narrative, saying that in writing the life of Tom Thumb "historians, biographers, and writers . . . are to behave as citizens of the world and pay no particular regard to any party, persuasion, or country whatsoever. And this we intend as an apology for our presuming to relate the following exploits of Tom Thumb, without declaring whether he was a whig or tory" (11). While denying specific political analogies, the narrator does not at all eliminate from the story political issues (and the associations they inspire).

20. Locke repeatedly stresses the importance of self-denial, of submitting bodily cravings to the rule of reason. See *Some Thoughts Concerning Education* (1694) in *The Educational Writings of John Locke*, ed. James L. Axtell (Cambridge: Cambridge University Press, 1968), sections 105–108.

21. The most illuminating study of the concept of representation, as it has developed since Hobbes, is Hanna Fenichel Pitkin, *The Concept of Representation* (Berkeley: University of California Press, 1967).

22. John Locke, *An Essay Concerning Human Understanding*, 1689, ed. Peter H. Nidditch (Oxford: Clarendon Press, 1979), book 2, chapter xxi, section 47. I treat this discussion of the role of judgment in Locke's definition of freedom in Chapter 1.

23. A Lover of Peace [Thomas Paine], "Thoughts on Defensive War," *The Pennsylvania Magazine; or, American Monthly Museum*, July 1775, 328–329. Paine served as editor of and one of the chief contributors to this magazine during 1775. On Paine's career with the *Pennsylvania Magazine*, see John Keane, *Tom Paine: A Political Life* (Boston: Little, Brown, 1995), 91–104.

24. If liberalism developed as an argument for the rights of each generation against the authority of the past, it ironically has produced a perhaps even stronger obligation to the future. This obligation sets the individual at continual odds between himself and others, between his own desires and sense of duty to others, especially children, even those unborn. In this context, the debates and terrorism surrounding the issue of abortion register a now long-standing American habit of defining ourselves in terms of future selves as we imagine them. Different Americans, of course, imagine different versions of the self, usually like themselves or selves they would like to be. Thus medical definitions of being may play a powerful role in the rhetoric and politics of abortion, but they are a pretext for authority in the debate rather than the issue at stake. Directed against the heritability of power, liberalism (as Locke conceived it and Paine elaborated it in *Common Sense* and later in *The Rights of Man*) eschews appeals to heritage, any invocations of the priority of the past. Instead, obligation to the future, to the unborn, is what has haunted liberalism since the eighteenth century. How liberals and their critics continue to struggle with the problem of different views of self is an important debate that Michael Sandal usefully has presented in *Liberalism and Its Critics* (New York: New York University Press, 1984). This collection includes essays by Isaiah Berlin, John Rawls, Ronald Dworkin, Robert Nozick, Charles Taylor, Michael Walzer, and Michael Oakeshott, as well as an excellent introduction by Sandal.

25. The opposite view of debt as an encumbrance of one generation upon another is more familiar and compelling to Americans of the early twenty-first century. Frances Ferguson has shrewdly explicated how the 1793 French Republic replaced the institution of heritable public offices with a heritable national debt, thus not at all abolishing the concept of heritability. In Ferguson's analysis (which is a clarification of Sade's writings), then, the French Revolution falls short of truly republican accomplishments as "the nationalized debt becomes the sign of the inevitable inequality of the modern state, whose contract is more binding precisely on account of its applying only to those who could not, by definition, have had any part in its formulation." See "Sade and the Pornographic Legacy," *Representations* 36 (Fall 1991): 1–21. Paine does not seem to acknowledge the inequity of all intergenerational debts as he argues for an American national debt. By emphasizing the benefits of debts for the inheritors, however, he does try to dispel the spectre of unchosen binding obligation that he has already denounced in Britain's policies toward the colonies.

26. Quoted in Wood, *Creation of the American Republic*, 378–379.

27. *Liberty Tree* was first printed as a concluding peroration to "Thoughts on Defensive War," by A Lover of Peace [Thomas Paine], in *The Pennsylvania Magazine; or, American Monthly Review* (July 1775): 328–329. The edition cited in this

chapter is *Liberty Tree, the Thomas Paine Reader,* ed. Michael Foot and Isaac Kramnick (London: Penguin, 1987), 63–64. Paine began work on his pamphlet in the fall of 1775 and *Common Sense* first appeared in January 1776.

28. Eric Foner has pointed out that Paine always considered the larger republican argument of *Common Sense* more important than the local call for American independence. Paine himself wrote in 1806 that "my motive and object in all my political works, beginning with *Common Sense,* have been to rescue man from tyranny and false systems and false principles of government, and enable him to be free." See *Tom Paine and Revolutionary America* (New York: Oxford, 1976), 75. After the American Revolution, the Liberty Tree became an important symbol in radical republican politics worldwide. It played a central role in French revolutionary imagery and festivals; see Lynn Hunt, *Politics, Culture, and Class in the French Revolution* (Berkeley: University of California Press, 1984), 52–86. In the nineteenth century, Hawthorne continues the identification of America with an oak tree when he organizes his children's book on colonial American history into a narrative told from the perspective of a rocking chair made from an old oak tree. Nathaniel Hawthorne, *Grandfather's Chair: A History for Youth* (Boston: E. P. Peabody, 1841).

29. This rhyme appears regularly in eighteenth-century editions of the *New England Primer* and is found in the Boston 1727 edition. The same rhyme appears in an 1880 edition quoted by Clifton Johnson in *Old-Time Schools and School-Books,* 81. As I note in Chapter 2, such specific references to British history often drop out or change over the course of the eighteenth century. In the wake of the Great Awakening, the letter *O* was used to designate the faithful Obadias rather than any political or royalist belief. But as Johnson notes, the political reference can return, even after the Revolution—more likely as a liberalization of Puritan pedagogy than as a return to respect for the British monarchy. The oak not surprisingly also appears in late-eighteenth-century alphabet rhymes as a reference to the Liberty Tree.

30. Jack Fruchtman, Jr., *Thomas Paine: Apostle of Freedom* (New York: Four Walls Eight Windows, 1994), 84–85. "The Forester," *Four Letters, The Complete Writings of Thomas Paine,* vol. 1, ed. Philip S. Foner (New York: Citadel, 1945). For more information on negative replies to *Common Sense,* especially the essays known as the *Cato Letters,* and on Paine's authorship of the *Four Letters,* see A. Owen Aldridge, *Thomas Paine's American Ideology* (Newark: University Press of Delaware, 1984), 179–190; 219–221.

31. Paine's faith in numbers expresses what was in the eighteenth century a new confidence in scientific measurements. Ian Hacking's study, *The Emergence of Probability: A Philosophical Study of Early Ideas about Probability, Induction, and Statistical Inference* (Cambridge: Cambridge University Press, 1975), reminds us that probability and statistics historically had to attain their status as respected registers of reality. Mary Poovey recently has explored fictive possibilities and pitfalls of the statistical in early-nineteenth-century scientific discourse. See "Figures of Arithmetic, Figures of Speech: The Discourse of Statistics in the 1830s," *Critical Inquiry* 19, no. 2 (Winter 1993): 256–276. Paine's own longtime interest in science is noted by most of his biographers. See, for example, John Keane's account of Paine's attendance of scientific lectures and associations with scientists in *Tom Paine: A Political Life,* 40–45.

32. Thomas Paine, *Letter to the Abbe Raynal,* in *The Thomas Paine Reader,* ed. Michael Foot and Isaac Kramnick (1782; London: Penguin, 1987), 147–166. Paine

makes the same point about changing perspective in his discussion of prejudice in *Common Sense*, 81–82.

33. This account of the identifications and concerns operating within sympathy initially follows and then interestingly departs from Adam Smith's delineation of sympathy as the projection of ourselves into another's distressed position: "By the imagination we place ourselves in his [the sufferer's] situation, we conceive ourselves enduring all the same torments, we enter as it were into his body, and become in some measure the same person with him, and thence form some ideas of his sensations, and even feel something which, though weaker in degree, is not altogether unlike them." Whereas Smith stresses the sympathizing observer's self-preoccupation with imagining himself suffering, Paine underscores the ways that imagined pains, whether of others or ourselves, can persist and thus sustain a social connection. Precisely because the sympathizer is in an imagined relation to the scene of suffering, he or she cannot get relief from the mental emanations of knowing about suffering. Paine thus assigns a huge burden to sympathizers as he discovers the vast scope that human suffering covers via the imagination. See Adam Smith, *The Theory of Moral Sentiments*, 1759, ed. D. D. Raphael and A. L. Macfie (Indianapolis: Liberty Classic, 1982), 9–23.

34. Many commentators have noted Paine's frequent usage of scripture. Isaac Kramnick finds this a typical feature of what he calls "bourgeois radicalism," which has its roots in dissenting Protestantism. See "Tommy Paine and the Idea of America," in *The American Revolution and Eighteenth-Century Culture: Essays from the 1976 Bicentennial Conference of the American Society for Eighteenth-Century Studies*, ed. Paul J. Korshin (New York: AMS Press, 1986), 75–91. Paine himself worked sporadically as a Methodist preacher among working-class groups in England. Jack Fruchtman characterizes Paine's reliance on Biblical language and allusions as his "homiletic style," an address specifically designed to appeal to lower- and middle-class audiences; see *Thomas Paine and the Religion of Nature* (Baltimore: The Johns Hopkins University Press, 1993), 4–15. It is interesting to recall that some of the middle-class audience who read drafts of *Common Sense* and contributed editorial suggestions included Benjamin Franklin and Benjamin Rush. Rush suggested the title. Upper-class admirers of the pamphlet included Washington and Jefferson. Some readers assumed that the anonymously published essay was authored by Jefferson. Fruchtman may be too quick to categorize the appeal of *Common Sense* in class terms. Eric Foner, like Kramnick, more convincingly sees Paine as enlisting "the Bible-based Protestantism of the majority of colonists in the cause of republicanism and independence" (80–81); see *Tom Paine and Revolutionary America* (New York: Oxford University Press, 1976).

35. The issue of representation that sparked the Revolutionary cause continued after the war to dominate debates about the forming of the American system of government. Paine's advocacy of representative bodies, in which he favored their differences from the actual bodies represented by them, differed from the logic of most visions that aligned the sovereignty of the people with schemes of representation; his view takes as a virtue the deficiency in representation (the fact that it can never exactly convey the views and will of the governed). Edmund S. Morgan presents an excellent and richly documented account of "the enigma of representation" for colonial Americans in *Inventing the People: The Rise of Popular Sovereignty in England and America* (New York: Norton, 1988).

36. Thomas Paine, *The Rights of Man*, ed. Henry Collins (London: Penguin,

1969), 282. In line with this logic of representational supplementation, Paine continues to display in *The Rights of Man* his fondness for charts, lists, and other numerical and verbal figures of measurement. See, especially, the chapter "Ways and Means."

37. Ibid., 203.

38. Ibid.

II. Introduction

1. *Locke's Conduct of the Understanding*, ed. Thomas Fowler (New York: Burt Franklin, 1971), 97. All subsequent references to this text will be noted parenthetically.

2. Locke, *Some Thoughts Concerning Education*, in *The Educational Writings of John Locke*, ed. James Axtell (Cambridge: Cambridge University Press, 1968), sections 174, 175.

3. Ibid., section 137.

4. Ibid., section 207.

5. Quoted in Robert Darnton, *Mesmerism and the End of the Enlightenment in France* (Cambridge, Mass.: Harvard University Press, 1968), 65–66.

6. Franz Mesmer, "On the Medicinal Usage of the Magnet" (1775) in *Mesmerism: A Translation of the Original Medical and Scientific Writings of F. A. Mesmer, M.D.*, trans. George J. Bloch (Los Altos, Calif.: William Kaufmann, 1980), 25–30.

7. For an account of the discourses of femininity emerging from the mesmerism debates in eighteenth-century France, see Lindsay Wilson, *Women and Medicine in the French Enlightenment: The Debate over Maladies des Femmes* (Baltimore: The Johns Hopkins University Press, 1993).

8. On the feminization of sensibility, see G. J. Barker-Benfield, *The Culture of Sensibility: Sex and Society in Eighteenth-Century Britain* (Chicago: University of Chicago Press, 1992); and Janet Todd, *Sensibility: An Introduction* (London: Methuen, 1986).

9. *Report of Dr. Benjamin Franklin, and Other Commissioners, Charged by the King of France, with the Examination of the Animal Magnetism, as Now Practiced at Paris*, trans. from the French (London: J. Johnson, 1785). During the American Revolution, Franklin had served as the American representative to France. After helping to negotiate the peace between Britain and the United States, Franklin stayed on in France, where he was highly respected as a scientist and diplomat. The other commissioners, all from the French Royal Academy of Sciences, included Jean-Sylvain Bailly, Jean-Baptiste le Roy, Gabriel de Borie, and Antoine Laurent Lavoisier. While the original edition of this translation held in the British Library attributes authorship to Franklin (without naming the translator), the original report in French, titled *Rapport des commissaires charges par le roi de l'examen du magnetisme animal* (Paris, 1784) is attributed to another member of the commission, J. S. Bailly. Since all of the commission members edited the report and some wrote ancillary essays, it is difficult to establish a sole author. In my remarks on the report, I will continue to cite Franklin as the primary author, with the understanding that the authorship is collective, a point that Franklin, who eshewed patents for his own inventions, would have perfectly appreciated. All further citations of the report will be to the London edition and will appear parenthetically. On Franklin

and mesmerism, see C. A. Lopez, *Mon Cher Papa: Franklin and the Ladies of Paris* (New Haven: Yale University Press, 1966), 168–175.

10. Mesmer, "On Magnetism" (1782) in *Mesmerism*, 33–38.

11. Mesmeric mergers did not strike all eighteenth-century observers as a form of subjection. Robert Darnton describes how French radicals detected democratic possibilities in mesmerism's production of connections between persons. See *Mesmerism and the End of the Enlightenment in France*, 107–125.

12. Mme. Millet, letter of 25 August 1784, quoted in James E. McClellan, III, *Colonialism and Science: Ste. Domingue in the Old Regime* (Baltimore: The Johns Hopkins University Press, 1992), 180. Nineteenth-century women developed a different account of mesmerism in which women could use it to serve their own desires. See, for example, Alex Owen, *The Darkened Room: Women, Power, and Spiritualism in Late Victorian England* (Philadelphia: University of Pennsylvania Press, 1990), and Judith Walkowitz, "Science of the Séance: Transgression of Gender and Genre," in *City of Dreadful Delight: Narratives of Sexual Danger in Late-Victorian London* (Chicago: University of Chicago Press, 1992), 171–189.

13. Jean Trembly to Charles Bonnet, September 1785, quoted in McClellan, *Colonialism and Science*, 181.

14. Ibid.

15. "Account of a Remarkable Conspiracy Formed by a Negro in the Island of St. Domingo," *New York Magazine* vol. 1, no. 5 (1796): 427–485.

16. Terry Castle makes a similar connection between psychoanalysis and eighteenth-century culture, viewing eighteenth-century formations such as sensibility, masquerade, and Gothics as making up the "invention of the uncanny." See her introduction to *The Female Thermometer: Eighteenth-Century Culture and the Invention of the Uncanny* (New York: Oxford University Press, 1996).

17. Benjamin Franklin, *The Autobiography and Other Writings*, ed. L. Jesse Lemisch (New York: New American Library, 1961), 30.

18. Olaudah Equiano, *The Interesting Narrative and Other Writings*, ed. Vincent Carretta (New York: Penguin, 1995), 68.

19. The prevailing concept of coverture defined woman's legal status as covered by the status of her male protector (father or husband). The American legal system closely followed the British system, delineated in Sir William Blackstone, *Commentaries on the Laws of England*, 4 vols. (Oxford: Clarendon Press, 1765–1769).

20. As I noted in the brief discussion of Phillis Wheatley in Chapter 1, nineteenth-century abolitionists such as Harriet Beecher Stowe and Lydia Maria Child routinely identified slaves as children due the rights of humanity. Slave narratives often make a religious version of this argument, stressing blacks as children of God. Like Wheatley, early American black writers such as John Marrant, Ukawsaw Gronniosaw, and Quobna Ottabah Cugoano all emphasize their membership in God's family. See *Black Atlantic Writers of the Eighteenth Century: Living the New Exodus in England and the Americas*, ed. Adam Potkay and Sandra Burr (New York: St. Martin's Press, 1995). For other and later examples, see *Black Women's Slave Narratives*, ed. William Andrews (Oxford: Oxford University Press, 1987), and *Spiritual Narratives*, ed. Susan Houchins (New York: Oxford University Press, 1988). The identification of entitlement with literacy that Equiano makes also becomes a standard feature of slave narratives, most notably in the *Life and Times of Frederick Douglass: His Early Life as a Slave, His Escape from Bondage, and His Complete History* (1892; New York: Collier Books, 1962), 78–79.

5. Coquetry and Its Consequences

1. Hannah Foster, *The Coquette* (1797), ed. Cathy N. Davidson (New York: Oxford University Press, 1986), 5. Subsequent references to this text will be cited parenthetically. Davidson provides a very informative historical account of *The Coquette* in *The Revolution and the Word: The Rise of the Novel in America* (New York: Oxford University Press, 1986), 110–150.

2. The spectre of the cruel parent who, perhaps even in the name of love, dictates or impedes his or her child's exercise of consent, whether in career or marital choice, haunts the emergence (as well as the continuance) of American culture and nationhood. In autobiographies, personal letters, sentimental and Gothic novels, sermons and newspapers, stories of the trials of filial independence abound in the post-Revolutionary as well pre-Revolutionary decades. Most dramatically personified by the Harlowe parents who abandon their daughter Clarissa for defying their marital plans for her, the cruel parents of sentimental and Gothic novels disregard the claims of their children to happiness and self-determination, and sometimes even to life. The indispensable treatment of representations of parental authority in eighteenth-century America is Fliegelman's *Prodigals and Pilgrims: The American Revolution against Patriarchal Authority* (Cambridge: Cambridge University Press, 1982).

3. Elizabeth Barnes, in *States of Sympathy: Seduction and Democracy in the American Novel* (New York: Columbia University Press, 1997), provides a very fine reappraisal of early American seduction novels that similarly attends to the politics of Foster's plot. Barnes also sees *The Coquette* as an examination of consent, or in her words, the liberal ideal of self-determination. Foster's project in *The Coquette* is "to see choice—and woman's choice in particular—through to the end, unmediated by the effects of seduction" and "come face-to-face with the limits of free will" (72). For Barnes, such a revelation is "a story that cannot be told" in American democratic society (72). In my own reading, the limits of free will openly preoccupy early American culture—this subject is a story repeatedly explored. Like Barnes's book, most recent criticism of *The Coquette* examines the novel in the context of sympathy or sentimentality. See Eva Cherniavsky, *That Pale Mother Rising: Sentimental Discourses and the Imitation of Motherhood* (Bloomington: Indiana University Press, 1995), 38–40; Julia Stern, *The Plight of Feeling: Sympathy and Dissent in the Early American Novel* (Chicago: University of Chicago Press, 1997), 71–151; Bruce Burgett, *Sentimental Bodies: Sex, Gender, and Citizenship in the Early Republic* (Princeton: Princeton University Press, 1998), 81–111. The social ethic of sympathy and the personal content and appeal of the sentimental mode usefully illuminate the sexual politics of novels like *The Coquette*, which so readily proffer analogies between public and private life. While I will not be invoking sympathy or sentimentality to explicate this novel, I see my own invocations of the discourses of consent and coquetry as complementary with these other critical approaches.

4. Although consent theory furnishes a justification of revolution, it still preserves the principle of cultural authority. So changing cultural authority, say from patriarchalism to republicanism, does not relieve consent of the presence of the conventional; rather, it redefines conventions. Thus the liberal republican principle of self-determination does not dispense with but rather relocates the source of authority for the individual. "The chief problem of the American revolution,"

Hannah Arendt observes, "turned out to be the establishment and foundation not of power but authority" (*On Revolution* [London: Penguin, 1963], 178). I am arguing that Lockean consent doctrine structures all forms of republicanism—conservative, moderate, liberal, radical—that appear in early American political and cultural life. That is, even what J. G. A. Pocock and others—e.g., Bernard Bailyn (*The Ideological Origins of the American Revolution* [Cambridge, Mass.: Harvard University Press, 1967]) and Gordon S. Wood (*The Creation of the American Republic* [Chapel Hill: University of North Carolina Press, 1969])—have identified as Americans' retrospective appeal to classical republicanism and rejection of liberal individualism can be read as part of a narrative of liberalism. The adventures of consent, documented in various forms, thus register the tangencies of as well as the tensions between liberalism and republicanism. In my reading, consent is one of the forms through which republicanism or republicanisms—and other interests—get articulated.

5. For Locke, individual freedom entails the individual's subjection to his own reason and rule. See my discussion in Chapter 1 of self-denial as the bedrock of child development in *Some Thoughts Concerning Education* (section 107). Charles Taylor similarly has noted that Locke's "theory of rational control of the self" and "ideal of rational self-responsibility" shape and permeate modern psychology (*Sources of the Self: The Making of the Modern Identity* [Cambridge, Mass.: Harvard University Press, 1989], 174). This model of self-control is not the panoptic design of socially self-regulating individuals that Foucault describes in *Discipline and Punish* (*Discipline and Punish: The Birth of the Prison*, trans. Alan Sheridan [New York: Vintage, 1977]), but a vision of the power of individual agency within social limits. In *Declaring Independence: Jefferson, Natural Language, and the Culture of Performance* (Stanford: Stanford University Press, 1993), Jay Fliegelman aptly describes the role of social limits upon individuals in late-eighteenth-century America as "soft compulsion," a compulsion that sometimes generated anxieties about individual agency.

6. See my Introduction, note 4, and Chapter 1 note 7, for a brief selective bibliography of debate on consent theory.

7. In a recent study of early American literary culture, Grantland S. Rice attributes coquetry to late-eighteenth-century American novelists themselves, arguing that they adopted "a formal posture of authorial evasiveness." Their practice of "literary coquetry" manifests to Rice "a strategic attempt to maintain the communicative and performative power of writing in a culture which was reconfiguring the printed word as a static literary good." *The Transformation of Authorship in America* (Chicago: University of Chicago Press, 1997), 10; see also 147–172. Rice interestingly accounts for the formal mixture of authorial solicitation and didacticism in seduction novels, but his structural explanation of style assumes a general sense of coquetry as a legitimately useful style. In Foster's case, I argue, the ultimate inadequacy of coquetry is the subject of her novel and critique.

8. As Cathy Davidson has noted, Foster bases her *History of Eliza Wharton* on the actual experiences of a woman named Elizabeth Whitman. In calling Eliza a coquette, Foster follows the popular press's view of Elizabeth Whitman. An editorial in the *Independent Chronicle* of September 11, 1788, for example, declared that "she aspired higher than to be a clergyman's wife; and having coquetted until past her prime, fell into criminal indulgences." The *Massachusetts Centinel* of September

20, 1788, described her as "vain and coquetish," qualities developed from having been "a great reader of romances" (quoted in Davidson's introduction to *The Coquette*).

9. While Rousseau's *The Social Contract* (trans. Maurice Cranston [London: Penguin, 1968]) is one of the great consent documents of the eighteenth century, most eighteenth-century Americans were much more familiar with his fiction and educational treatise. See Paul Merrill Spurlin, *Rousseau in America, 1760–1809* (Birmingham: University of Alabama Press, 1969). As I will show, Rousseau's account of woman in *Emile; or, The Education*, trans. Allan Bloom (New York: Basic Books, 1979) can also be read as a treatise about—or purifying vison of—consent.

10. Modesty occupies a prominent place in eighteenth-century advice literature and fiction, as Ruth Yeazell has demonstrated in *Fictions of Modesty* (Chicago: University of Chicago Press, 1991). While modesty ideally expressed self-control, the very self-denials involved in the practice of self-control could entail the dishonesty that Rousseau discovered. Thus false modesty appears very like coquetry, and feminist critics of Rousseau such as Mary Wollstonecraft accordingly disassociate women from the exaggerations of both coquetry and modesty. See *A Vindication of the Rights of Woman, with Strictures on Political and Moral Subjects* (1792; reprint ed. Carol H. Poston, New York: W. W. Norton & Co., 1974).

11. In his arresting reading of the aesthetics of beholding in Rousseau's presentation of women in *Letter to D'Alembert on the Theatre*, Michael Fried suggests that woman acts at once as an agent in and the object of beholding (see *Absorption and Theatricality: Painting and the Beholder in the Age of Diderot* [Berkeley: University of California Press, 1980], 167–171). Thus Rousseau can be understood as transforming the theatrical paradigm in which woman is the spectacle viewed into a textual paradigm in which woman both reads and is read. I am arguing that Rousseau's account of women in *Emile* similarly attributes a textuality to women and moreover works to simplify interpretation of that text by designating a standard female intention and equipping men with a standard understanding of that intention.

12. Here I see Rousseau reverting from what Michael Fried has characterized as a textual paradigm to a theatrical paradigm in which sight is privileged, though also oriented by a cultural account of what the sight of women means. My reading of the eyewitness or witness as the corroborator of custom and law follows the stipulatory logic of rape that Frances Ferguson delineates in "Rape and the Rise of the Novel," *Representations* 20 (Fall 1987): 88–112.

13. Catharine Macaulay, *Letters on Education* (1790), reprinted in *The Feminist Controversy in England, 1788–1810*, ed. Gina Luria (New York: Garland Publishing, 1974), 406.

14. Mary Wollstonecraft, *An Historical and Moral View of the Origin and Progress of the French Revolution and the Effect It Produced in Europe* (1794; reprint with an introduction by Janet M. Todd, Delmar, N.Y.: Scholars' Facsimiles and Reprints, 1975), 29–30.

15. Quoted in Jan Lewis. "The Republican Wife: Virtue and Seduction in the Early Republic," *William and Mary Quarterly* 44 (1987): 698.

16. Ian Watt and subsequent critics have established the novel's integral relation to the project of substantiating individual experience as well as the novel's feminization of that project. For illuminating feminist expositions of that femini-

zation, which eighteenth-century women writers immediately grasped, see Nancy Miller, *The Heroine's Text* (New York: Columbia University Press, 1981), and Claudia Johnson, *Equivocal Beings: Politics, Gender, and Sentimentality in the 1790s* (Chicago: University of Chicago Press, 1995). The evidentiary activity of novelistic enterprise demonstrates the political utility of the novel, in contrast to Nancy Armstrong's view of the novel as an instrument in maintaining "an apolitical realm of culture within the culture as a whole" (*Desire and Domestic Fiction: A Political History of the Novel* [New York: Oxford University Press, 1987], 48). Novelistic goals and strategies of representation may be political or apolitical; they emerge in conjunction with liberal political philosophies that they may or may not endorse. Alexander Welsh has recently advanced the understanding of the novel's representational purposes in his compelling analysis of the relation of the novel's evidentiary techniques to British legal and cultural formulations of circumstantial evidence. See *Strong Representations: Narrative and Circumstantial Evidence in England* (Baltimore: The Johns Hopkins University Press, 1992).

17. The novelistic obsession with the subject of female consent and chastity emerges from and exemplifies the eighteenth-century feminization of virtue, which supplanted the classical republican identification of virtue with manliness described by J. G. A. Pocock in *Virtue, Commerce, and History: Essays on Political Thought and History, Chiefly in the Eighteenth Century* (Cambridge: Cambridge University Press, 1986), and Hanna Fenichel Pitkin, *Fortune Is a Woman: Gender and Politics in the Thought of Niccolo Machiavelli* (Berkeley: University of California Press, 1984). A number of feminist historians have documented and amplified this description. See, for example, Ruth Bloch, "The Gendered Meanings of Virtue in Revolutionary America," *Signs* 13 (1987): 37–58; Linda Kerber, *Women of the Republic: Intellect and Ideology in Revolutionary America* (New York: Norton, 1986); Jan Lewis, "The Republican Wife: Virtue and Seduction in the Early Republic," *William and Mary Quarterly* 44 (1987): 689–721; and Rosemarie Zagarri, *Writing in the New Nation: Prose, Print, and Politics in the Early United States* (New Haven: Yale University Press, 1991). That actual sexual practices did not match sexual and gender ideals is clear from Nancy Cott's informative study of eighteenth-century Massachusetts divorce records. See "Eighteenth-Century Family and Social Life Revealed in Massachusetts Divorce Records," in *A Heritage of Her Own: Toward a New Social History of American Women*, ed. Nancy F. Cott and Elizabeth H. Pleck (New York: Simon & Schuster, 1979), 107–135. As late-eighteenth-century republicanism feminized virtue—in the figures of the Republican Mother and Republican Wife described by Kerber and Lewis—it also forwarded a misogynistic tradition of blaming women for social ills, inadequacies, and excesses. The vivid appearances of such misogyny in the career of radical republicanism in late-eighteenth-century France have been richly treated in Joan Landes, *Women and the Public Sphere in the Age of the French Revolution* (Ithaca: Cornell University Press, 1988), and Lynn Hunt, ed., *Eroticism and the Body Politic* (Baltimore: The Johns Hopkins University Press, 1991). Carol Kay provocatively argues that the sentimentalization of virtue in republicanism in fact signifies a remasculinization of moral virtue ("Canon, Ideology, and Gender: Mary Wollstonecraft's Critique of Adam Smith," *New Political Science* 15 [1986]: 63–76).

18. The legal concept of coverture is detailed in Sir William Blackstone's *Commentaries on the Laws of England* (Oxford: Clarendon Press, 1765–1769), which the

American legal system followed closely. The implications of coverture for women in England and America have been closely examined and explicated by Susan Staves in *Married Women's Separate Property in England, 1660–1833* (Cambridge, Mass.: Harvard University Press, 1990), and Marylynn Salmon, *Women and the Law of Property* (Chapel Hill: University of North Carolina Press, 1986).

19. The question of whether consent can ever serve women is the ongoing subject of feminist debates. Some feminist readers of Locke see his generational and familial model of consensuality as a paradigm that potentially includes and encourages the concept of female consent and citizenry. See Melissa Butler, "Early Liberal Roots of Feminism: John Locke and the Attack on Patriarchy," in *Feminist Interpretations and Political Theory*, ed. Mary Lyndon Shanley and Carole Pateman (University Park: Pennsylvania State University Press, 1991), 74–94; and Linda Nicholson, *Gender and History* (New York: Columbia University Press, 1986). Other feminists, such as Carole Pateman and Catherine Mackinnon, have developed provocative critiques of the androcentrism and misogyny of liberal consent theory. Pateman regards consent as a "hypothetical social contract" premised on the actual subordination and repression of women; she thus renames it "the sexual contract." See Pateman, *The Disorder of Women: Democracy, Feminism, and Political Theory* (Stanford: Stanford University Press, 1989); and MacKinnon, *Feminism Unmodified: Discourses on Life and Law* (Cambridge, Mass.: Harvard University Press, 1987). From my perspective, in which consent is a hypothetical but functional construct often identified with a certain hypothesis about female biology, consent represents a desire by men as well as women that could be masculinist or feminist. How persons choose to tell and use the consent story shapes the character of consent. Historically, consent primarily has served masculinist interests though it also has figured prominently in the development of Anglo-American feminism since Wollstonecraft. I elaborate on the deployments of liberal individualism by Wollstonecraft and twentieth-century anorectics and feminists in "Anorexia, Humanism, and Feminism," *Yale Journal of Criticism* 5 (Fall 1991): 189–215.

20. See readings of *The Coquette* by Davidson, *Revolution and the Word*; Kristie Hamilton, "An Assault on the Will: Republican Virtue and the City in Hannah Webster Foster's *The Coquette*," *Early American Literature* 24 (1989): 135–151; and Carroll Smith-Rosenberg, "Domesticating 'Virtue': Coquettes and Revolutionaries in Young America," in *Literature and the Body: Essays on Populations and Persons*, ed. Elaine Scarry (Baltimore: The Johns Hopkins University Press, 1988), 160–184.

21. Caroline Dall, *The Romance of the Association; or, One Last Glimpse of Charlotte Temple and Elizabeth Wharton* (Cambridge, Mass.: John Wilson and Son, 1875), 17. Mary C. Crawford, *Romance of Old New England Churches* (Boston: L. C. Page & Company, 1904); Charles K. Bolton, *The Elizabeth Whitman Mystery* (Peabody, Mass., 1912).

22. Davidson, *Revolution and the Word*, 149.

23. Roberto Unger elegantly describes this paradox of liberal psychology and politics—that individual freedom depends upon some social constraint, even as it contends with and sometimes against it—as the antinomy between reason and desire. In my exposition of Lockean liberalism, there is no antithesis between the realms of reason (constraint) and desire (individuality), for they are integral to each other. See Unger, *Knowledge and Politics* (New York: The Free Press, 1975).

24. In *Revolution and the Word*, Cathy Davidson also sees Eliza's experience with Boyer as her "ruin," but attributes this ruin to the "negation of female self" that Boyer's sermonizing rejection of Eliza emblematizes (146). Carroll Smith-Rosenberg attributes Eliza's downfall to "the desire for independence coupled with the wish to rise socially" that propel her toward the rake Sanford ("Domesticating 'Virtue,'" 169). My reading, which focuses on the question of coquetry and its relation to consent, offers different, though complementary, terms in which to understand the sense of limitation as well as the desire for freedom that the novel projects. Larzar Ziff has usefully pointed out the integral relation between economic difficulties and sexual falls in early American seduction novels; see his *Writing in the New Nation: Prose, Print, and Politics in the Early United States* (New Haven: Yale University Press, 1991), 71–75. Smith-Rosenberg and Ziff read seduction novels as registering the anxieties attendant upon liberal economic individualism. While I agree with this general account, I think that Foster's portrayal of Eliza invokes economic differences and desires less to develop a socioeconomic analysis of her desire than to employ the formula of seduction tales (of which economic difference is a standard convention) in order to illuminate the various and variable interests that consent represents. It is worth noting in this context that Locke views money as a sign of universal consent.

25. Mary Wollstonecraft, *Thoughts on the Education of Daughters: With Reflections on Female Conduct, in the More Important Duties of Life* (1787; facsimile edition, New York: Garland Publishing, 1974), 28.

26. Here I concur with those critics who align the novel's female chorus with patriarchal values. See, for example, Smith-Rosenberg, "Domesticating 'Virtue,'" 178; Stern, *Plight of Feeling*, 90–91.

27. Mary C. Crawford recites the epitaph engraved on the Elizabeth Whitman tomb in *The Romance of Old New England Churches* (Boston: L. C. Page & Company, 1904), 11–12.

28. Julia Stern likewise notes that "Foster short-circuits any efforts to draw political conclusions [about the virtuous women and wives in the novel] by killing off every child born within its pages" (*Plight of Feeling*, 134).

29. Foster is not the only novelist of her era to raise questions about the function of pregnancy in seduction narratives. Susanna Rowson closes *Charlotte Temple* with the survival of Charlotte's illegitimate daughter Lucy, who is adopted by Charlotte's parents (*Charlotte Temple: A Tale of Truth* [Philadelphia: Printed for M. Carey, 1794]). Whatever different experience might be imagined for the innocent offspring of a seduced woman is qualified, however, in the sequel *Charlotte's Daughter*, where Rowson follows the life of Lucy Temple until her engagement to a man who turns out to be her half-brother (*Charlotte's Daughter; or, The Three Orphans* [Boston: Richardson & Land, 1828]). The lovers/siblings separate and renounce marriage. A similar situation of a family destroyed by seduction and potential incest appears in William Brown, *The Power of Sympathy; or, The Triumph of Nature, Founded in Truth* (1789), in *The Power of Sympathy and The Coquette*, ed. William S. Osborne (Albany: New College and University Press, 1970). The Fatal Effects of Seduction, to borrow the words of the title of a 1789 play (Anon. [Bennington, Vt.: Haswell & Russell, 1789]), thus overtake the life of the family as well as that of the fallen woman. This concern with the fate of the family links female consent to the exogamous project of furthering the society—illicit female consent is imagined to

generate endogamy and extinction, undoing a patriarchal order. Disallowing life to all offspring, *The Coquette* removes the threat of incest as well as the force of the incest threat as a principle of regulating women's consent. In *States of Sympathy*, 19–39, Elizabeth Barnes effectively demonstrates that incest is the logical extension of the ideal of familial relations presented in early American novels; the novels both incite and censure connections between already connected individuals. In light of Barnes's point on the novelistic conventionality of incest, Foster's forestalling of the possibility of incest appears a powerful statement against both the novelistic convention and the social order that the convention upholds.

6. The Quixotic Fallacy

1. Ludwig Bemelman's *Madeline* series, which first appeared in 1939, has become such a beloved classic of twentieth-century children's literature that the stories currently appear in the increasingly favored electronic media: television, video, and CDs. The original Madeline story can be found in Ludwig Bemelmans, *Madeline* (New York: Puffin, 1977).

2. Ian Watt notes this evidentiary function of novelistic literary representation when he compares "the novel's mode of imitating reality" to the testimony presented to a jury in a court of law. See *The Rise of the Novel: Studies in Defoe, Richardson, and Fielding* (Berkeley: University of California Press, 1957), 31–32. Alexander Welsh has recently further elaborated on the similarities between narrative realism and rules of evidence in *Strong Representations: Narrative and Circumstantial Evidence in England* (Baltimore: The Johns Hopkins University Press, 1992).

3. John Trumbull, "The Progress of Dullness," *The Satiric Poems of John Trumbull*, ed. Edwin T. Bowden (Austin: University of Texas Press, 1962), 88.

4. On the pervasiveness of the figure of the deluded reader in early American discussions of fiction, see James D. Hart, *The Popular Book: A History of America's Literary Taste* (Berkeley: University of California Press, 1950), 51–54; Linda Kerber, *Women of the Republic: Intellect and Ideology in Revolutionary America* (New York: Norton, 1986), 236–246; and Cathy Davidson, *The Revolution and the Word: The Rise of the Novel in America* (New York: Oxford University Press, 1986), 45–54. Janet Todd finds the case of the misguided reader to be a standard scenario of the late-eighteenth-century "attack on sensibility"; see *Sensibility: An Introduction* (London: Methuen, 1986), 129–146. In an informative essay on early American reading practices, Robert B. Winans usefully points out the "essential irrelevance" of the opposition to novel-reading to both American printers and readers—see "The Growth of a Novel-Reading Public in Late-Eighteenth-Century America," *Early American Literature* 9 (1975): 267.

5. Monroe Beardsley and W. K. Wimsatt, Jr., "The Affective Fallacy," in W. K. Wimsatt, Jr., *The Verbal Icon: Studies in the Meaning of Poetry* (Lexington: University Press of Kentucky, 1954), 21–39. Beardsley and Wimsatt define the affective fallacy as "a confusion between the poem and its *results* (what it *is* and what it *does*)." Such faulty reading "begins by trying to derive the standard of criticism from the psychological effects of the poem and ends in impressionism and relativism" (21). In their attempt to purge criticism of irrelevant and subjective emotions, Beardsley and Wimsatt assert that poems themselves relay "the most precise emotive report" of their culture. Thus, "though cultures have changed and will change,

poems remain and explain" (39). The quixotic fallacy, I think, illustrates the impossibility of such a project to keep emotion within the precincts of the poem. If the quixote is a faulty reader who mistakes the relation between literature and life—who does not understand what fiction is—she nevertheless is absolutely loyal to the authority of the literary representation that Beardsley and Wimsatt uphold. We might say that she takes too literally the precise emotive report of what she reads.

6. Royall Tyler, *The Algernine Captive; or, The Life and Adventures of Dr. Updike Underhill Six Years a Prisoner among the Algernines*, 2 vols. (1797; New Haven: College & University Press, 1970), 46.

7. Tabitha Gilman Tenney, *Female Quixotism: Exhibited in the Romantic Opinions and Extravagant Adventures of Dorcasina Sheldon* (1801), eds. Jean Nienkamp and Andrea Collins (New York: Oxford University Press, 1992), 6, 4. Subsequent citations of this novel will appear parenthetically throughout the chapter.

8. Noah Webster, "On the Education of Youth in America" (1788) in *A Collection of Essays and Fugitive Writings* (1790; New York: Scholars' Facsimiles & Reprints, 1977), 30.

9. Tyler, *Algernine Captive*, 28.

10. Judith Sargent Murray, "Thoughts on Clarissa Harlowe," in *The Gleaner: A Miscellaneous Production*, vol. 2 (Boston: I. Thomas and E. T. Andrews, 1798), 66. On the reception of *Clarissa* in eighteenth-century America see Hart, *Popular Book*, 55–57, and Jay Fliegelman, *Prodigals and Pilgrims: The American Revolution against Patriarchal Authority* (Cambridge: Cambridge University Press, 1982), 83–89. Fliegelman concludes from the American embrace of the novel that "Clarissa was to the eighteenth century what the maid of Orléans had been to the fifteenth: a martyred heroine who had led a revolutionary cause" (89). In an intriguing study of the reception and function of *Clarissa*, Leonard Tennenhouse has shown how American abridgments expanded or deleted certain sections in order to stress specifically American ideas of identity. In the Americanized *Clarissa*, for example, more space and hope is given to the possibility of Clarissa being saved by her uncle Mordred, suggesting alternative organizations of familial authority based on guardianship rather than direct bloodlines. In Tennenhouse's view, this change does not support revolutionary ideology but rather strengthens the concept of British identity now rerooted in a different and perhaps better familial ground. See "The Americanization of Clarissa," *Yale Journal of Criticism* 2, no. 1 (1998): 177–196.

11. Benjamin Rush, "Thoughts upon Female Education," in *Essays, Literary, Moral, and Philosophical* (1798; reprint ed. Michael Moranze, Schenectady, N.Y.: Union College Press, 1988), 48; Murray, "Thoughts on Clarissa Harlowe," 65.

12. Murray, "Thoughts on Clarissa Harlowe," 64.

13. Just a few of the many early American novelists who announce in their prefaces the truth of the narratives that follow are Anon., *Amelia; or, The Faithless Briton* (1798); Charles Brockden Brown, *Ormond; or, The Secret Witness* (1799); William Hill Brown, *The Power of Sympathy* (1789); Hannah S. Foster, *The Coquette* (1797) and *The Boarding-School; or, Lessons of a Preceptress to Her Pupils* (1798); Susanna Rowson, *Charlotte Temple* (1792); Tabitha Tenney, *Female Quixotism* (1801); and Royall Tyler, *The Algernine Captive* (1797). For a more extensive list, see Herbert Ross Brown, *The Sentimental Novel in America, 1780–1860* (Durham: Duke University Press, 1940), 9–12; and Henri Petter, *The Early American Novel*

(Columbus: Ohio State University Press, 1971), 57. As Michael T. Gilmore remarks, "No genre was more insistent about its pretension to be an objective chronicle of actual occurrences." See "The Literature of the Revolutionary and Early National Periods," *The Cambridge History of American Literature*, vol. 1, ed. Sacvan Bercovitch (Cambridge: Cambridge University Press, 1994), 623.

14. Michael Warner, *The Letters of the Republic: Publication and the Public Sphere in Eighteenth-Century America* (Cambridge, Mass.: Harvard University Press, 1990), 175–176.

15. Davidson is referring to Abigail Adams's famous letter to John Adams bidding him to remember women's rights and roles in the new nation. See *The Revolution and the Word: The Rise of the Novel in America*, ix. Davidson's extensively researched literary history is indispensable to the reappraisals of the early American novel now taking place.

16. This is not to deny Warner's thesis about the crucial role of print in the formation of the American nation but to assert that novelistic representation does not (necessarily) depart from the public aims of other literary forms. It is also important to remember that all printed matter engages the imaginative processes of individuals, which by definition operate personally, sometimes in isolation. So I would not at all exclude the novel from the project of imagining the American republic, but underscore its particular displays of the public-private nexus that all representation involves. In *Political Constructions: Defoe, Richardson, and Sterne in Relation to Hobbes, Hume, and Burke* (Ithaca: Cornell University Press, 1988), Carol Kay usefully reminds us that the twentieth-century critical custom of aligning the novel with an individualism opposed to "discourses about public things that might have an impact on political life"—a habit of thinking about the novel initiated by Ian Watt—overlooks how eighteenth-century novels do conduct political discourse: "The relation of the novel to the political is the animating problem continually meditated and redefined by each major eighteenth-century artist" (9). Kay is describing the works of Defoe, Richardson, and Sterne, which define the British novelistic tradition from which the early American novel emerges. Within this tradition, the first American novels can be seen as conducting their own particular meditations on and redefinitions of politics. Moreover, as Nancy Armstrong and Leonard Tennenhouse provocatively suggest in *The Imaginary Puritan: Literature, Intellectual Labor, and the Origins of Personal Life* (Berkeley: University of California Press, 1992), early American colonial narratives help shape the British novel and thus the novelistic discussion of politics.

17. Scholars of the history of the book, attentive to the material facets of print publication, distribution, and reception, attest to the social character of eighteenth-century literacy in America, as indicated by social libraries (which were commercial societies run by printers and publishers), lending libraries, personal letters, family practices, and group readings. My understanding of reading in eighteenth-century America has benefitted from several valuable studies. See William Gilmore, *Reading Becomes a Necessity of Life: Material and Cultural Life in Rural New England, 1780–1835* (Knoxville: University of Tennessee Press, 1988); David D. Hall, *Cultures of Print: Essays in the History of the Book* (Amherst: University of Massachusetts Press, 1996); Kenneth Lockridge, *Literacy in Colonial New England: An Enquiry into the Social Context of Literacy in the Early Modern West* (New York: Norton, 1974); Robert B. Winans, "The Growth of a Novel-Reading Public in

Late Eighteenth-Century America," *Early American Literature* 9 (1975): 267–275; and the essays collected in Cathy Davidson's *Reading in America: Literature and Social History* (Baltimore: The Johns Hopkins University Press, 1989). Janice Radway has demonstrated the persistence of such social habits of reading in her study of contemporary romance reading circles; see *Reading the Romance: Women, Patriarchy, and Popular Literature* (Chapel Hill: University of North Carolina Press, 1984). For more general histories of the book, see Lucien Febvre and Henri-Jean Martin, *The Coming of the Book: The Impact of Printing, 1450–1800,* trans. David Gerard (London, 1976) and Elizabeth Eisenstein, *The Printing Press as an Agent of Change: Communications and Cultural Transformations in Early Modern Europe,* 2 vols. (New York: Cambridge University Press, 1979). My understanding of early American literacy also has been enhanced and amplified by Jay Fliegelman's important study of the performative features of Jefferson's Declaration of Independence in *Declaring Independence: Jefferson, Natural Language, and the Culture of Performance* (Stanford: Stanford University Press, 1993), and by David S. Shields's informative exploration of eighteenth-century American social spaces of conversations such as coffeehouses, taverns, salons, balls, card games, clubs, and colleges in *Civil Tongues and Polite Letters in British America* (Chapel Hill: University of North Carolina Press, 1997). Clearly, the select societies examined by Shields do not include all American inhabitants, and reflect class, gender, and racial hierarchies long present in the colonies. As William Gilmore points out, all histories of literacy since the landmark work of Febvre and Eisenstein on the impact of the emergence and proliferation of print tend to argue about cultural agency and authority (*Reading Becomes a Necessity of Life,* 1). Literacy can appear the privileged possession of certain classes or institutions, such as the aristocracy, the clergy, or the state. At the same time, as Natalie Zemon Davis has observed (1975), ordinary people can remain independent of specific orders of literacy, practicing their own imaginative and practical representational relations. In arguing for the simultaneously social and private character of the early American novel, and denying its function as either a primarily conservative or subversive engine, I am following Davis in stressing the particular and often unpredictable dynamics, inflected by historical circumstances and cultural habits, that can emerge in imaginative encounters. Davis's argument appears in "Printing and the People," in *Society and Culture in Early Modern France,* ed. Natalie Zemon Davis (Stanford: Stanford University Press, 1975).

18. In a recent study of changing notions of character in the novel, Deidre Shauna Lynch states that despite the historical personalization and privatization of the concept of character, "our transactions with characters remain profoundly social experiences" (*The Economy of Character: Novels, Market Culture, and the Business of Inner Meaning* [Chicago: University of Chicago Press, 1998], 20). I would extend this description to include our transactions with novelistic representation in general.

19. Many scholars have documented the emergence of the feminine domestic sphere in the United States. Nancy Cott's *The Bonds of Womanhood: "Women's Sphere" in New England, 1780–1835* (New Haven: Yale University Press, 1977) supplies a model treatment of how the private and public are intertwined in American experience, and especially in the experiences of women.

20. These antinomies are the well-known polarities presented by historical theses about the republicanism of the early national period. Most powerfully artic-

ulated in the work of J. G. A. Pocock, Bernard Bailyn, and Gordon Wood, the republican thesis holds that the United States arose from a republican ideology hearkening back to Roman models of civic organization, which place the state before the individual. See J. G. A. Pocock, *The Machiavellian Moment: Florentine Political Thought and the Atlantic Republican Tradition* (Princeton: Princeton University Press, 1975), and *Virtue, Commerce, and History* (New York: Cambridge University Press, 1985); Bernard Bailyn, *The Ideological Origins of the American Revolution* (Cambridge, Mass.: Harvard University Press, 1967); and Gordon Wood, *The Creation of the American Republic, 1776–1787* (Chapel Hill: University of North Carolina Press, 1969). For other contributions on republicanism, see the scholars cited in note 15 of the Introduction. Literary historians, long embarrassed by what have seemed the aesthetic limitations of early American fiction, have found this paradigm to be a convenient standard for measuring the significance of early American novels. Thus recent readings have tended to take the historical or sociological character of the novels as their aesthetics, to think of these novels in terms of their republican or individualist affinities. Following Warner and Davidson, critics have been producing new readings of the early American novel that emphasize its political performance, particularly with respect to gender issues. See, for example, Elizabeth Barnes, *States of Sympathy: Seduction and Democracy in the American Novel* (New York: Columbia University Press, 1997); Shirley Samuels, *Romances of the Republic: Women, the Family, and Violence in the Literature of the Early American Nation* (New York: Oxford University Press, 1996); and Julia A. Stern, *The Plight of Feeling: Sympathy and Dissent in the Early American Novel* (Chicago: University of Chicago Press, 1997). While the paradigm of historical republicanism usefully illuminates the historical context, and sometimes content, of the novel, critical reliance on this paradigm risks overlooking the actual aesthetic choices and configurations through which the novels express their particular politics or points of view.

21. Janet Todd, for example, has demonstrated how both radical and conservative cultural critics in late-eighteenth-century Britain charged each other with excesses of literary sensibility (*Sensibility*, 130–137).

22. Bakhtin's characterization of novels as heteroglossic—composed of different speeches, bearing "a multi-languaged consciousness"—usefully captures the multiplicity of novelistic discourse. Thus readers of widely divergent beliefs can discover points of identification within the same novel. *Don Quixote*, inevitably, is one of the exemplary texts in Bakhtin's theory of the novel; see *The Dialogic Imagination*, ed. Michael Holquist, trans. Caryl Emerson and Michael Holquist (Austin: University of Texas Press, 1981), 11.

23. Mrs. Leanora Sansay, *Laura* (Philadelphia: Bradford & Insheep, 1809).

24. The preeminent example is John Cleland's *Memoirs of a Woman of Pleasure*, a narrative so identified with its narrator that it came to be known by her name, Fanny Hill.

25. John Locke, *Of the Conduct of the Human Understanding* (1697), ed. Thomas Fowler (New York: Lenox Hill/Burt Franklin, 1971), 102.

26. John Locke, "Some Thoughts Concerning Reading and Study for a Gentleman" (also titled "Mr. Locke's Extempore Advice), appendix 3 in *Some Thoughts Concerning Education*, eds. John W. and Jean S. Yolton (Oxford: Clarendon Press, 1989), 325–326. This manuscript, dictated by Locke to Samuel Bold, was first published in 1720 in Pierre Desmaizeaux's *Collection of Several Pieces by Mr. Locke*. The

original text is in the British Library (MS Sloane 4290, folios 11–14). Locke presents related advice on reading in *Some Thoughts Concerning Education*, 211–214.

27. Locke, *Conduct of the Human Understanding*, 97.

28. Alicia Sheridan Lefanu, *Lucy Osmond* (New York, 1804); and Sukey Watson [or Eliza Vicery], *Emily Hamilton* (Worcester: Isaiah Thomas, 1803). Other female quixotes appear in Charles Brockden Brown, *Ormond* (New York: Hocquet Caritat, 1799); William Hill Brown, *The Power of Sympathy* (Boston: Isaiah Thomas and Company, 1789); Hannah Foster, *The Boarding School* (Boston: Isaiah Thomas and Company, 1798); and Maria Edgeworth, "Letters of Caroline and Julia," in *Letters for Literary Ladies* (London, 1795), 5–6.

29. Hugh Henry Brackenridge, *Modern Chivalry*, 1793–1815, ed. Claude M. Newlin (New York: Hafner Publishing Company, 1962), 256. I follow Christopher Looby in thinking the structure of *Modern Chivalry* "fundamentally true to Cervantes" (*Voicing America: Language, Literary Form, and the Origins of the United States* [Chicago: University of Chicago Press, 1996], 243). For a different reading, which takes Farrago's servant Teague O'Regan as the quixotic figure, see Joseph H. Harkey, "The Don Quixote of the Frontier: Brackenridge's *Modern Chivalry*," *Early American Literature* 8 (1973): 193–203.

30. Sexual difference develops an increasing significance over the course of the eighteenth century as particular notions of women are formulated and instituted as scientific knowledge. see Thomas Laqueur, *Making Sex: Body and Gender from the Greeks to Freud* (Cambridge, Mass.: Harvard University Press, 1990), especially 149–192. Numerous historians have recorded the emergence of a new rhetoric about womanhood during the early national period in the United States: Ruth Bloch, "The Gendered Meaning of Virtue in Revolutionary America," *Signs* 13 (Autumn 1987): 37–58; Kerber, *Women of the Republic*, 265–288; Jan Lewis, "The Republican Wife: Virtue and Seduction in the Early Republic," *William and Mary Quarterly* 44 (1987): 689–721; and Rosemary Zagarri, "Morals, Manners, and the Republican Mother," *American Quarterly* 44 (1992): 192–216.

31. Erich Auerbach notes the probably most famous example of the quixote's own influentiality: the incident in *Don Quixote* in which the servant Sancho Panza adopts the quixotic mode of seeing the world. In order to rouse his master from despair, Sancho insists that a strange ugly peasant woman is in fact an enchanted form of Dulcinea, Quixote's imagined beloved. See *Mimesis: The Representation of Reality in Western Literature*, trans. Willard D. Trask (Princeton: Princeton University Press, 1953), 334–354.

32. Benedict Anderson has insightfully linked the presence of local common beliefs and practices with the formation of nations. In the Americas, for example, the Creole populations shared languages with their European ruling nations yet developed separate national identities because these residents came to be strongly connected by their geography, internal commerce, and local circulation of print media (mainly newspapers). See *Imagined Communities: Reflections on the Origin and Spread of Nationalism* (London: Verso, 1983), 37–65.

33. Mikkel Borch-Jacobsen illustrates this point in his explication of the communal role that African tribes take in curing mad or possessed individuals. Tribal members observe and mime the individual's identifications, thus translating the individual condition into a wider social condition. The oddity of the individual state disappears as its internal social dynamic is generalized. See "Mimetic Efficacity," in

The Emotional Tie (Stanford: Stanford University Press, 1995), 98–120. For another intriguing account of sociability in madness, see Terry Castle's study of the homo-erotic connections facilitated in the experience of folie à deux. Castle examines two Englishwomen's shared delusion that they encountered the ghosts of Marie Antoi-nette and members of her court in "Contagious Folly: An Adventure and Its Skep-tics," in *The Female Thermometer: Eighteenth-Century Culture and the Invention of the Uncanny* (New York: Oxford University Press, 1995), 190–214.

34. Michel Foucault, *The Order of Things: An Archaeology of the Human Sciences* (New York: Vintage, 1973), 48–49.

35. In their readings of Lennox's *Female Quixote*, Catherine Gallagher (*Nobody's Story* [Berkeley: University of California Press, 1994], 165–195), Janet Todd (*The Sign of Angellica: Women, Writing, and Fiction, 1660–1800* [New York: Colum-bia University Press, 1989], 151–160), and Laurie Langbauer (*Woman and Romance: The Consolations of Gender in the English Novel* [Ithaca: Cornell University Press, 1989], 62–92) present a variety of feminist arguments about quixotism, as do read-ings of Tenney's *Female Quixotism* by Davidson (*Revolution and the Word*, 186–192) and Cynthia Miecznikowski—"The Parodic Mode and the Patriarchal Imperative: Reading the Female Reader(s) in Tabitha Tenney's *Female Quixotism*," *Early American Literature* 25, no. 1 (1990): 34–45.

36. The social mimeticism of consent that I am describing here differs sig-nificantly from Sacvan Bercovitch's familiar concept of consensus in American cul-ture, articulated most forcefully in *The Office of the Scarlet Letter* (Baltimore: The Johns Hopkins University Press, 1992), and *The Rites of Assent: Transformations in the Symbolic Construction of America* (New York: Routledge, 1993). According to Bercovitch, American society works by consensus, a general agreement most mani-fest in instances of dissent. Hester Prynne, who returns to the community that out-lawed her, is Bercovitch's exemplary figure of affirmative dissent. Dissent, then, is never really dissent. While I think Bercovitch is right to see how American soci-ety regularly incorporates forms of dissent, I regard this process as an unpredict-able method of liberal society rather than a determinant structure or force. It is crucial to note the quite real historical changes, for better or worse, that different incorporations of dissent effect at different moments. Even though consent en-tails conformity, notions and compositions of conformity can change. The Cana-dian Bercovitch interestingly describes his first encounter with American consen-sus in this way: "I felt like Sancho Panza in a land of Don Quixotes. It was not just that the dream [i.e., the American dream] was a patent fiction. It was that the fiction involved an entire hermeneutic system" ("The Ritual of Consensus," in *Rites of Assent*, 29). In my view, this description captures perfectly the common sense of the specific social compact, in all its pervasiveness and artificiality, under and within which Americans operate. A person from a different culture quite natu-rally finds American society a strange system with its own peculiar standards of meaning.

37. Catherine Gallagher argues that eighteenth-century novels most effec-tively claim readers' sympathies because they elicit feelings for fictional persons, for nobodies. By this account, Dorcasina seems an insensitive reader. See *Nobody's Story*, 165–195.

38. For another reading of the antidemocratic logic of *Female Quixotism*, see

Linda Frost, "The Body Politic in Tabitha Tenney's *Female Quixotism,*" *Early American Literature* 32 (1997): 113–134.

39. Maria Edgeworth, "Angelina; or L'Amie Inconnue," in *Moral Tales for Young People*, vol. 2 (London: J. Johnson, 1801). Subsequent citations of this story in the chapter will appear parenthetically. Edgeworth is one of the British (Anglo-Irish, actually) authors whose writings were very popular among early American readers.

40. Judith Sargent Murray, *Story of Margaretta* (1798) in *Selected Writings of Judith Sargent Murray*, ed. Sharon M. Harris (New York: Oxford University Press, 1995), 165.

41. Murray, "Thoughts on Clarissa Harlowe," 63.

42. Borch-Jacobsen, "Mimetic Efficacity," 104.

43. Tenney's husband was Dr. Samuel Tenney, a physician who served three terms (1800–1816) as a U.S. Senator from New Hampshire. He opposed the presidential election of Republican Thomas Jefferson and supported the continuation of the Federalist Alien and Sedition Act. While wives often hold their own political views, Tenney's correspondence as well as political sentiments expressed in *Female Quixotism* suggest that she at least respected Federalist positions. See Jean Nienkamp and Andrea Collins, Introduction to *Female Quixotism*, xxiv–xxvi.

44. Jennifer Nedelsky provides a detailed account of how thinking about property figured in the forming of the Constitution. See *Private Property and the Limits of American Constitutionalism: The Madisonian Framework and Its Legacy* (Chicago: University of Chicago Press, 1990), 67–95.

45. The successful counterview is expressed in Madison's discussion of factions in *Federalist*, no. 10. Unlike Morris, Madison sees economic and class interests as variously intersecting with other interests on different occasions. Madison finds the large size of the American republic a deterrent to any one faction's or interest's prevailing over the populace. Hanna Pitkin furnishes an excellent analysis of the American paradoxical imagination of a government representing individual interests, how "by definition, no one can really act for another." See *The Concept of Representation* (Berkeley: University of California Press, 1967), 190–208.

46. Dorcasina and Betty refer to Paine's *The Age of Reason* (1795), his republican critique of institutionalized religion. Paine had eloquently defended the French Revolution in his earlier *The Rights of Man* (1791). By the end of the eighteenth century, the American association of Paine with the French Revolution and its excesses superseded memories of him as an American patriot and the author of *Common Sense*.

47. Erich Auerbach has remarked on "the admiration [that] has been accorded to Don Quixote by almost all readers" (*Mimesis*, 343). The tendency to see the quixote as heroic or admirable is also encouraged by Charlotte Lennox in her depiction of her absurdly behaving heroine Arabella as beautiful and good-hearted. Tenney, interestingly, refuses to endow Dorcasina with beauty, but she does endow her with notable "ornaments"—the virtues of "piety and charity" (15). Her community loves her for these qualities, and it is their desire to protect her generosity from being imposed upon that moves them to oppose her quixotic schemes.

48. Bakhtin, *Dialogic Imagination*, 419–422.

49. William B. Warner, *Licensing Entertainment: The Elevation of Novel Reading in Britain, 1684–1750* (Berkeley: University of California Press, 1998), 277.

Epilogue

1. See Walter Lippman, *Public Opinion* (New York: Harcourt, Brace, and Company, 1922); Edward Bernays, *The Engineering of Consent* (Norman: University of Oklahoma Press, 1955); Noam Chomsky, "The Manufacture of Consent," in *The Chomsky Reader*, ed. James Peck (New York: Pantheon, 1987), 136.

2. Olaudah Equiano, *The Interesting Narrative and Other Writings*, ed. Vincent Carretta (New York: Penguin, 1995). The Rowlandson and Panther captivity narratives, as well as accounts of similar experiences undergone by other early American women—Hannah Dustan, Elizabeth Hanson, Jemima Howe, Mary Kinnan, Mary Jemison, and Elizabeth Godfrey—have been reprinted in a very useful volume, *Women's Indian Captivity Narratives*, ed. Kathryn Zabelle Derounian-Stodola (New York: Penguin, 1998).

3. Susanna Rowson, *Slaves in Algiers* (Philadelphia: Matthew Carey, 1795); Royall Tyler, *The Algernine Captive; or, The Life and Adventures of Dr. Updike Underhill Six Years a Prisoner among the Algernines* (1797; New Haven: College & University Press, 1970). For an informative discussion of 1790s white slavery literature, see Benhilde Montgomery, "White Captives, African Slaves: A Drama of Abolition," *Eighteenth-Century Studies* 27 (Summer 1994): 615–630.

4. Anonymous [attributed to John McGowan], *The French Convert: Conversion of a Noble French Lady* (Boston: Rogers & Fowle, 1744). This book was reprinted by Peter Stewart of Philadelphia in 1791, 1794, and 1798.

Acknowledgments

The writing of this book took me to many places and introduced me to different critical interests and new colleagues. It is a pleasure to remember all those new as well as old conversants who participated in the process of thought that became this book. Comments, questions, and suggestions at various times from Jonathan Arac, Nancy Armstrong, Bill Brown, Lawrence Buell, Robert Caserio, Rob Corber, Kenneth Dauber, Frances Ferguson, Stanley Fish, Jay Fliegelman, Catherine Gallagher, Claudia Johnson, Catherine Jurca, Carol Kay, Celeste Langan, Christopher Looby, Deidre Lynch, Sandra Macpherson, Walter Benn Michaels, Donald Pease, Elizabeth Renker, Elaine Scarry, Gordon Schochet, Carroll Smith-Rosenberg, Simon Stern, Mark Strand, Jane Thrailkill, Judith Walkowitz, and Michael Zuckerman have helped shape this book, perhaps in ways quite unrecognizable to themselves. I thank them all for their intellectual attentiveness and generosity. I also am most grateful to my anonymous readers at Harvard University Press whose richly informed and insightful responses helped refine the book.

In a book that takes quite seriously Locke's point that judgment is an empirical process, the result of an individual's engagement with her environment, it is fitting also to mention the influence and sustenance of certain places: the Place des Vosges in Paris, the Dingle Peninsula, the footpaths from Carbis Bay to St. Ives and from Shanklin to Ventnor,

Chez Panisse, Becky Johnson's first-grade classroom, and my garden. In these places and in the less pleasant yet still stimulating spaces of the London Tube, hospital waiting rooms, Tai Kwon Do studios, and Little League fields, I worked out my arguments. My sense of the limits of consent stems at least in part from the alternately enabling and impeding features of my surroundings.

Without question, libraries provided the most directly helpful environments. This book owes a great deal to the hospitality and expertise of the librarians at the British Library, Oxford's Bodleian Library, the American Antiquarian Society, the Huntington Library, the New York Public Library, the Pierpont Morgan Library, The Columbia University Rare Book Library, the Free Library of Philadelphia, the Library Company of Philadelphia, and the Boston Public Library. I am especially grateful to Jenna Loosmore at the American Antiquarian Society, Lisa Libbey at the Huntington, and Roberta Zonghi at the Rare Book Room of the Boston Public Library for their help in finding usable illustrations. Anna Lou Ashby at the Pierpont Morgan shared her own exhaustive research on Aesop's fables.

Fellowships from the National Endowment for the Humanities and the University of Utah Tanner Humanities Center, as well as grants from the University Research Council, provided me with the time and funds to work at these libraries. My excellent research assistants Ron Carpenter, Tanya Radford, Emily Summerhays, and Rebecca Summerhays energetically searched for materials and checked references. I could not have completed this book without the wonderful childcare provided by Kashka Celinska, Jade Lidz, and Tanya Radford.

Lindsay Waters has been an exemplary editor, a provocative and searching interlocutor. His critical engagement with this project greatly enhanced the process of completing it. I also was fortunate to have a superb copy editor, Julie Carlson, who read every page with a keen eye, sensitive ear, and sympathetic intelligence. Kimberly Steere at Harvard University Press expertly assisted in the material labors of transforming the manuscript into a book.

Earlier, briefer versions of Chapters 3, 5, and 6 have appeared as articles: "Fables and the Forming of Americans," *Modern Fiction Studies* 18 (Spring 1997): 115–143; "Consent, Coquetry, and Consequences," *American Literary History* 9, no. 4 (Winter 1997): 625–652; "The Quixotic Fallacy," *NOVEL: A Forum on Fiction* 32, no. 2 (Spring 1999): 250–

273; copyright NOVEL Corp. © 1999. I thank the Johns Hopkins University Press, Oxford University Press, and *NOVEL* for giving me permission to reprint these essays in revised form.

My parents patiently read and usefully commented upon every chapter. As always, I profoundly appreciate their encouragement and interest. The companionship of Howard Horwitz, my most challenging and helpful reader, has immeasurably enriched this book and the time of writing it. My deepest gratitude goes to him and to our son, Devon, for providing me with ever interesting conditions of thought. This book is dedicated to them and to the memory of Carol Kay, whose response I shall always miss.

Index

DATE DUE

HIGHSMITH #45115